Introduction

The **Design Project Tutorial** is intended to introduce a new user of **SolidWorks99®** to the application of the software in a project-oriented environment. All learning is cumulative and coordinated as the elements and outcomes of a mechanical Design Project take shape.

The text includes thirty *Exercises* and nine groups of *Design Project Assignments*. The Exercises introduce new commands and operations, and they include very thorough step-by-step instructions which maximize learning efficiency. Generally, each Exercise is short in scope, and most can easily be completed in less than thirty minutes.

After new skills are acquired using the Exercises they are immediately reinforced in the ensuing Design Project Assignments (DPA's). The sequence of new skills acquisition through Exercises followed by reinforcement with DPA's is repeated five times throughout the text.

DPA's contain less thorough instructions than Exercises because they are intended to test and reinforce learning from the Exercises. They also require more time and effort as they simulate application of solid modeling to a design project in the workplace.

All of the DPA's concentrate on the various stages of design for a single complex assembly. Design of any complex assembly in the "real world" naturally progresses from part models to part drawings to assemblies, and this sequence is reflected in the DPA's. Learning of this sequence is more important than the learning of individual commands and operations, and it is intuitively refelected in the overall layout of the text.

Since Exercises provide skills which are applied during the DPA's they too can be seen to be integral with the overall Design Project. This reality will satisfy users who are frustrated by seemingly unrelated, incoherent and uncoordinated activities. In other words, the objective of the text is to complete the Design Project, but the Design Project cannot be accomplished without first tackling the Exercises.

Design Project Introduction

The *Air Handler Assembly* is the coordinating Design Project. Its components and sub-assemblies will be created sequentially as the text progresses.

The top-level *Air Handler Assembly* contains one each of two sub-assemblies:
        Motor Sub-Assembly
        Blower Sub-Assembly

In turn, the Motor Sub-Assembly contains the following parts and quantities:
- (1) Motor
- (1) Driver Shaft
- (2) Snap Rings
- (1) Cover

And the Blower Sub-Assembly contains the following parts and quantities:
- (1) Lower Housing
- (1) Upper Housing
- (1) Impeller

The top-level assembly, sub-assemblies, and subcomponents are shown and identified within general and exploded views on the following pages.

DESIGN PROJECT TUTORIAL

MOTOR Sub-Assembly

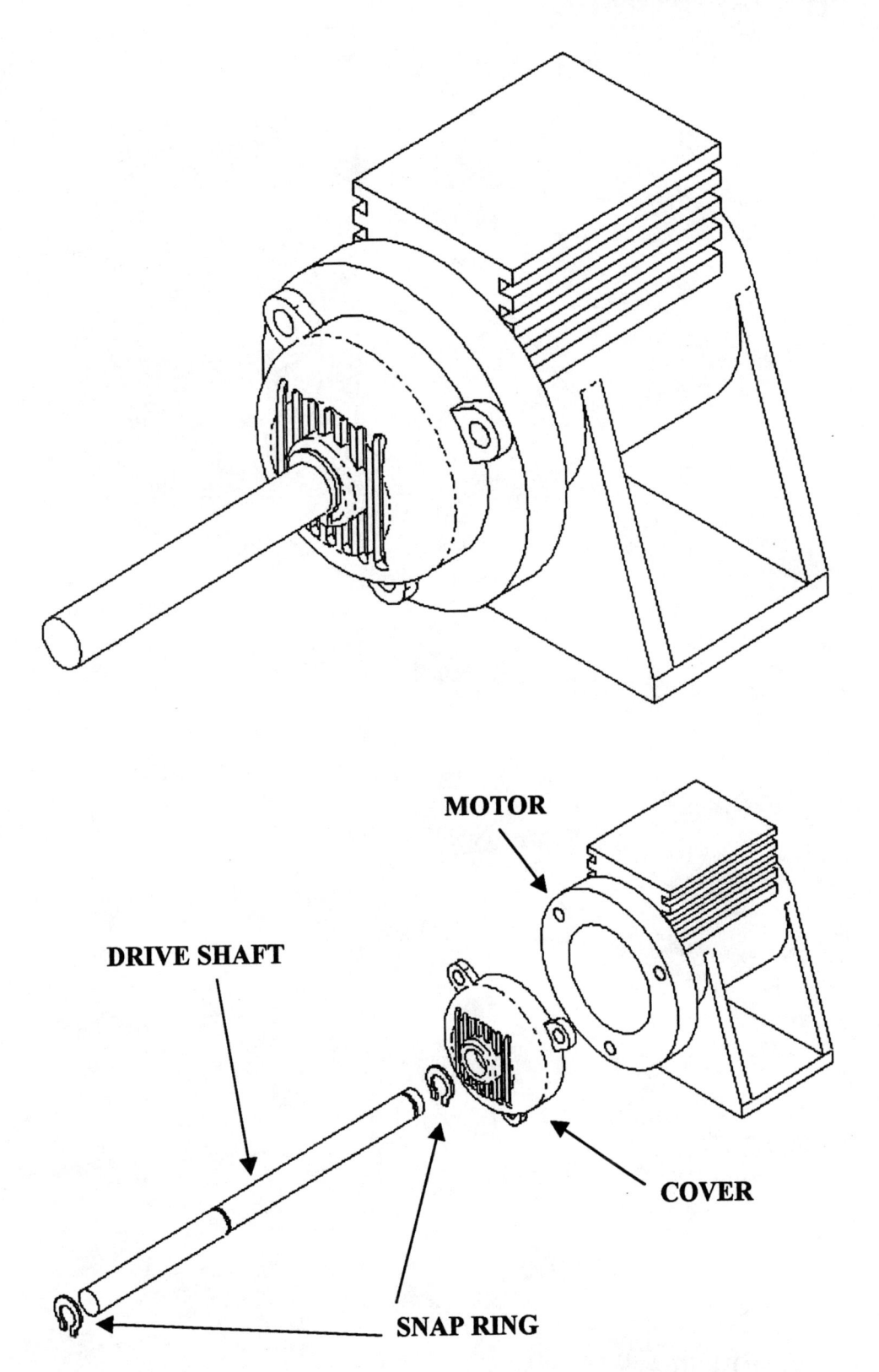

MOTOR

DRIVE SHAFT

COVER

SNAP RING

DESIGN PROJECT TUTORIAL

BLOWER Sub-Assembly

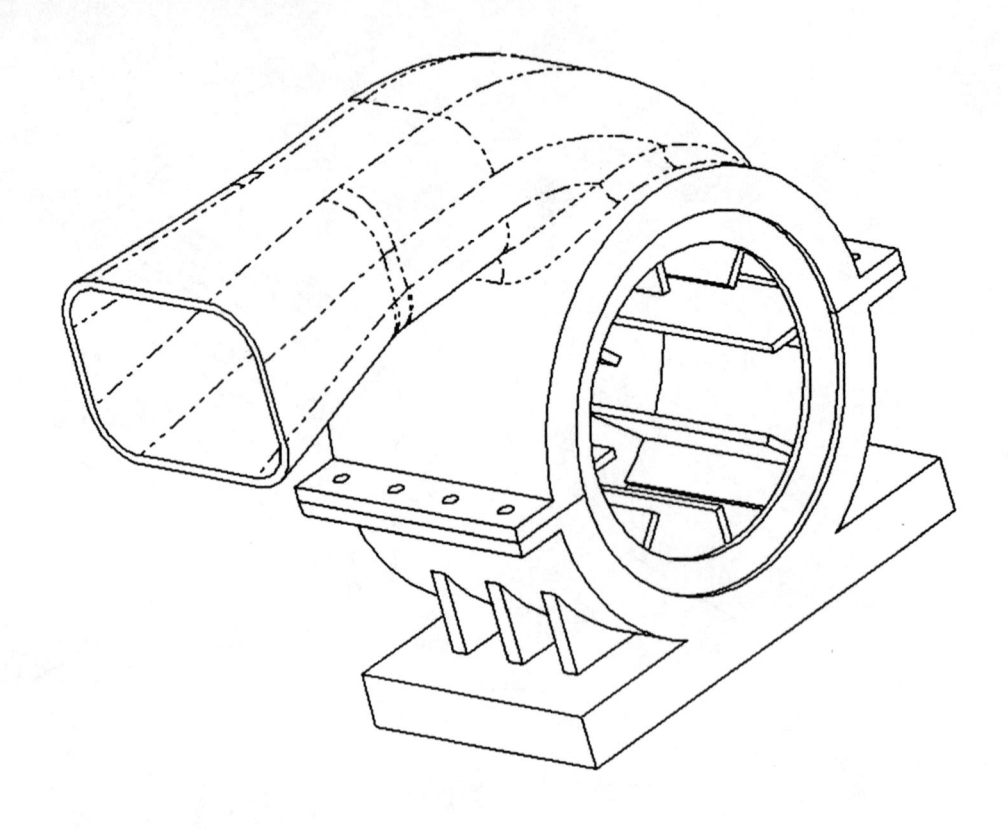

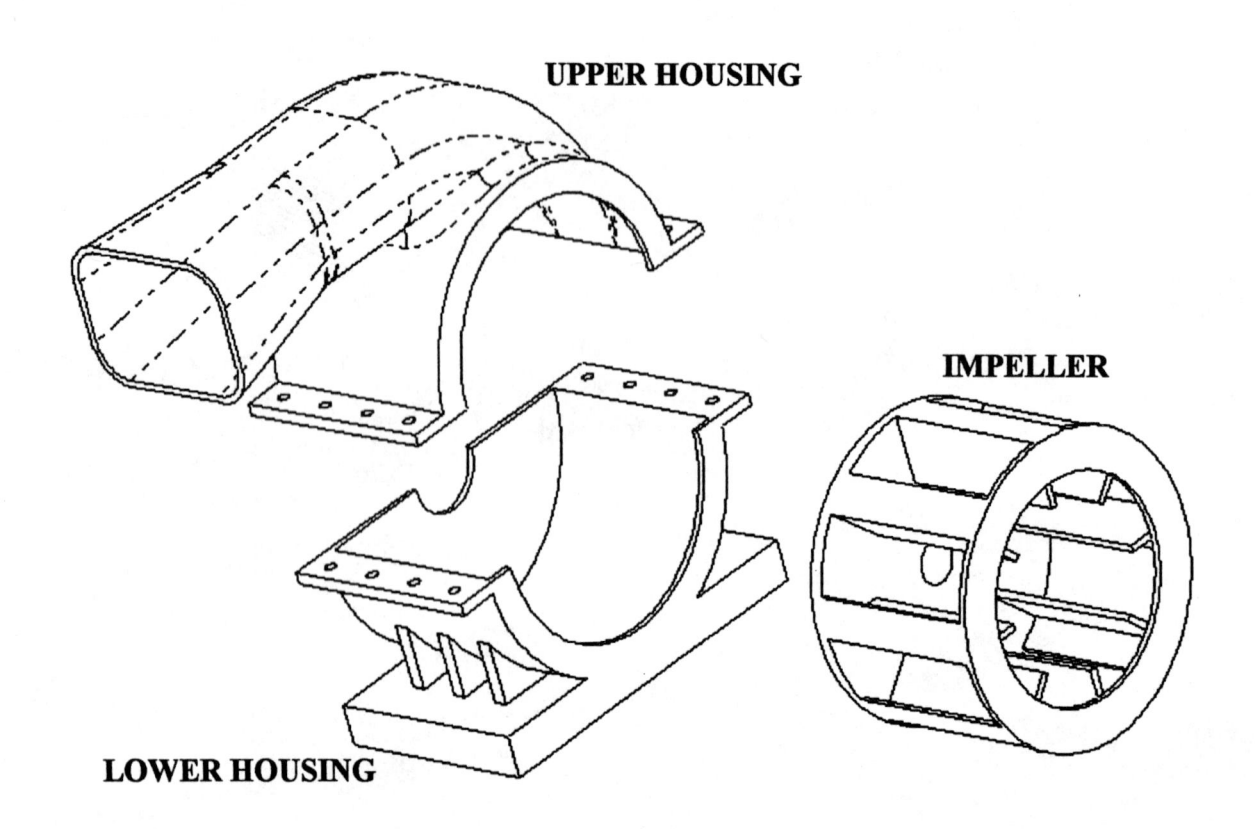

UPPER HOUSING

IMPELLER

LOWER HOUSING

iv

DESIGN PROJECT TUTORIAL

AIR HANDLER (top level) Assembly

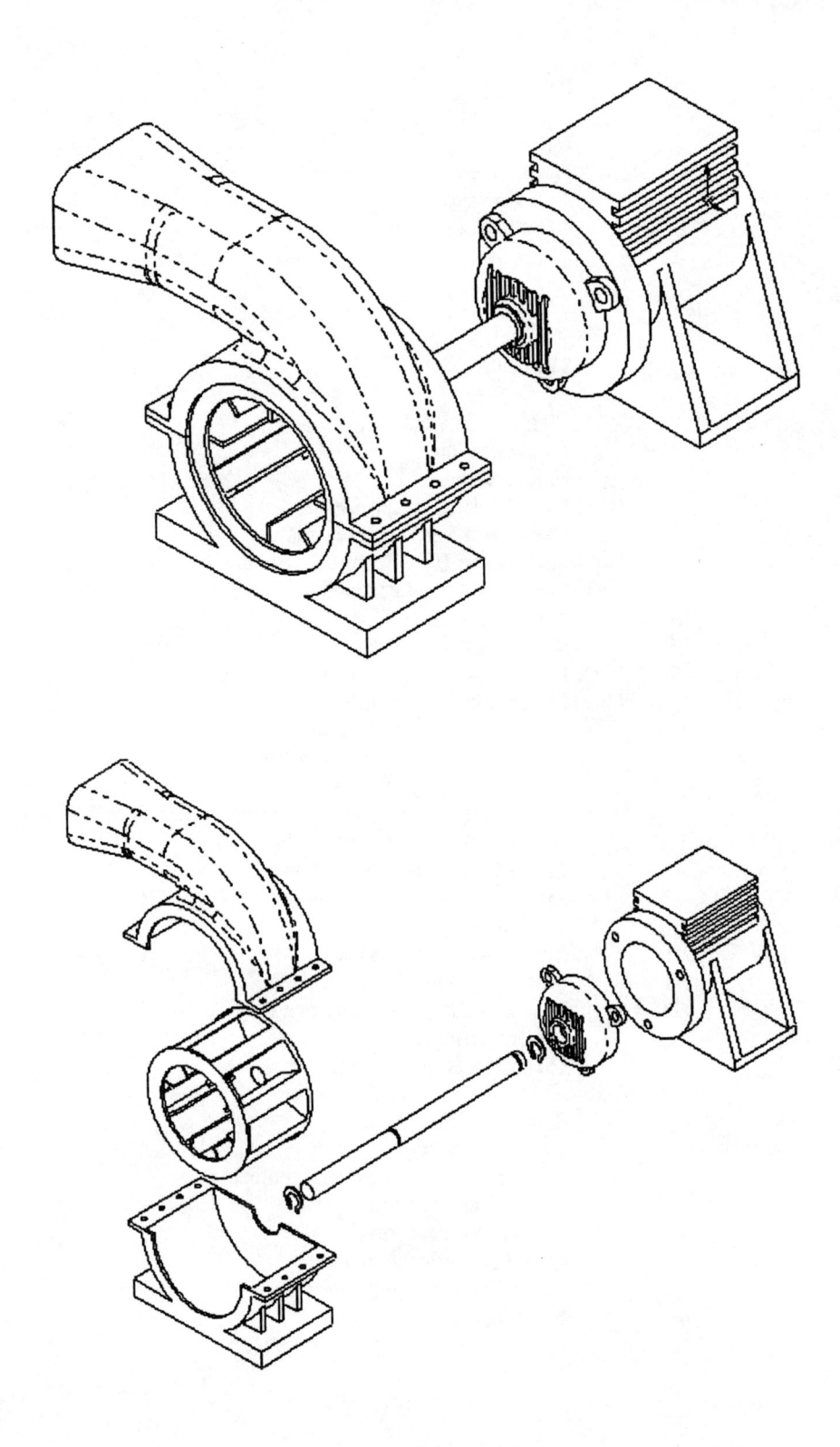

Table of Contents

Prefatory Item	Page Number
Introduction	i
Design Project Introduction	ii
Text Conventions	viii
Acknowledgements	ix

Tutorial Exercise	Design Project Assignment	Title	
1		Chamfer Creation	1-1
2		Fillet Creation	2-1
3		Hole Creation	3-1
4		Extruded Boss & Cut Creation	4-1
5		Cylindrical Base Feature Creation	5-1
6		Rectangular Base Feature Creation	6-1
7		Construction Plane Creation	7-1
	1A	Drive Shaft, partial part	D1-1
	1B	Motor, partial part	D1-2
	1C	Lower Housing, partial part	D1-4
8		Library Feature Creation	8-1
9		Library Feature Application	9-1
10		Geometric Relations in Sketches	10-1
11		Model and Sketch Editing	11-1
12		Feature Suppression, Reorder, and Insertion with Rollback	12-1
13		Feature Conflicts & Conflict Resolution	13-1
14		Linear Pattern in One Direction	14-1
15		Linear Pattern in Two Directions & Pattern Redefintion	15-1
	2A	Drive Shaft, complete part	D2-1
	2B	Snap Ring, complete part	D2-2
	2C	Motor, part modifications	D2-5
	2D	Lower Housing, part modifications	D2-8
	2E	Cover, partial part	D2-9
16		Creating a Base Sweep	16-1
17		Creating a Revolved Boss Loft	17-1
18		Creating a Basic Drawing	18-1
19		Detailed Drawing	19-1
20		Circular Pattern: Impeller, complete part	20-1
	3A	Upper Housing, partial part	D3-1
	3B	Cover, complete part	D3-7
	4A	Snap Ring drawing, partial	D4-1
	4B	Drive Shaft drawing, complete	D4-2
	4C	Motor drawing, partial	D4-3

Table of Contents, continued

Tutorial Exercise	Design Project Assignment	Title	Page Number
21		Mirror All	21-1
22		Feature Mirror	22-1
23		Equations & Properties	23-1
24		Part Configurations & Design Tables	24-1
25		Assembly Creation	25-1
26		Exploded View Creation	26-1
	5A	Motor, part modifications	D5-1
	5B	Upper Housing, part complete	D5-3
	5C	Lower Housing, part complete	D5-4
	5D	Impeller, blade spacing equation	D5-7
	6A	Motor Subassembly, complete	D6-1
	6B	Blower Subassembly, complete	D6-3
27		Assembly Modifications, Inquiries, and Drawings	27-1
28		Use of Layout Sketches and Part Creation within an Assembly	28-1
29		Creating an SLA file	29-1
30		Part Modeling Review	30-1
	7A	Motor, part complete	D7-1
	8A	Motor Drawing, complete	D8-1
	9A	Air Handler Assembly, complete	D9-1

Appendices

A	SolidWorks99® Menu Options	A-1
B	Software Configuration	B-1
C	Contents of Accompanying 3.5" Diskette	C-1

Text Conventions

The default software settings are listed in Appendix B. It is recommended to implement these minor changes before beginning the first exercise.

NOMENCLATURE	MEANING
Insert ▼ Pattern/Mirror ▶ Linear Pattern...	This is a sequence of menu selections that leads to execution of a single command, e.g., *Linear Pattern* in this example. See Appendix A for a complete description of embedded menus within SolidWorks.
OK **Esc** **Enter** **Ctrl** **Shift**	The bold *Arial* font shows that a button, either on the keyboard or in a software window, is to be pressed.
Click **Select** **Toggle** **Pick**	Select the prescribed item with a single push of the left mouse button.
Double click	Select the prescribed item with a double push of the left mouse button.
Right click	Push the right mouse button once.
Bold face type	Bold face type generally indicates the choice of selections from a flipdown list, an icon to be pressed, or a numerical value to be entered.
Italics type	Italics general refers to an area where a selection is to be entered, not the entry or selection itself.

Preface

This text is intended to introduce a new user to solid modeling with SolidWorks 99 using step-by-step tutorial instructions. This first edition does not contain chapter introductions, supplemental exercises, or review questions, but these may be added in subsequent editions.

Acknowledgements

All models were produced using SolidWorks 99, a copyrighted product of SolidWorks Corporation. Portions of SolidWorks 99 software are copyrighted by D-Cubed Limited, Softsource, Spatial Technology, Inc., and Summit Software Co.

All images in the text, except certain drawing images, were produced using Corel Photo House, version 1.00.170, by Corel Corporation. Text documents were produced using Microsoft Word 2000 by Microsoft Corporation. Certain drawing images were enhanced using AutoCAD LT97 by Autodesk.

Many part configurations and part names are borrowed from "Autodesk Mechanical Desktop Tutorial Student Version 1" by Jacob Halim, as published by Orange Software Publishing of Fountain Valley, CA, and from "Pro/ENGINEER Basic Design Training Guide Version 18" by Parametric Technology Corporation of Waltham, MA, and self-published.

©2000 by Donald E. Coho, York, PA, USA. All right reserved. This document may not be copied, photocopied, reproduced, transmitted, or translated in any form or for any purpose without the express written consent of the publisher, Schroff Development Corporation.

Exercise 1 - Chamfer Creation

In this exercise you will create chamfers on an edge using two different dimensioning methods, called **Angle-Distance** and **Distance-Distance**.

2 Edges
Angle-Distance
(Step 1)

4 Edges
Distance-Distance
(Step 2)

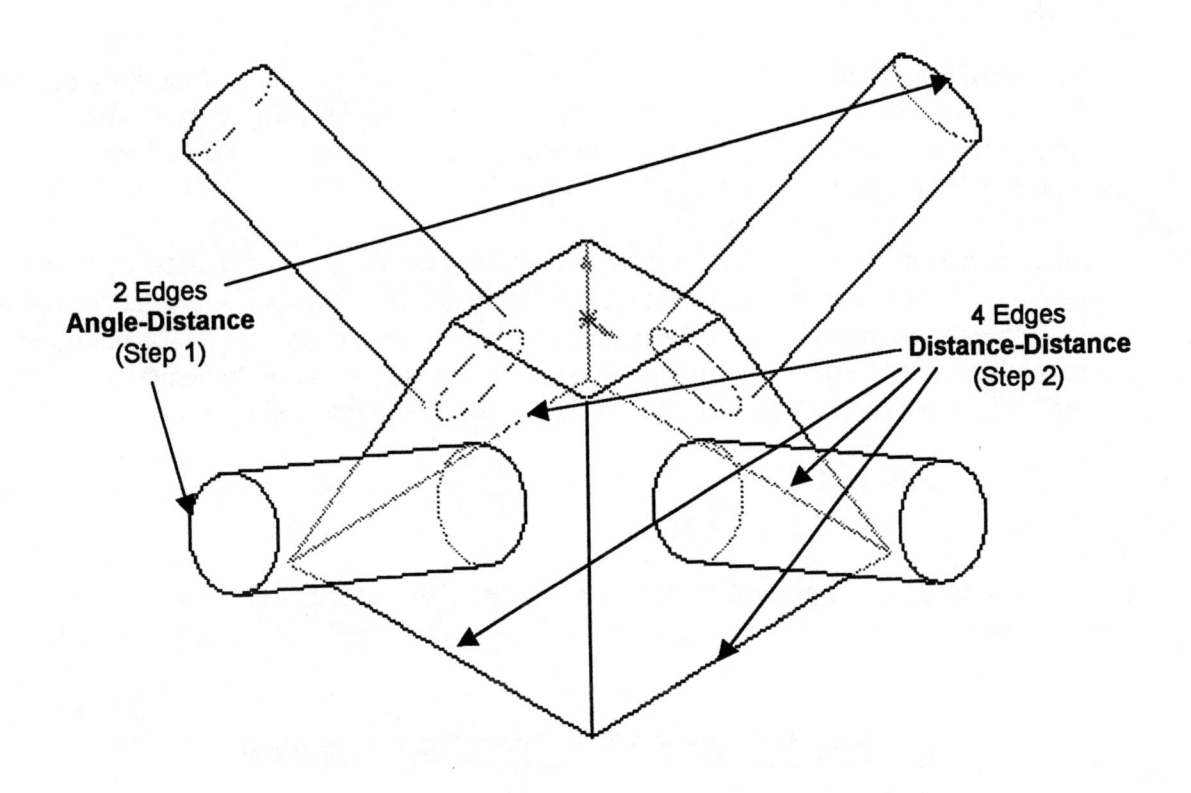

Figure X1-1

Step 1: Open the file WIDGET.SLDPRT and add the first chamfers to the model. They will be located at the two edges of the circular extrusion using the *Angle-Distance* chamfer type as shown on Figure X1-1.

A. Open the part file widget.SLDPRT using **File ▼ Open...** or the tool: from the *Standard Toolbar*.

B. Observe the contents of the *FeatureManager* design tree at the left side of the part window.

DESIGN PROJECT TUTORIAL

C. Guide the mouse pointer around over top of the model image. The normal mouse pointing arrow will be accompanied by either a vertical line or a waving flag at various positions over the model.

The vertical line means that the current location of the mouse pointer will result in the selection of an edge. The waving flag means that the current location of the mouse pointer will result in the selection of a surface or "face." The outline of the edge or face will be highlighted as cyan color.

D. Select (with a left click) the circular <u>edge</u> at the top of the front left cylindrical extrusion (see Figure X1-1). Hold down the **CTRL** button on the keyboard and select the circular edge at the top of the right rear cylindrical extrusion (holding down the **CTRL** button adds entities to the current selection set and allows a single operation to be performed on many entities at once). Both of the edges should be highlighted in blue.

E. Press the **Chamfer** tool: to reveal the *Chamfer Feature* dialog.

F. Select **Angle-Distance** as the *Chamfer Type*, enter **1.00in** as the *Distance* by clicking inside the window and editing the text, enter **45deg** as the *Angle*, and depress the **OK** button.

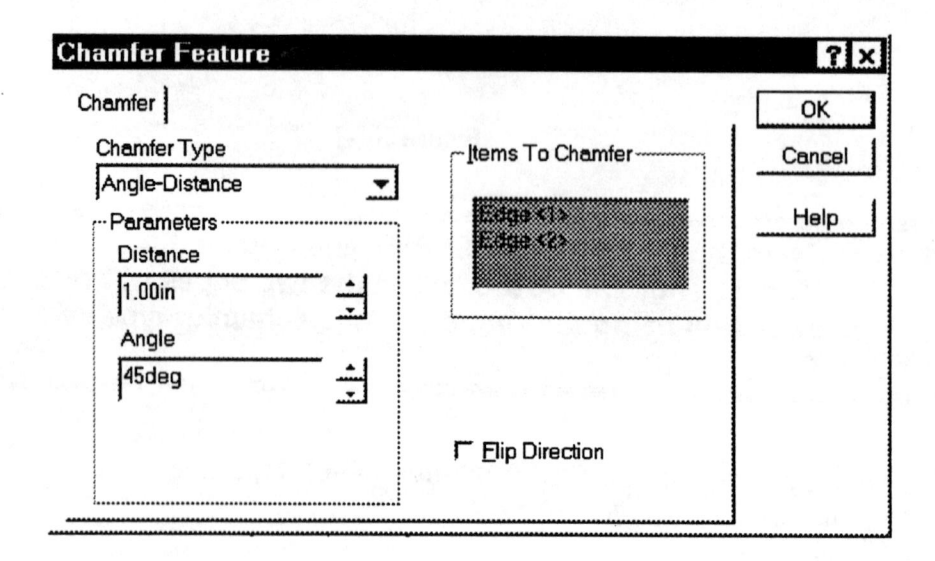

DESIGN PROJECT TUTORIAL

| Step 2: | The second chamfer will be added to the four edges at the bottom of the model using the *Distance-Distance* chamfer type, as shown on Figure X1-1. |

A. Select (with a left click) the four edges to be chamfered around the bottom surface of the part (see Figure X1-1) (remember to hold down the **CTRL** button for the second, third, and fourth edge selection).

B. Again press the **Chamfer** tool to reveal the *Chamfer Feature* dialog.

C. Select **Distance-Distance** as the *Chamfer Type*, enter **1.00in** as the *Distance 1* by clicking inside the window and editing the text and enter **2.00in** as the *Distance 2*.

You may have wondered, "How will the software decide in which direction to apply the distances?" Drag and drop the *Chamfer Feature* dialog into a position where you can see an olive colored preview arrow (Figure X1-2).

The *Distance 2* will be applied in the direction shown by this preview arrow. If the preview arrow points upward along one of the inclined surfaces the *Distance 2* will be measured along the inclined surfaces as shown on Figure X1-3, and the *Distance 1* will applied perpendicular along the bottom surface of the part.

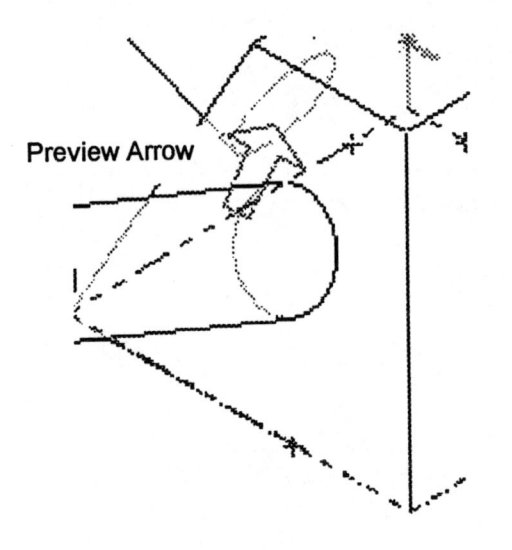

Figure X1-2

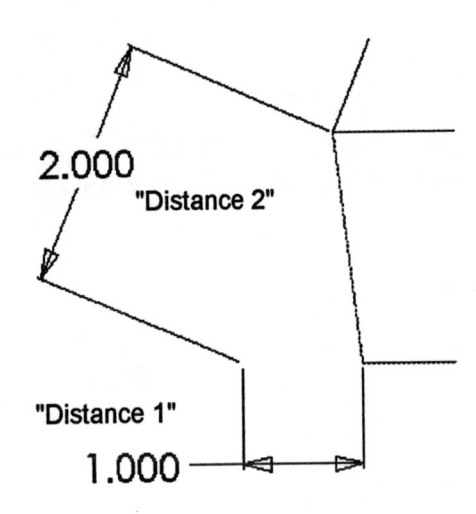

Figure X1-3

DESIGN PROJECT TUTORIAL

D. If your preview arrow is pointing horizontally into the bottom surface of the part, instead of upward along one of the inclined surfaces, then change the *Distance 1* to **2.00in** and change the *Distance 2* to **1.00in.**

E. Press the **OK** button within the *Chamfer Feature* dialog to finalize the feature.

The final model should look like this:

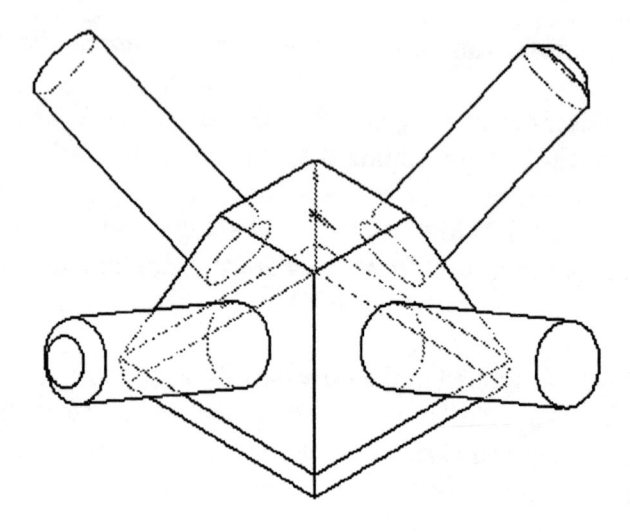

Figure X1-4

You may save the modified file to your own personal media (3.5" diskette, ZIP® disk, etc.) using the **File ▼ Save As...** command if you wish.

End of Exercise 1.

DESIGN PROJECT TUTORIAL

Exercise 2 - Fillet Creation

In this exercise you will create four simple fillets and rounds using the **Fillet** command. The difference between a "fillet" and a "round" is a matter of semantics--a round applies to an external edge and a fillet applies to an internal edge, but both are created using the **Fillet** command.
The first and second rounds are created using a **Constant Radius** fillet type. The third round is created on four edges using a **Variable Radius** fillet type, and the fourth round will be created by taking advantage of a helpful software capability, called "Propagate to Tangent Faces."

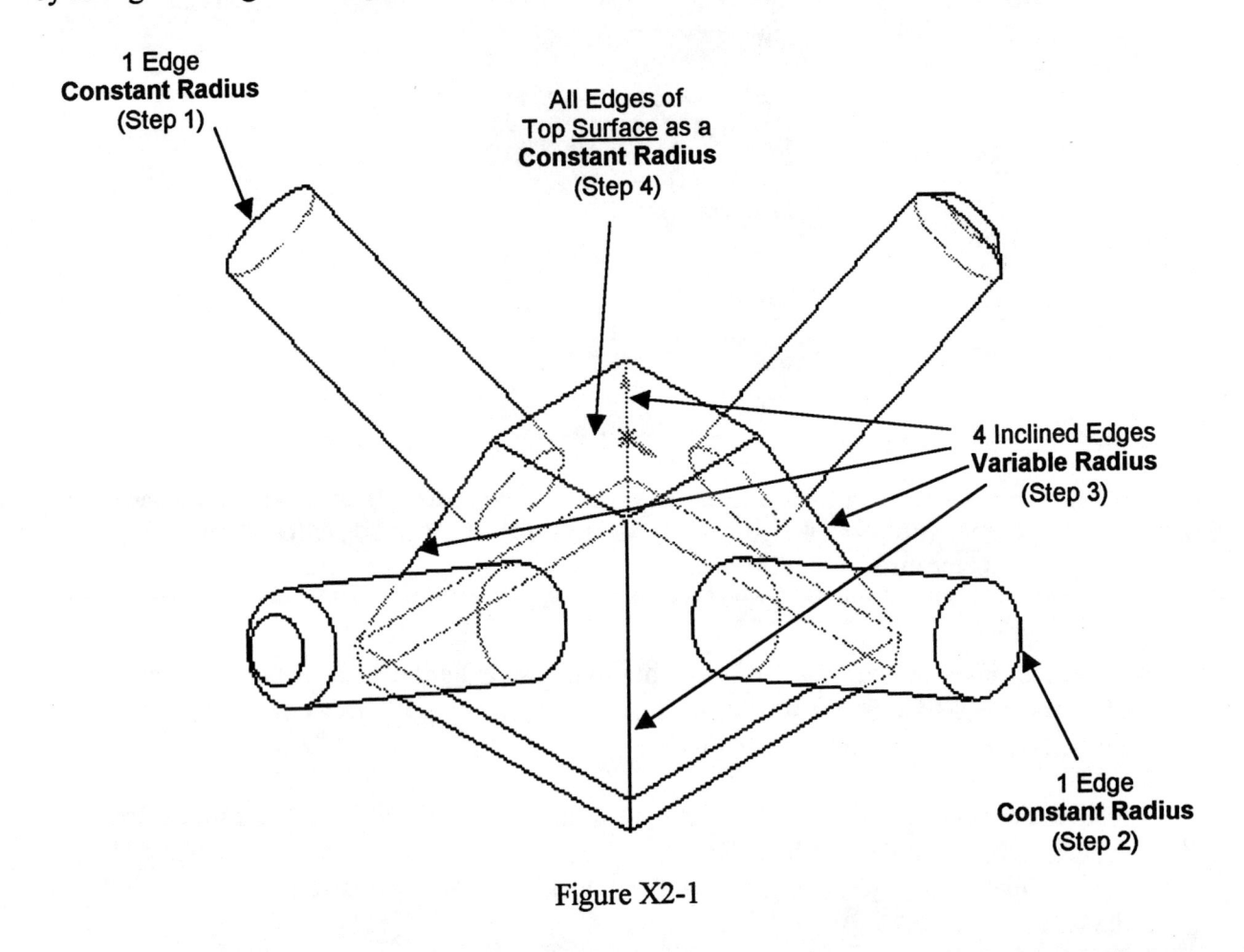

Figure X2-1

Step 1: Add the first edge round as a simple *Constant Radius* type with a radius value of 1.50in.

A. Open the file `widget.sldprt`.

B. Select (with a left click) the single circular edge at the top of the left rear cylindrical extrusion and press the **Fillet** tool: to reveal the *Fillet Feature* dialog.

C. Select **Constant Radius** as the *Fillet Type*, enter **1.50in** as the *Radius* value. See Figure X2-2 for the desired appearance of the left side of the dialog, check your inputs and selections, and press the **OK** button to create the fillet.

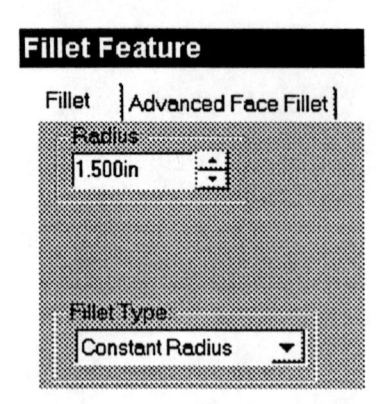

Figure X2-2

Step 2: Add the second edge round as a simple *Constant Radius* type with a radius value of 1.25in.

A. Select the single circular edge at top of the front right cylindrical extrusion, press the **Fillet** tool, select **Constant Radius** as the *Fillet Type*, enter **1.25in** as the *Radius* value, and press the **OK** button to create the fillet.

B. Note in the *FeatureManager* design tree, near the bottom, that **Fillet1** and **Fillet 2** now appear in the feature list, or hierarchy. Select **Fillet1** in the *FeatureManager* and notice how the fillet is highlighted in green on the model. Next select **Fillet2** to highlight it on the model.

C. Right Click with the mouse pointer over top of **Fillet 2** in the *FeatureManager* design tree. Select **Edit Definition** and change the *Radius* value to **1.00in** and press the **OK** button. The model quickly and automatically updates to the new radius value.

DESIGN PROJECT TUTORIAL

Step 3: Create four simple rounds at once as the *Variable Radius* type. Note the four vertical edges for this step from Figure X2-1. The radius at the bottom of each edge will be 0.00in, and the radius at the top of each edge will be 2.00in.

A. Select the four vertical inclined edges (remember to hold down the **CTRL** button on the keyboard as you select the second, third, and fourth edges to add them to the selection set).

B. Click on the **Fillet** tool and change the *Fillet Type* to **Variable Radius.** Note the change in appearance in the *Items to Fillet* area of the dialog--the *Vertex List* has been added to the pre-existing *Edge Fillet Items*.

C. Scroll up and down in the *Vertex List* window using the **Scroll Up** and **Scroll Down** arrow buttons [⇕]. How many vertices show in the window? A separate radius value can be stored for each of the eight vertices. How many edges show in the *Edge Fillet Item* window, and how does the number of edges relate to the number of vertices?

D. Click on **V1** and type **0.00in** in the *Radius* window. Do not press the **Enter** key after typing the radius value because this action will finalize the creation of the rounds.

E. Click on **V2** and type **2.00in** in the *Radius* window.

F. Enter a *Radius* value of **0.00in** one-at-a-time for **V3, V5,** and **V7.** Use the **Scroll Down** arrow button [▼] to see the higher numbered vertices.

G. Enter a *Radius* value of **2.00in** one-at-a-time for **V4, V6,** and **V8.**

H. Check the *Radius* values for each vertex by scrolling up or down to view the entire *Vertex List*. The odd-numbered vertices should have a *Radius* value of **0.00in**, and the even-numbered vertices should have a *Radius* value of **2.00in**. If these are all correct then press the **OK** button to create the rounds. Your model should look like Figure X2-3:

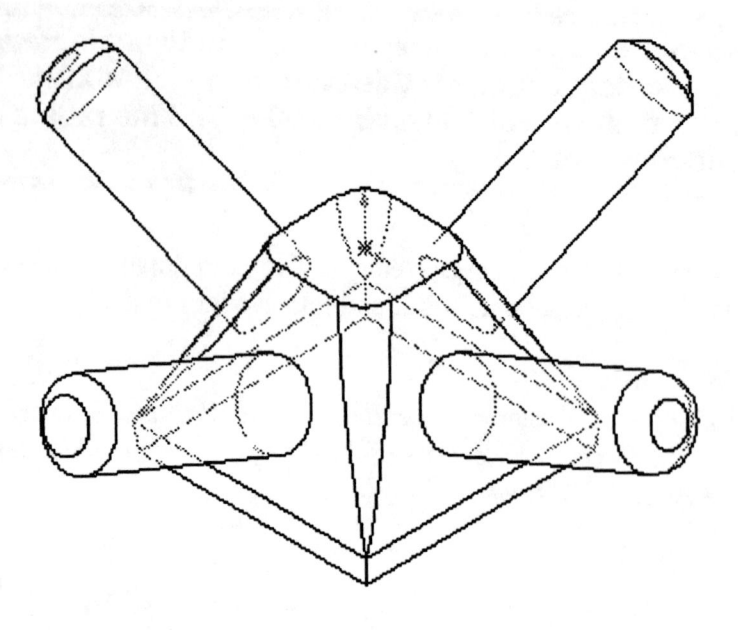

Figure X2-3

Step 4: Add the fourth edge round as a simple *Constant Radius* type with a radius value of 1.50in by selecting only *one* edge.

A. Select any one of the four straight edges or any one of the four corner radii that form the boundary of the top surface of the object. Press the **Fillet** tool and enter a *Radius* value of **1.50in.**

B. Note that the **Propagate to Tangent Faces** checkbox is enabled (checked) by default. This selection will allow the round to extend itself or "propagate" to the other seven boundary edges of the top surface.

C. Press the **OK** button.

The final model should look like Figure X2-4:

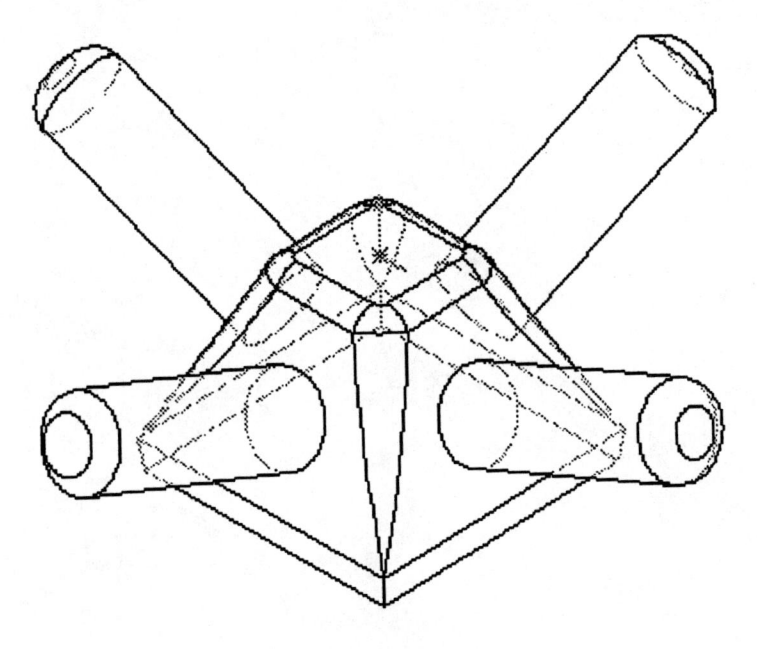

Figure X2-4

End of Exercise 2.

Exercise 3: Hole Creation

In this exercise you will create cylindrical and conical holes using several different depth options. The starting point part consists of a rectangular base feature, four fins, an Inlet pipe and a 270° Disk.

You will create a total of ten holes using four different types of holes (counterbored, tapered, countersunk, and straight) and five different definitions of "depth." The completed model is shown in Figure X3-11.

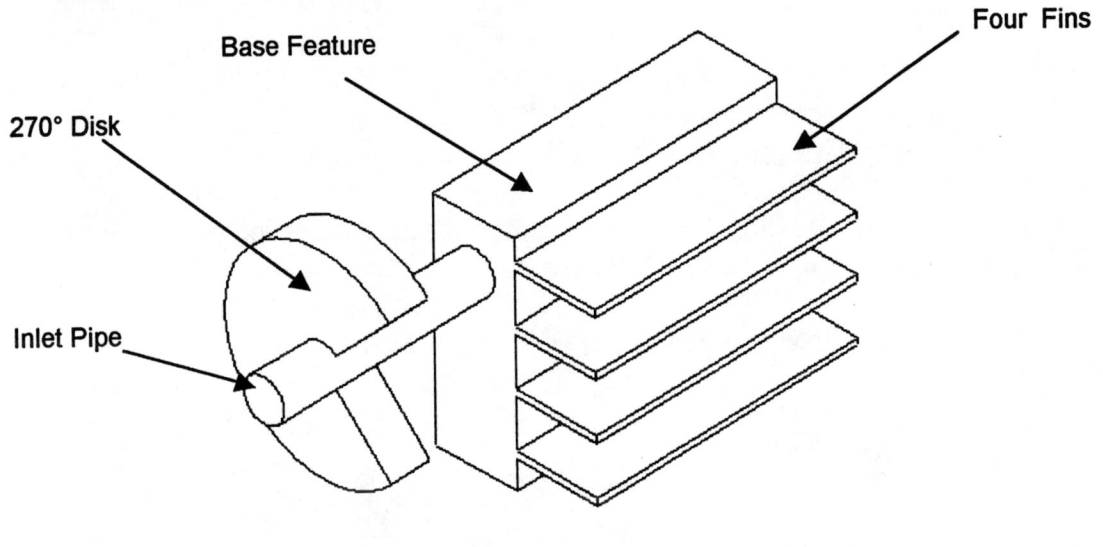

Figure X3-1

Step 1: Open the file HOLES.SLDPRT and add the first hole the model through all of the fins with a single feature definition.

A. Open the part file `holes.sldprt`.

B. Pick a placement point on the top of the uppermost fin as shown on Figure X3-2:

DESIGN PROJECT TUTORIAL

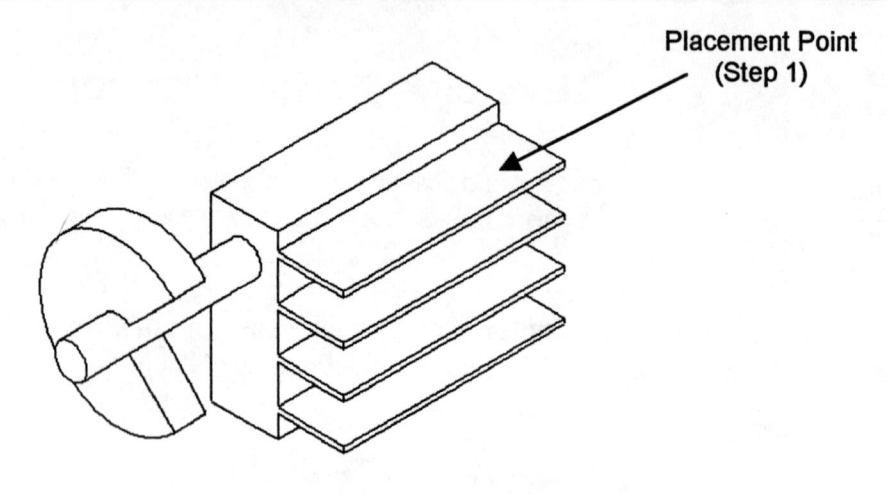

Figure X3-2

C. Select **Insert ▼ Features ▸ Hole ▸ Simple...** or the *Hole* tool:

D. Select **Through All** as the *Type* of hole in the *Hole Feature* dialog box, enter the *Diameter* as **1.500in**, and depress the **OK** button.

The hole is immediately created as shown in Figure X3-3:

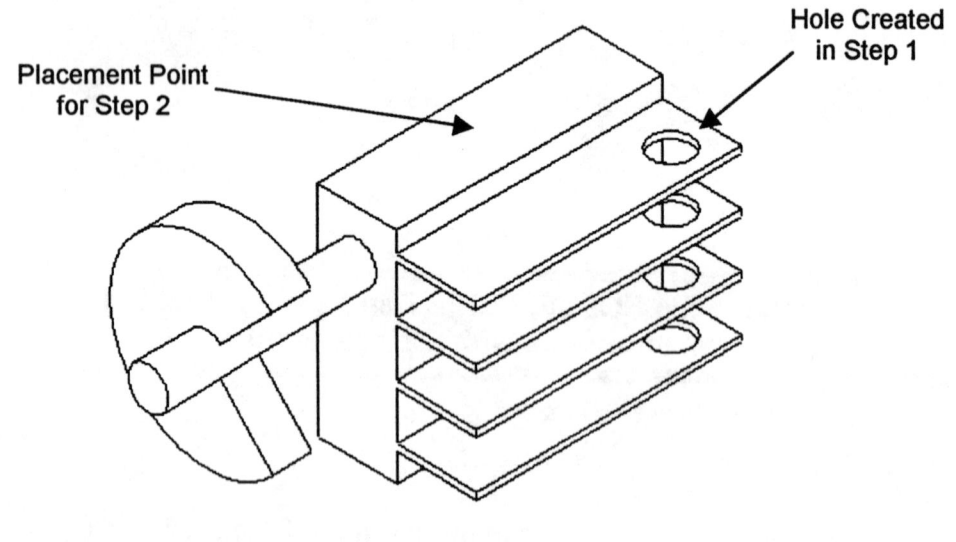

Figure X3-3

Step 2:   Create the second hole as a blind counterbored hole into the top of the *Base* feature.

A. Pick a placement point on the top of the base feature as shown on Figure X3-3.

DESIGN PROJECT TUTORIAL

B. Select **Insert ▾ Features ▸ Hole ▸ Wizard...** or the *Hole Wizard* tool:

C. Select **Counterbored** as the *Hole Type* from the flipdown menu and **Blind** as the *End Condition Type* in the *Hole Definition* dialog box. Input the following dimensional values by double clicking on the existing value, entering the new value, and pressing the **Enter** key:

        1.250in.   Diameter
        5.000in.   Depth
        2.500in.   C-Bore Diameter
        1.000in.   C-Bore Depth

Then press the **Next** button in the *Hole Definition* dialog and the **Finish** button in the *Hole Placement* dialog. The hole is immediately created as shown in Figure X3-4:

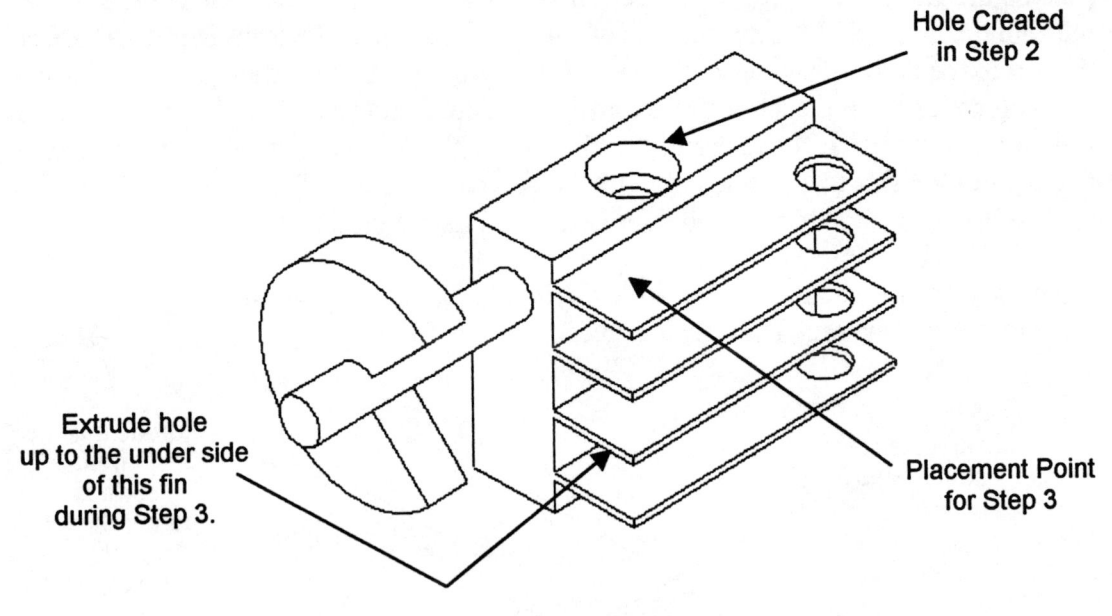

Figure X3-4

Step 3: Create the third hole passing through only three of the four fins with a single feature definition.

A. Pick a placement point on the top of the uppermost fin as shown on Figure X3-4.

B. Select **Insert ▾ Features ▸ Hole ▸ Wizard...** or the *Hole Wizard* tool:

DESIGN PROJECT TUTORIAL

C. Select **Tapered** as the *Hole Type* from the flipdown menu and **Up to Surface** as the *End Condition Type* in the *Hole Definition* dialog box. Input the following dimensional values by double clicking on the existing value, entering the new value, and pressing the **Enter** key:

           1.000in.   Minor Diameter
[**4.250in.**   Depth (do not change this one)]
           3.000in.   Major Diameter

D. **Click** inside the *Face* window and move the *Hole Definition* dialog box off to the side of the model image by "dragging and dropping" its *Title Bar* because you will be picking entities on the model and will need the dialog box to the side.

E. Move the mouse pointer to the upper surface of the third fin from the top (See Figure X3-4) but do not select yet. If you select with a left click on the top of the third fin the hole will not penetrate the whole way through it. Instead, **Right Click** over the top of the third fin and pick the **Select Other** option. Immediately, a small mouse tool will appear with the letter "Y" over the left mouse button and the letter "N" over the right mouse button. If the underside surface of the third fin is outlined with a blue dashed line then **Left Click (Y)** to select it. Otherwise, **Right Click (N)** until that underside surface becomes highlighted, and then **Left Click (Y)** to select it.

F. Then press the **Next** button in the *Hole Definition* dialog and the **Finish** button in the *Hole Placement* dialog. The hole is immediately created as shown in Figure X3-5:

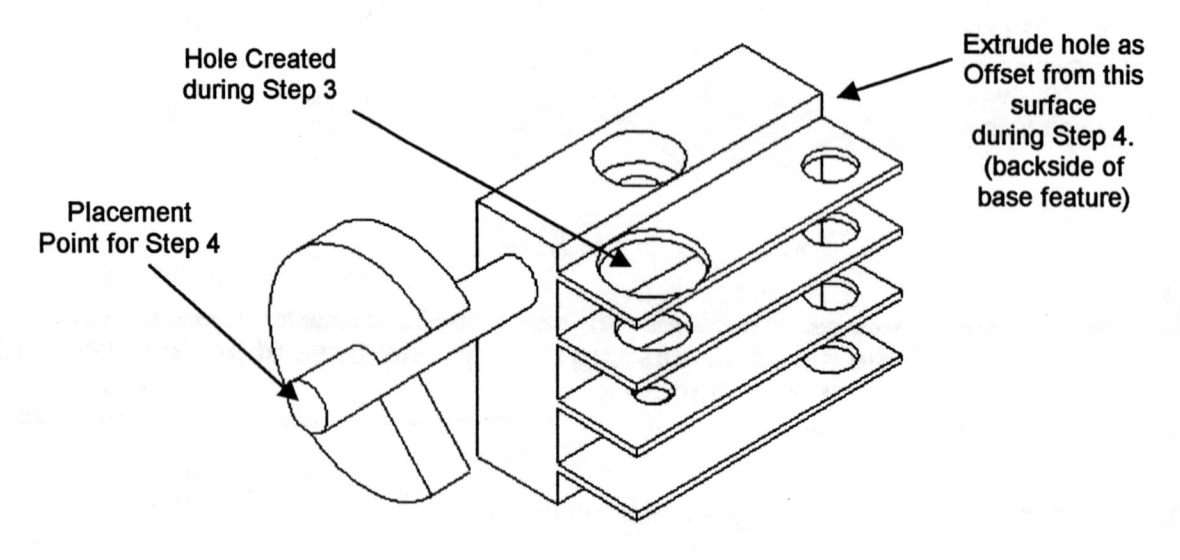

Figure X3-5

DESIGN PROJECT TUTORIAL

Step 4: **Create the fourth hole on the axis of the Inlet Pipe.**

A. Pick a placement point on the end of the Inlet Pipe as shown on Figure X3-5.

B. Select **Insert ▼ Features ▶ Hole ▶ Simple...** or the *Hole* tool:

C. Select **Offset from Surface** as the *Type* of hole in the *Hole Feature* dialog box, enter the *Offset* as **6.000in.**, and enter the *Diameter* as **0.500in.**

D. **Click** inside the *Selected Items* window and move the *Hole Feature* dialog box off to the side of the model image by "dragging and dropping" its *Title Bar*.

Point the mouse *anywhere* over the back surface of the Base Feature as shown in Figure X3-5. You will need to use *Select Other* again. Just right click over the hidden surface and then use **Left Click (Y)** and **Right Click (N)** as you did before until the back surface of the Base Feature is highlighted in blue.

E. Depress the **OK** button in the *Hole Feature* dialog box. The hole is immediately created as shown in Figure X3-6:

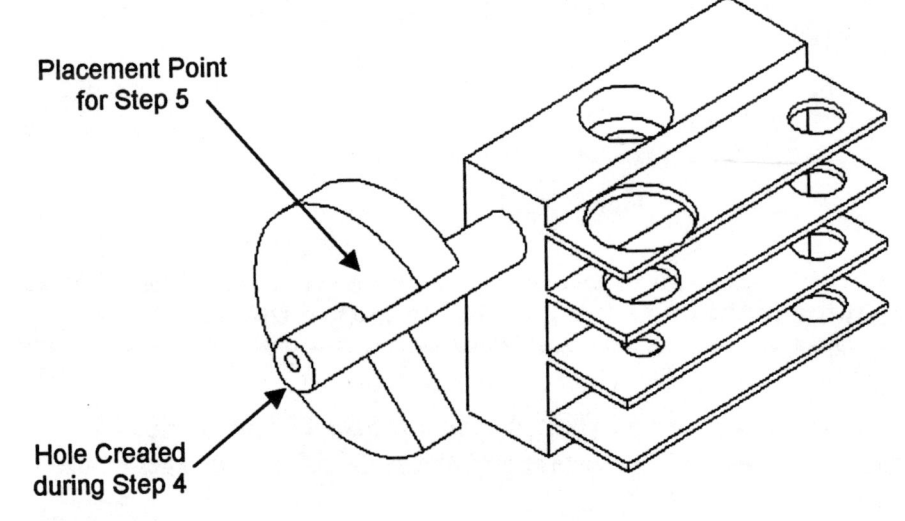

Figure X3-6

Step 5: **Create the final hole in the 270° Disk.**

A. Pick a placement point on the front of the 270° Disk as shown on Figure X3-6.

B. Select **Insert ▼ Features ▶ Hole ▶ Wizard...** or the *Hole Wizard* tool:

DESIGN PROJECT TUTORIAL

C. Select **Countersunk** as the *Hole Type* from the flipdown menu and select **Up to Next** as the *End Condition Type* in the *Hole Definition* dialog box. Input the following dimensional values by double clicking on the existing value, entering the new value, and pressing the **Enter** key:

	1.250in.	Diameter
[	1.500in.	Depth (do not change this one)]
[	82.00deg	C-Sink Angle (do not change this one)]
	2.000in.	C-Bore Depth

D. Then press the **Next** button in the *Hole Definition* dialog and the **Finish** button in the *Hole Placement* dialog. The hole is immediately created as shown in Figure X3-7:

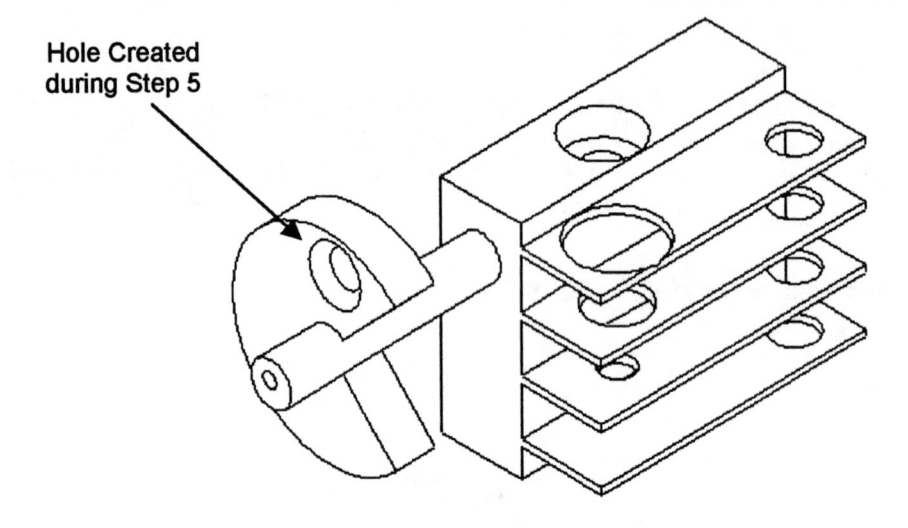

Hole Created during Step 5

Figure X3-7

Step 6: Constrain the location of the hole in the end of the Inlet Pipe.

During this Exercise all of the holes have been created in an *unconstrained* condition. This means that the locations of the hole centerlines are approximate, based upon inexact mouse picks on the placement surfaces.

Let's say that the concentricity of the hole in the Inlet Pipe to its outside surface is critical to the part design. Constraining this relationship between the hole and the outside surface of the Inlet Pipe will ensure the satisfaction of the stated design intent.

A. **Right Click** over *Hole4* (or whatever is the name of your hole in the Inlet Pipe) on the *FeatureManager* design tree and select **Edit Sketch** from the popup menu.

DESIGN PROJECT TUTORIAL

B. There are three different ways to change your direction of viewing a part or assembly. To change to a **Front** view of the part we can simply click the **Front** tool on the *View* toolbar:

Alternatively, we can press the **Spacebar** on the keyboard or select **View ▼ Orientation** to access the *View Orientation* dialog:

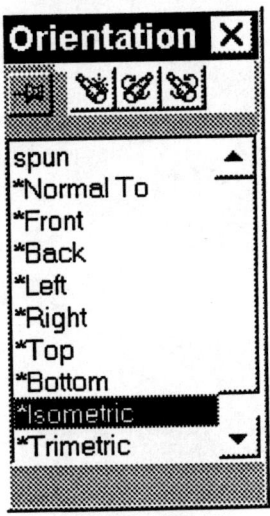

Figure X3-8

You can simply **double click** on one of the named views in this dialog to change the direction of viewing the part.

C. Zoom in on the end of the Inlet Pipe by selecting **View ▼ Modify ▶ Zoom to Area** and dragging a small rectangle centered around the end of the Inlet Pipe. Alternatively, the **Zoom to Area** tool: can be depressed to activate the zoom command.

Press **ESCAPE** if you lose control of the zooming operation. Use the **Pan** and **Zoom to Fit** command tools if you get lost.
Undo will always reverse an undesired action or result:

3-7

The result of the your zoom command should resemble Figure X3-9:

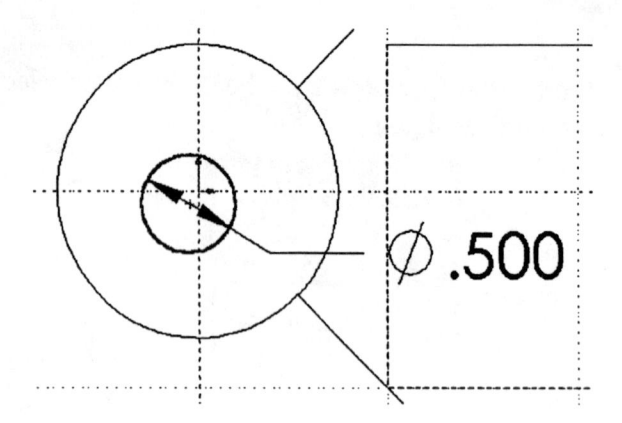

Figure X3-9

The actual position of your blue circle will depend upon the accuracy with which you picked the placement point in Step 4.

Note the inexact location of the hole and that the hole circumference is shown in blue. A feature which shows in blue is not fully constrained. Since your objective is to fully constrain the hole you will have succeeded when the hole circumference shows in the fully constrained color, black.

Click on the **Zoom to Area** tool again or press **Esc** to de-activate this feature.

D. Go to the **View▼** pulldown menu. If *Temporary Axes* is not already checked then **click** on it once to turn them on.

E. Select (**left click**) on the center point of the blue circle. Hold down the **CTRL** button and select the axis (center line) of the Inlet Pipe. Both should now be selected.

F. Click on the **Add Relations** tool: to reveal the *Add Geometric Relations* dialog box.

DESIGN PROJECT TUTORIAL

G. Select the **Coincident** radio button, press **Apply**, and press **Close:**

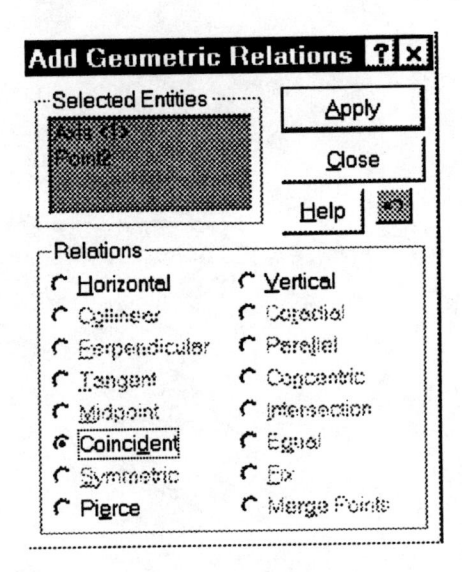

Figure X3-10

The model will rebuild with the hole and outside surface of the Inlet Pipe in a concentric relationship. The hole should now be black.

H. Click the **Sketch** tool: to end the sketch modification.

I. Select **View ▼ Orientation...** and **Double Click** on *Isometric* to return to a pictorial view of the model or **click** on the tool:

The final model should look like Figure X3-11:

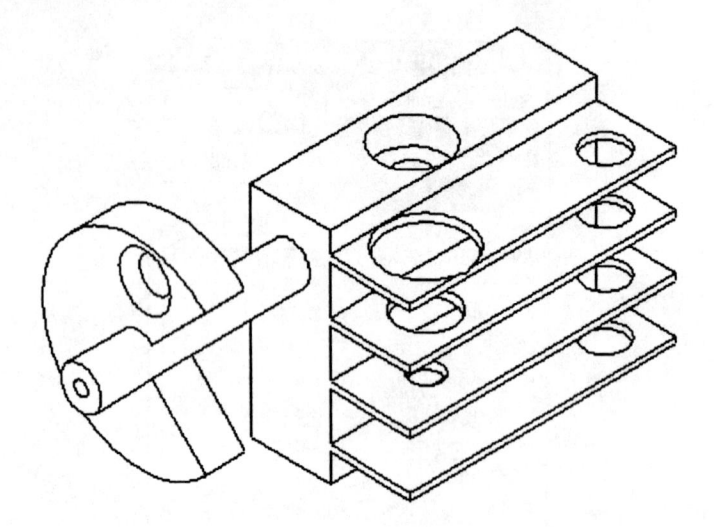

Figure X3-11

End of Exercise 3.

Exercise 4: Extruded Boss and Cut Creation

The first feature of any part, which creates its initial volume and mass, is called the *base* feature. After the creation of this *base* feature, a *boss* adds material and a *cut* removes material from a part.

In the previous three exercises we only performed operations which removed material from a given part. In this exercise we will create one extruded cut and one extruded boss on a given base feature using sketched profiles.

Sketch profiles allow the creation of both simple and complex geometries. Unlike the process of creating chamfers, rounds, and cylindrical holes, where creativity and uniqueness were extremely limited, the creation of sketched features frees the design process.

This freedom arises from the many options for sketched feature creation:
- Choice of sketching plane or surface
- Actual shape of the feature's cross-section (as sketched)
- Size and location of the feature's cross-section (as dimensioned and constrained)
- Type of feature (base, boss, or cut)
- Method of feature generation (extrusion, revolution, or a more complex method)
- Defining attributes for the extrusion or revolution of the sketch [directions and depths (for extrusions) or angular extents (for revolutions)]

Figures X4-1 and X4-2 show the "before" and "after" appearances of the part:

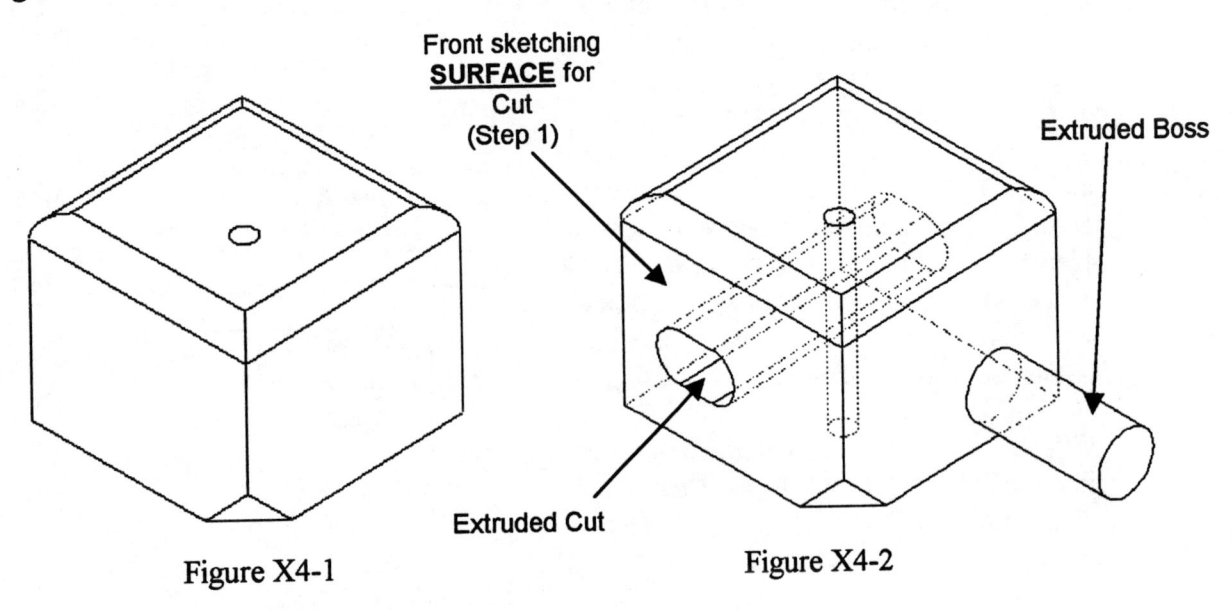

Figure X4-1

Figure X4-2

| Step 1: | Open the file BOSS_CUT.SLDPRT and prepare for sketching the cross-section of the *Extruded Cut*. |

A.   Open the file `boss_cut.SLDPRT`.

DESIGN PROJECT TUTORIAL

B. Select the front <u>surface</u> of the object (watch for the *waving flag* cursor).

C. Toggle the **Sketch** tool:

D. Select **View, Orientation...** and double click on **Front** *or* click the tool:

Step 2: Become familiar with the *Sketch* toolbar, draw a centerline, and draw the horizontal top and bottom lines of the cut using mirroring.

Four of the command tools from the **Sketch** toolbar are very likely to be used during this Step. Their functions are mainly self-explanatory with the possible exception of **Mirror Objects.**

With a single centerline selected and highlighted, clicking the **Mirror Objects** tool will cause all objects sketched on one side of the centerline to be mirrored to the opposite side of the centerline. Please note that sketching objects which cross over from one side of the centerline to the other side is undesirable.

Sketch a **Line**

Sketch a **Tangent Arc**

Sketch a **Centerline**

Mirror Objects (during sketching)

A. Click the **Centerline** tool and sketch the centerline approximately in the center of the object face as shown in Figure X4-4. Watch for the "**H**" inferencing on the mouse pointer which indicates that the sketched centerline is assumed to be horizontal.

B. With the centerline still highlighted in green click the **Mirror Objects** tool. Then select **Line** and draw a horizontal line either above or below the centerline.

C. Click the **Mirror Objects** tool to deactivate mirroring.

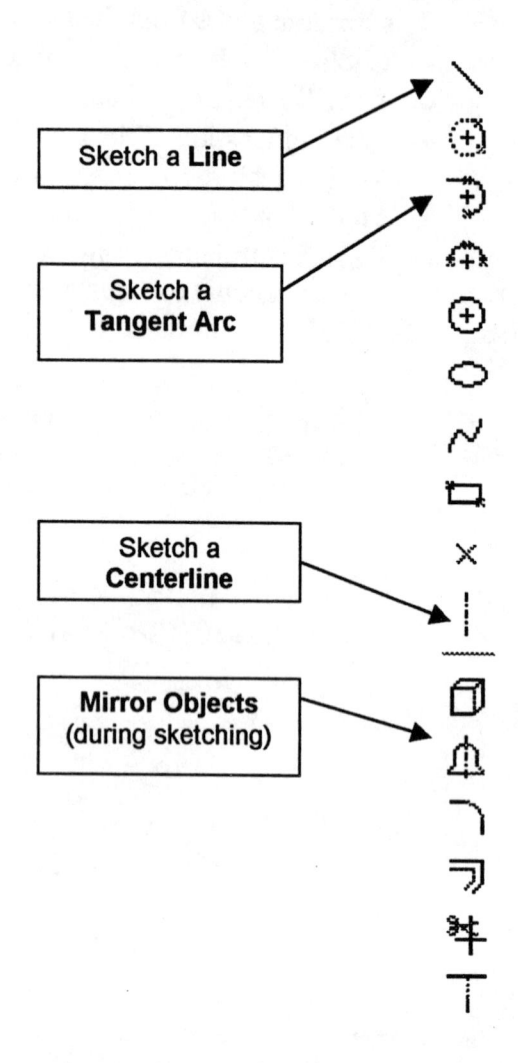

Figure X4-3

DESIGN PROJECT TUTORIAL

Step 3: Draw the semicircular sides of the Cut cross-section.

A. Click the **Tangent Arc** tool and draw one arc by dragging it from the end of one line segment to the end of the other line segment. Watch for the pointer inferencing (in this case a tiny square) that tells you when the end of a straight line has been found.

B. Draw the other arc.

C. Click **Tangent Arc** again to deactivate the command.

The sketch should look much like Figure X4-4:

Mirrored *Lines*
(Step 2B)

Centerline
(Step 2A)

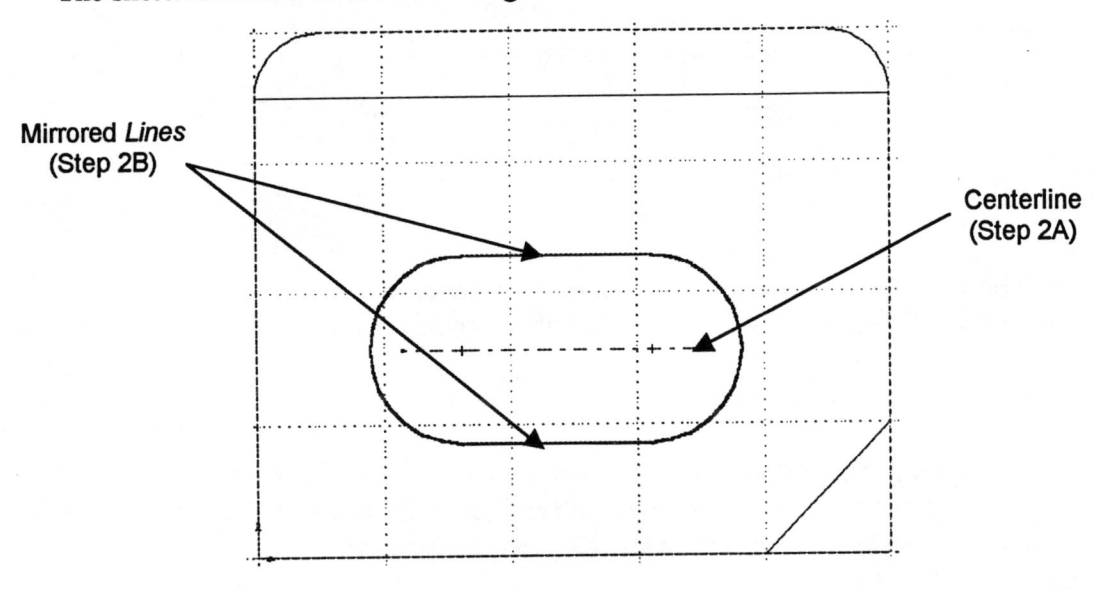

Figure X4-4

Step 4: Dimension the sketch.

A. Click the **Dimension** tool: to activate the dimensioning features. Remember that each dimension requires three left mouse picks: the two dimension origin points and the location for the dimension text. For the cut several of the dimensions will begin or end at the <u>arc centers</u>.

4-3

DESIGN PROJECT TUTORIAL

B. Create the four dimensions shown on Figure X4-5:

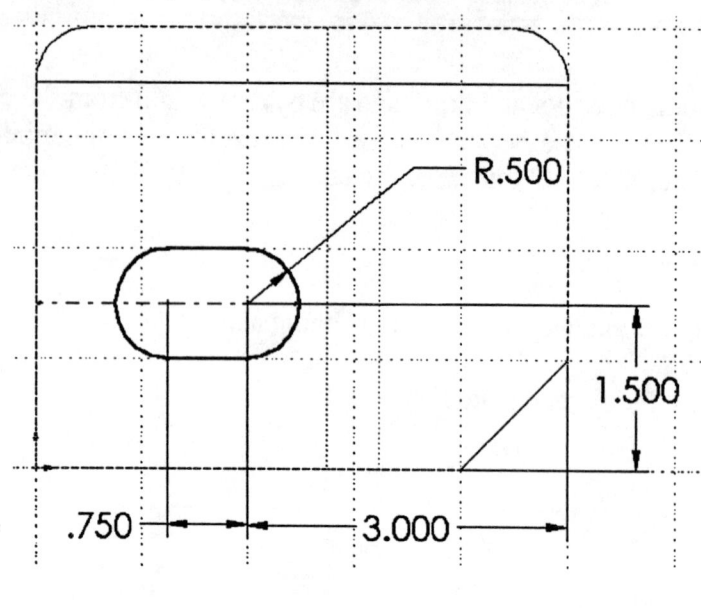

Figure X4-5

Don't be concerned if the dimension values do not match upon first creation--they almost certainly will not, and we will modify the values quickly and easily.

C. Click the **Dimension** tool again to deactivate dimensioning.

D. **Double Click** on the text of one of the dimensions to reveal the **Modify** dialog box. Type in the correct value for the dimension and press **Enter** to update the value and redraw the sketch. Alternatively, you can press the green check mark on the **Modify** dialog box to enter the change.

E. **Modify** the three remaining dimensions in the same way.

Step 5: Finalize the Extruded Cut and add it to the model.

A. Click the **Extruded Cut** tool: to finalize feature creation.

B. Select the **Type** as **Through All** and press the **OK** button.

DESIGN PROJECT TUTORIAL

The extruded cut is created as shown in Figure X4-6:

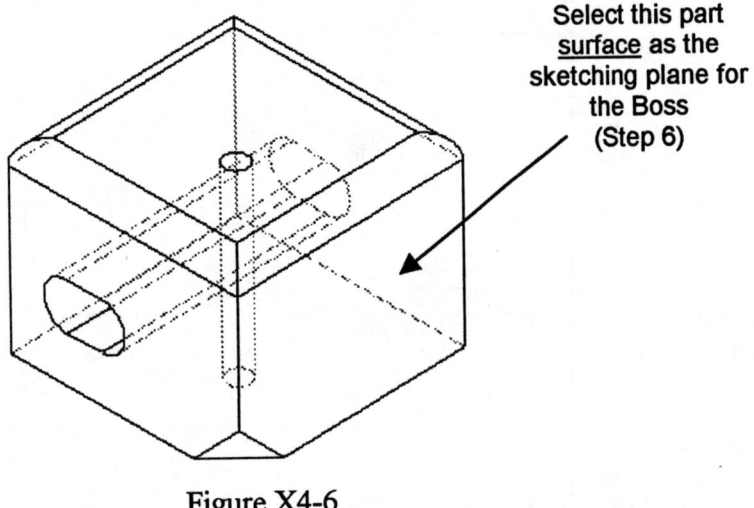

Select this part <u>surface</u> as the sketching plane for the Boss (Step 6)

Figure X4-6

Step 6: Sketch the circular boss.

A. Select the right side of the part and click the **Sketch** tool to activate sketching mode. See Figure X4-6.

B. Select **View▼ Orientation...** and double click **Right** to obtain a "straight on" view of the sketching plane or click the **Right** viewing tool:

C. Click the **Circle** tool, draw one circle by dragging from its center to a point on its circumference, click **Circle** again to turn it off, and click on the **Dimension** mode tool.

D. **Dimension** the circle as shown on Figure X4-7. Click **Dimension** again (to turn off this mode) and **Modify** the dimension values to **1.500in**, **1.250in**, and **3.000in**.

DESIGN PROJECT TUTORIAL

Figure X4-7

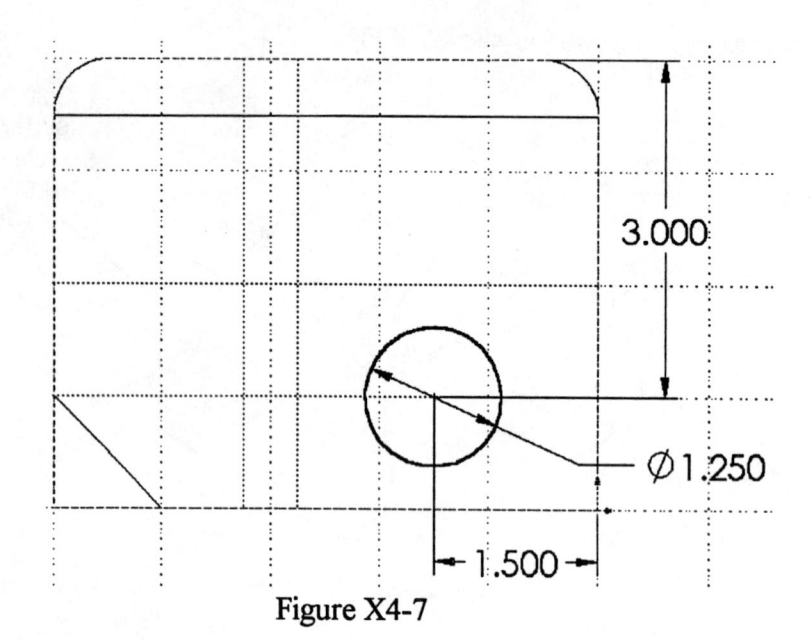

Step 6: Extrude the circular boss.

A. Click the **Extruded Base/Boss** tool:

B. Select the **Type** as **Blind** and enter the **Depth** as **3.000in.**

C. Switch to an **Isometric** view of the part by clicking the **Isometric** tool:

D. **Drag** the **Extrude Feature** dialog box slightly to the side and observe the brown-colored direction preview circle. If it shows that the extrusion will extend into the part instead of away from the base feature select the **Reverse Direction** checkbox to change the direction of extrusion.

E. Press the **OK** button to create the circular boss.

DESIGN PROJECT TUTORIAL

The object will now look like Figure X4-8:

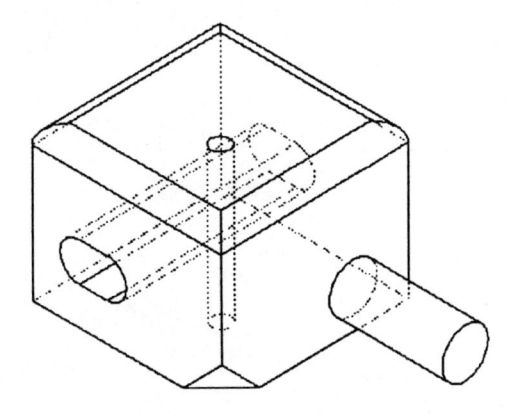

Figure X4-8

Step 7: Shade the model.

A. Toggle through the four different options on the **View** toolbar and observe how the display of the part changes.

The rightmost display mode tool activates the **Shaded** mode. This mode gives the most lifelike, solid appearance to the object.

B. Save the modified file using **File ▾ Save As...** on your personal media (floppy or Zip® disk) for use in Exercise 7.

End of Exercise 4.

Exercise 5: Cylindrical Base Feature Creation

In this exercise we will create an Extruded Base feature starting with a default **New** part.

Step 1: Create a *New* part, *Show* the default features, and obtain an *Isometric* view of the default features.

A. Click on the **New** tool:

B. Select **Part** from the *New* dialog and press **OK** to create the default features for the new part:

C. In the *FeatureManager* design tree right click over the **Front** default construction plane and select **Show** from the popup menu. Also *show* the **Right** and **Top** construction planes. Note that the origin is shown by default.

D. Activate an **Isometric** view of the now-visible model default features by clicking the tool:

E. Select **Tools ▼ Options** and the **Grid/Units** tab. Disable the **Snap to Grid (or Points)** checkbox in the *Snap Behavior* heading of the tab. Check to make sure that the *Units* are **millimeters**. Then press **OK**.

Note that the Top, Front, and Right construction planes, Origin, and Annotations folder are contained in *every* single part model. For this reason they are called *default features*. These features do not possess mass or volume, but they simplify the creation of features that do.

Step 2: Create the *Extruded Base* feature by sketching on the *Front* plane.

Click on the **Sketch** mode tool: and change the view orientation to **Front**. By default, sketching for the *Base* feature begins automatically on the *Front* plane. If you had wanted, for some reason, to begin the *Base* feature by sketching on one of the other two planes then you could have simply selected the plane in the *FeatureManager* design tree or selected it within the graphics window.

Step 3: Sketch a circle as the shape to be extruded.

Sketch a **Circle** by activating the tool on the *Sketch* toolbar. Draw the circle by dragging from as close to the origin as you can get outward until the circle diameter is approximately 1/2 the height of the **Front** plane.

If you began the dragging operation to create the circle close enough to the origin a **Coincident** relation, between the **Origin** and the circle's center, will be created automatically for you.

Step 4: Dimension the circle.

Click on the **Dimension** mode tool, click on the perimeter of the circle, and pick a point outside of the circle for the dimension text. The circle should turn black to indicate that it is fully *constrained*. Click on the **Dimension** mode tool again to deactivate it.

DESIGN PROJECT TUTORIAL

Step 5: *Modify* **the circle diameter.**

Double click on the dimension text. **Modify** the diameter value to **20.00mm**. **Enter** the change. The sketch as shown in Figure X5-4 is ready for extrusion:

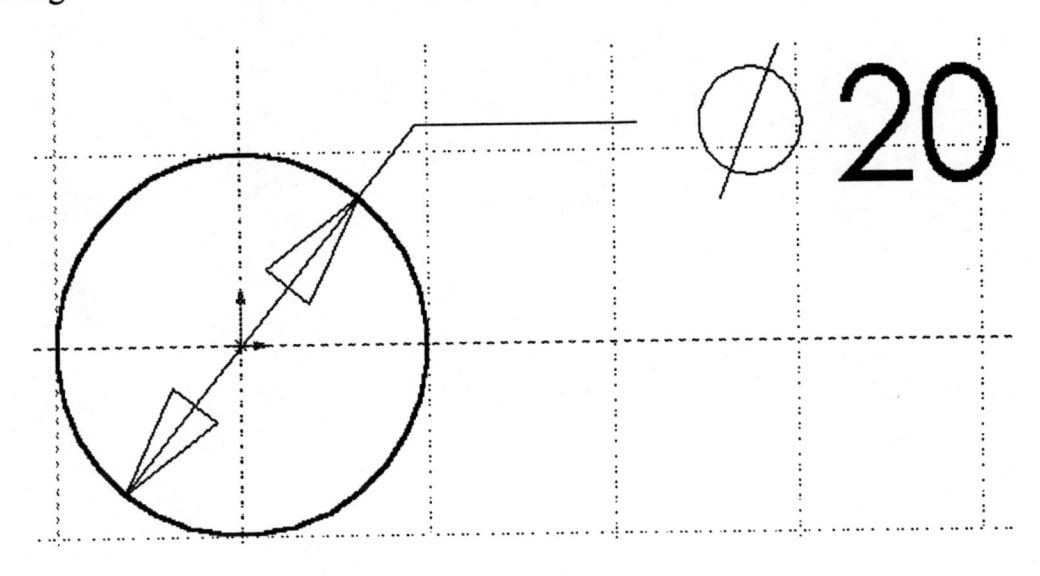

Figure X5-4

Step 6: **Complete the** *Extruded Base* **feature with a blind depth of 175.00mm.**

A. Click the **Extruded Boss/Base** tool:

B. Select the *Type:* as **Blind,** enter a *Depth:* value of **175.00mm,** and press the **OK** button to create the feature.

C. **Shade** the model if it isn't already.

D. **Save** the part as `cyl_base.sldprt`.

End of Exercise 5.

Exercise 6: Rectangular Base Feature Creation

In this exercise we will create a part whose first solid Extruded Base feature is a rectangular extrusion.

Step 1:	Create a *New* part, *Show* the default features, and obtain an *Isometric* view of the default features.

A. Click the **New** tool:

B. Select **Part** from the New dialog and press **OK** to create the default features for the new part:

C. In the *FeatureManager* design tree right click over the **Front** default construction plane and select **Show** from the popup menu. Also show the **Right** and **Top** construction planes. Note that the origin is shown by default.

D. Select **View ▼ Orientation...** and activate an **Isometric** view of the now-visible model default features or simply click the tool:

E. Select **Tools ▼ Options** and the **Grid/Units** tab. Disable the **Snap to Grid (or Points)** checkbox in the *Snap Behavior* heading of the tab. Check to make sure that the *Units* are **millimeters**. Then press **OK**.

Step 2:	Create the *Extruded Base* feature by sketching on the *Front* plane. The feature will be created as a *Midplane* type of extrusion.

Click the **Sketch** mode tool: and change the view orientation to **Front**. By default, sketching for the *Base* feature begins automatically on the *Front* plane.

DESIGN PROJECT TUTORIAL

Step 3: Sketch a rectangle as the shape to be extruded.

Sketch a **Rectangle** by activating the tool: on the **Sketch** toolbar. Draw the rectangle by dragging from as close to the origin as you can get upward and outward until the rectangle fills approximately 3/4 of the upper right quadrant of the **Front** plane.

If you began the dragging operation to create the rectangle close enough to the origin **Coincident** relations, between the **Right** plane and the left edge of the rectangle and the **Top** plane and bottom edge of the rectangle, will be created for you.

Step 4: Dimension the rectangle.

Click on the **Dimension** mode tool, click on the right vertical edge of the rectangle, and pick a point to the right of the rectangle for the dimension text. **Dimension** the top edge of the rectangle. The rectangle should turn black to indicate that it is fully *constrained*. Click on the **Dimension** mode tool again to deactivate it.

Step 5: *Modify* the dimensions of the rectangle.

Double click on the dimension text. **Modify** the height value to **75.00mm** and the width value to **100.00mm**. **Enter** the change. The sketch as shown in Figure X6-4 is ready for extrusion:

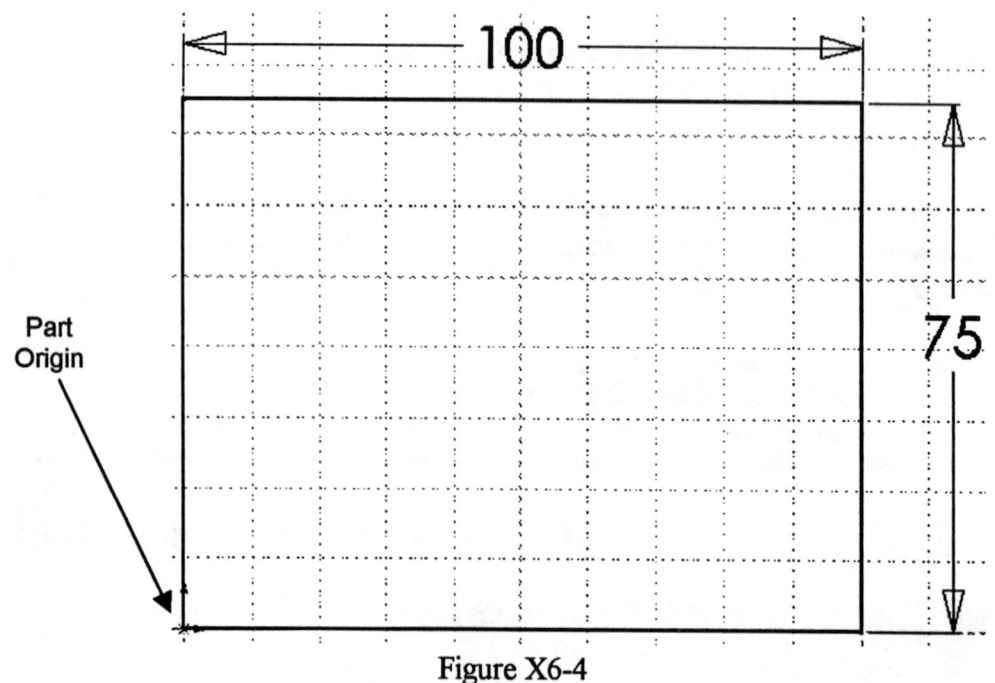

Figure X6-4

6-2

DESIGN PROJECT TUTORIAL

As necessary, click on **Zoom to Fit** to restore a full view of the sketched and dimensioned rectangle.

Step 6: **Complete the *Extruded Base* feature with a *MidPlane* depth of 125.00mm.**

A. Click the **Extruded Boss/Base** tool:

B. Select the *Type*: as **Midplane.**

C. Enter a *Depth*: value of **125.00mm.**

D. Press the **OK** button to create the feature.

E. To see the effect of using **Midplane** select a **Right** view:

F. Return to an **Isometric** view:

G. **Shade** the model if it isn't already.

H. Save the file as `rect_base.sldprt`.

End of Exercise 6.

DESIGN PROJECT TUTORIAL

Exercise 7: Construction Plane Creation

Construction Planes have the same characteristics as their counterpart from Euclidean geometry. They do not contain any mass or weight, and they are infinitely thin. However, they are very useful as an aid for creating many features, and a few features cannot be created at all without them.

A second cylindrical *Boss* which intersects the first cylindrical *Boss* at a right angle will be added to the part from Exercise 4. This extrusion will be sketched like the *Cut* and *Boss* from that earlier Exercise.

The new *Boss* will not be sketched on a default construction plane. Instead, an entirely new construction plane will be created for the sketch.

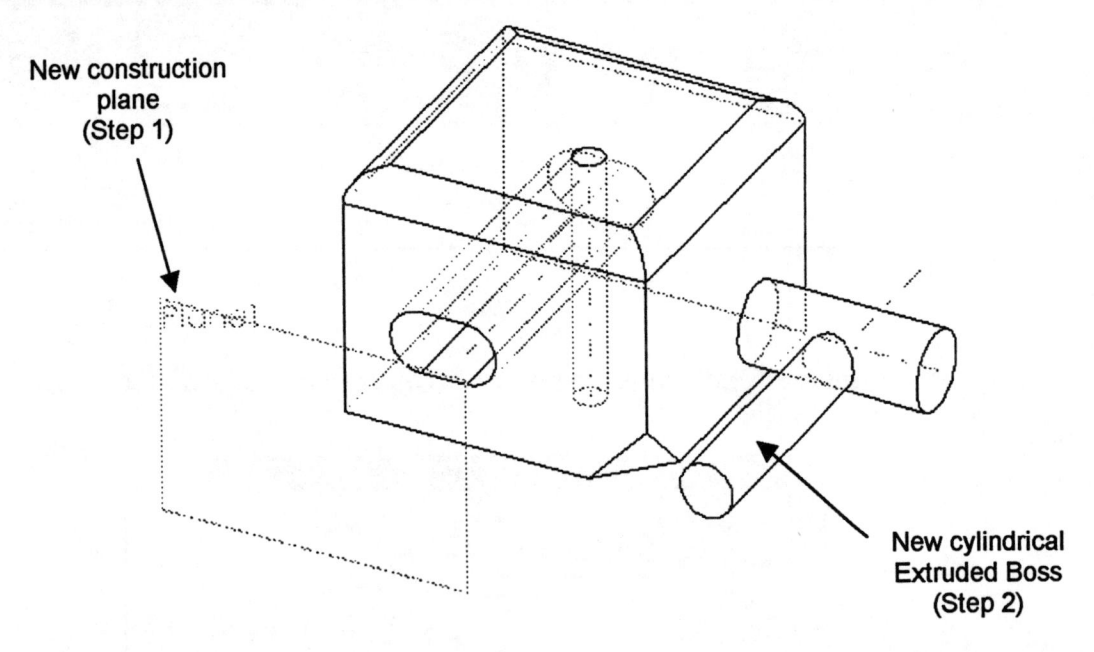

Figure X7-1

Step 1: Open the CON_PLANE.SLDPRT file and add the new construction plane for sketching the second cylindrical *boss*.

A. Open your file `boss_cut.SLDPRT` from Exercise 4, if you saved it, or open the file `con_plane.SLDPRT` if you didn't save it.

B. Change to an **Isometric** view orientation if necessary:

DESIGN PROJECT TUTORIAL

C. Activate the *Reference Geometry* toolbar if it isn't already by selecting **View ▼ Toolbars ▶ Reference Geometry**. The tool bar looks like this:

D. Select **Insert ▼ Reference Geometry ▶ Plane...** or on the *Reference Geometry* toolbar click the tool:

to reveal the **Specify Construction Plane: Step 1 of 2** dialog, shown as Figure X7-2.

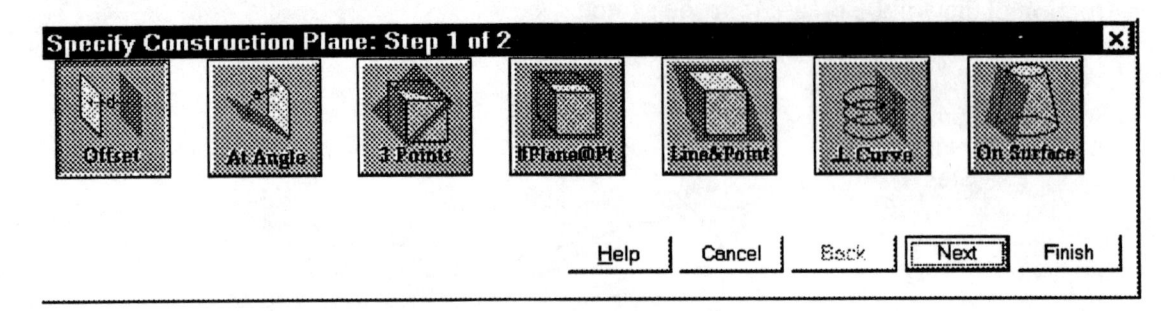

Figure X7-2

E. Press the **Offset** and **Next** buttons to reveal the *Offset Plane: Step 2 of 2* dialog.

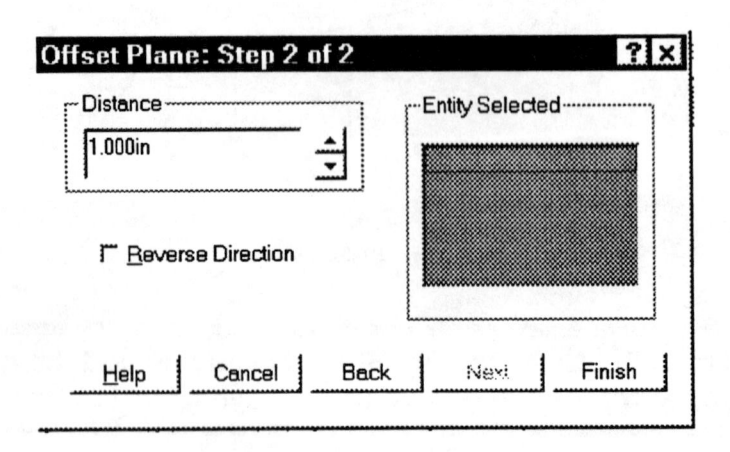

Figure X7-3

F. Enter the *Distance* as **1.000in** and click inside the **Entity Selected** window.

DESIGN PROJECT TUTORIAL

G. Select the front surface of the *Base* feature as indicated on Figure X7-4. Do not select the *Front* reference plane--this is a different surface altogether:

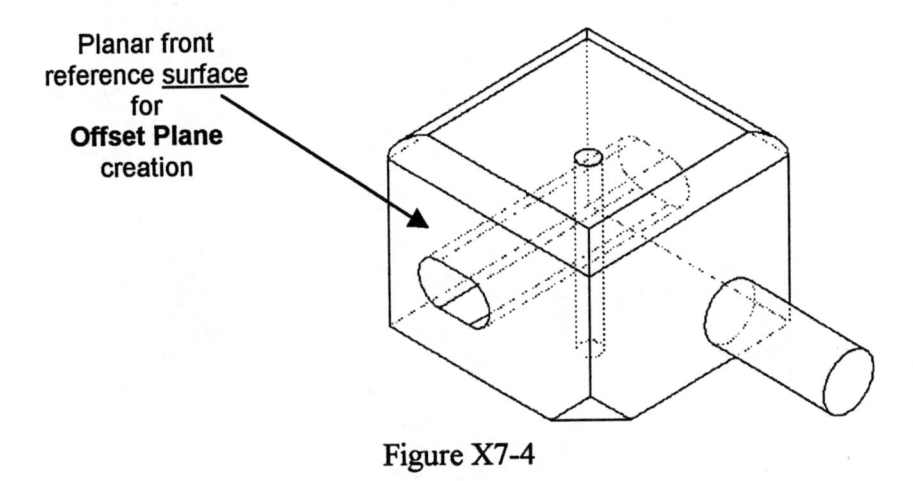

Planar front reference <u>surface</u> for **Offset Plane** creation

Figure X7-4

H. Switch to a **Right** view orientation and observe the brown preview plane. Check and uncheck the **Reverse Direction** box to see the two options for the direction of offset.

I. With the brown preview plane out in front of the *Base* feature press **Finish** and return to an **Isometric** view orientation.

J. Note the new **Plane1** in the *FeatureManager* design tree and in the graphics window.

| **Step 2:** | **Sketch, Dimension, and extrude the cylindrical boss.** |

A. Switch to a **Front** view orientation:

B. With the new *Plane1* selected (highlighted in green) enter **Sketch** mode.

C. Select **View ▼ Temporary Axes** to show the axis line for the cylindrical *boss*. We turned these on because we want the axis of the first extrusion and the center of the circle we are about to sketch to be **Coincident**.

7-3

DESIGN PROJECT TUTORIAL

D. Drag a **Circle** with its center on the axis of the first *Boss*, **Dimension** its diameter and location, and **Modify** the dimension values as shown on Figure X7-5. Note the change in the sketched circle's color from blue to black--what does this signify?

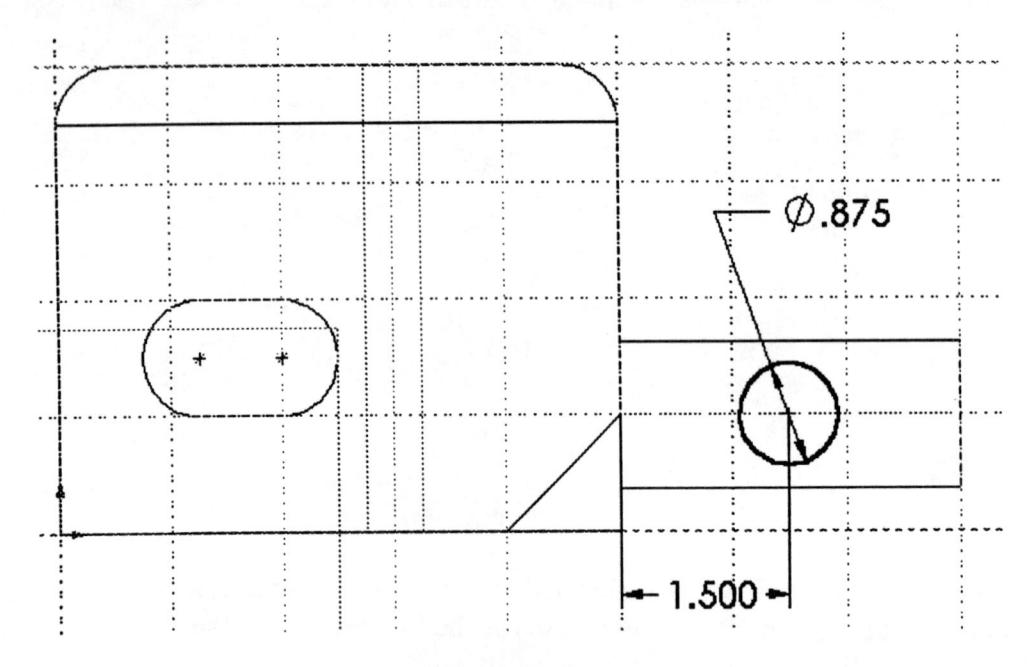

Figure X7-5

E. Click on the **Extruded Base/Boss** tool.

F. Select the *Type* as **Up to Surface** and pick inside the **Selected Items** window.

G. Select the external surface of the first *Boss* and press the **OK** button.

H. A *Trimetric* view orientation of the completed part will look like Figure X7-1.

End of Exercise 7.

DESIGN PROJECT TUTORIAL

Design Project Assignment 1

Seven different parts will be created and assembled in the nine Design Project Assignments. In this first assignment we will partially complete three parts:
- A. DRIVE_SHAFT
- B. MOTOR
- C. LOWER_HOUSING

Assignment 1A: Begin the DRIVE_SHAFT Part

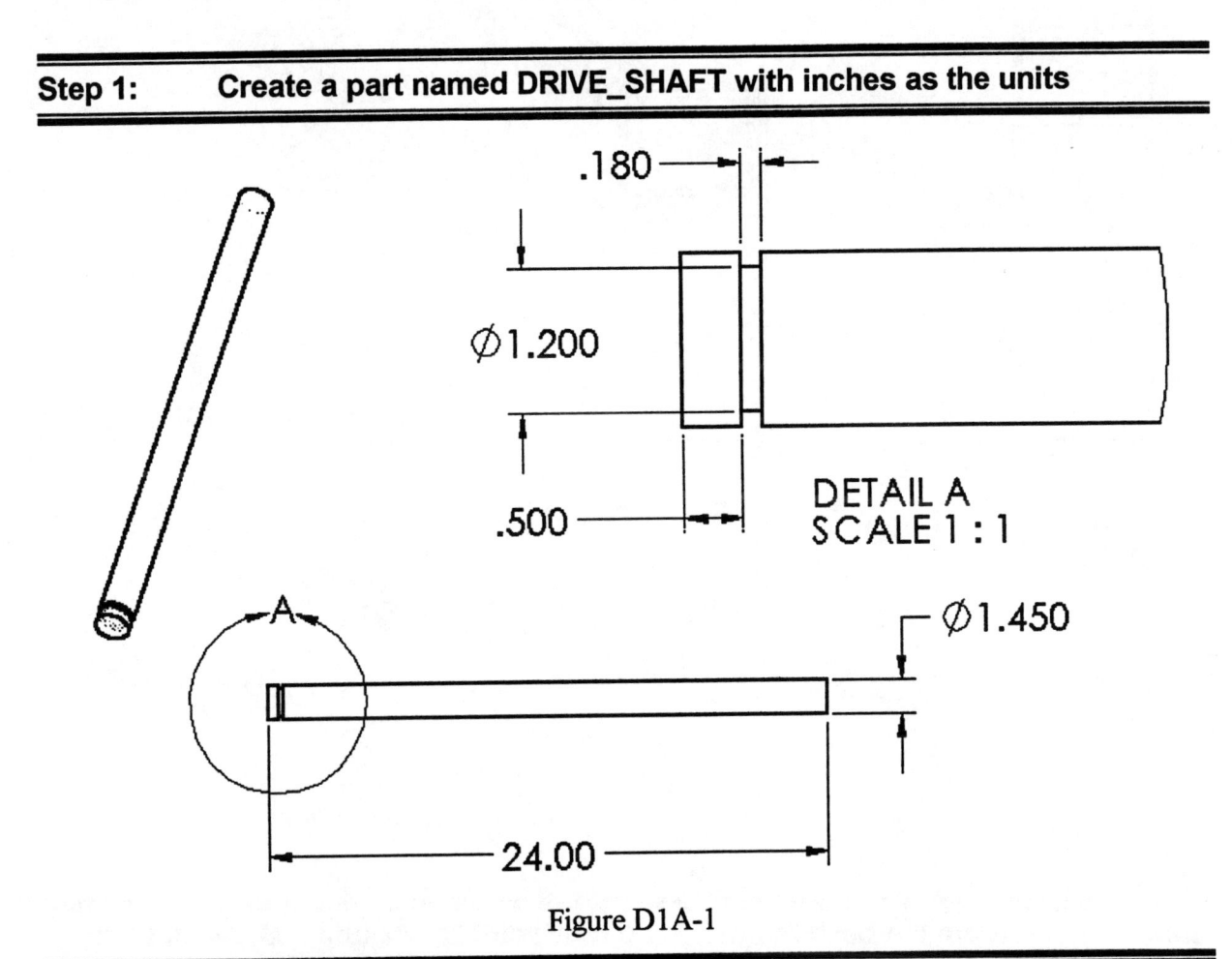

Step 1:	Create a part named DRIVE_SHAFT with inches as the units

Figure D1A-1

Step 2:	Create the base feature of the shaft by extruding a Ø 1.45in. by a length of 24.00in.

Step 3:	Add a revolved cut feature, to be used as a snap ring groove, as shown in Detail A. (Note: a second snap ring groove will be added to the model later.)

DESIGN PROJECT TUTORIAL

Step 4: Save and close the part file.

Assignment 1B: Begin the MOTOR Part

Step 1: Create a part named MOTOR with inches as the units.

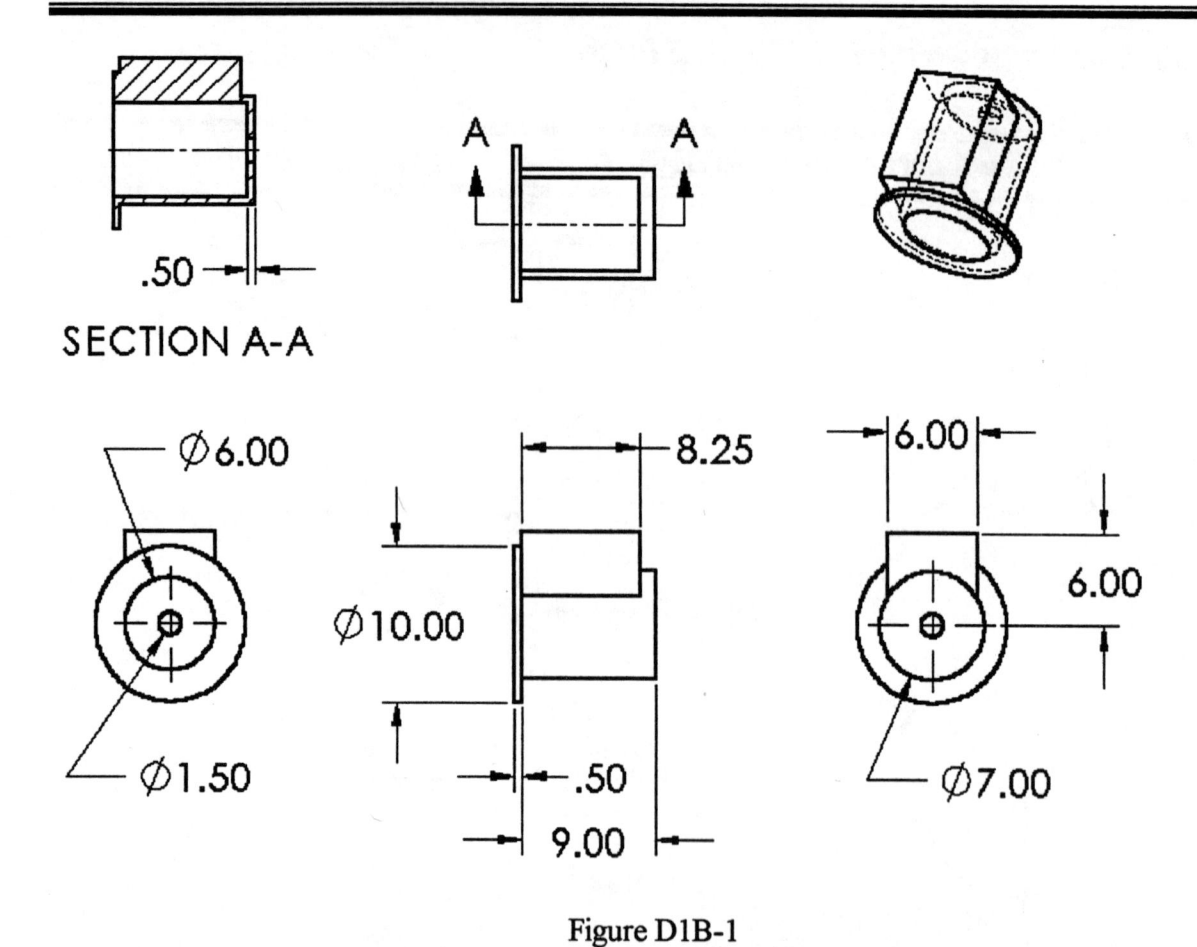

Figure D1B-1

Step 2: Create the base feature. You may want to extrude a Ø7.00in. circle by a depth of 9.00in.

D1-2

Step 3:	Add a boss to be used as a wiring housing. This housing must be rectangular and measure 8.25in. x 6.00in. in the top view. The height of the housing must be 6.00in., measured from the center of the motor.

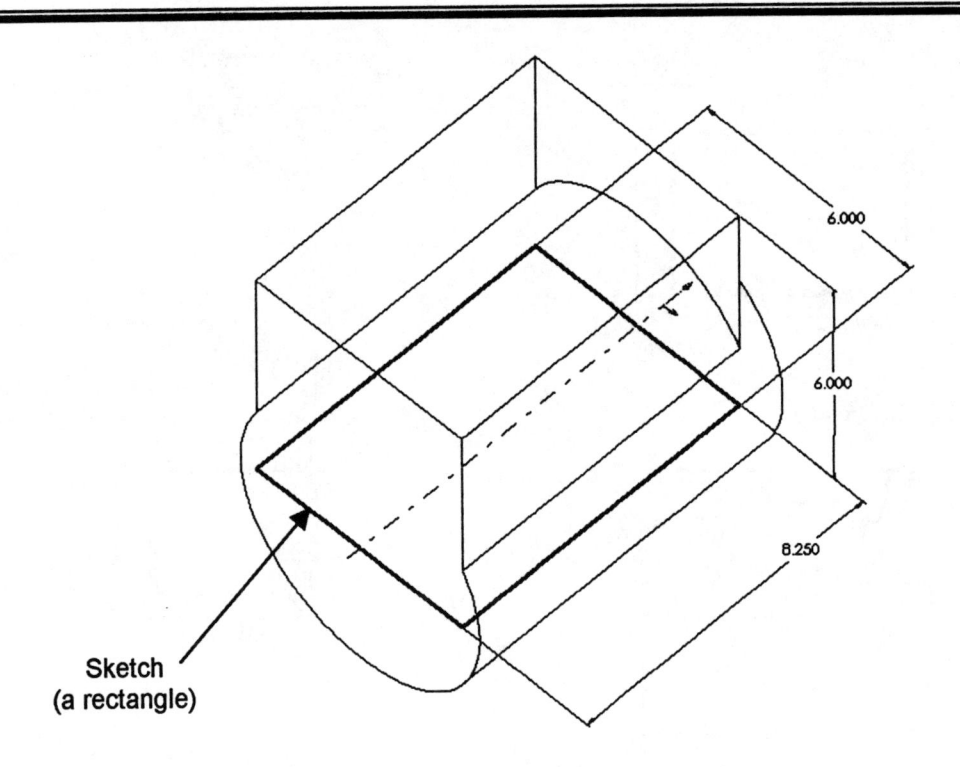

Figure D1B-2

Step 4:	Add a Ø 10.00in. bolting flange to the front surface of the model with a thickness of 0.50in. Refer to Figure D1B-1.

Step 5:	Hollow out a space in the model to receive the motor armature. The new feature should be Ø 6.00in. and leave a wall thickness of 0.50in. at the back of the motor, as shown on Section A-A of Figure D1B-1.

Step 6:	Add a Ø 1.50in. hole to the back of the motor.

Step 7:	Save and close the part file.

DESIGN PROJECT TUTORIAL

Assignment 1C: Begin the LOWER_HOUSING Part

Step 1: Create a part named LOWER_HOUSING with inches as the units.

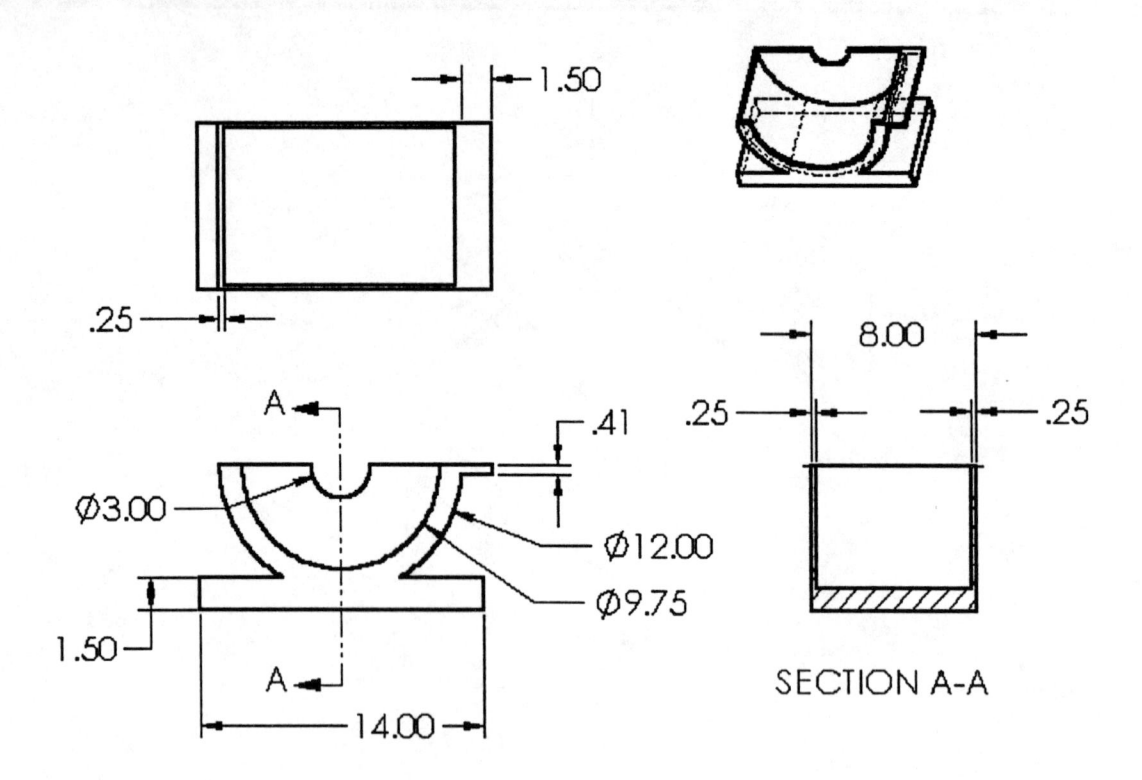

Figure D1C-1

Step 2: Create the base feature. You may want to extrude a Ø 12.00in. diameter semi-circle by a depth of 8.00in.

Step 3: Add a feature, 1.50in. x 0.41in., that extends through the total depth of the housing. Later, this lip, or flange, will be used to bolt the two housing halves together.

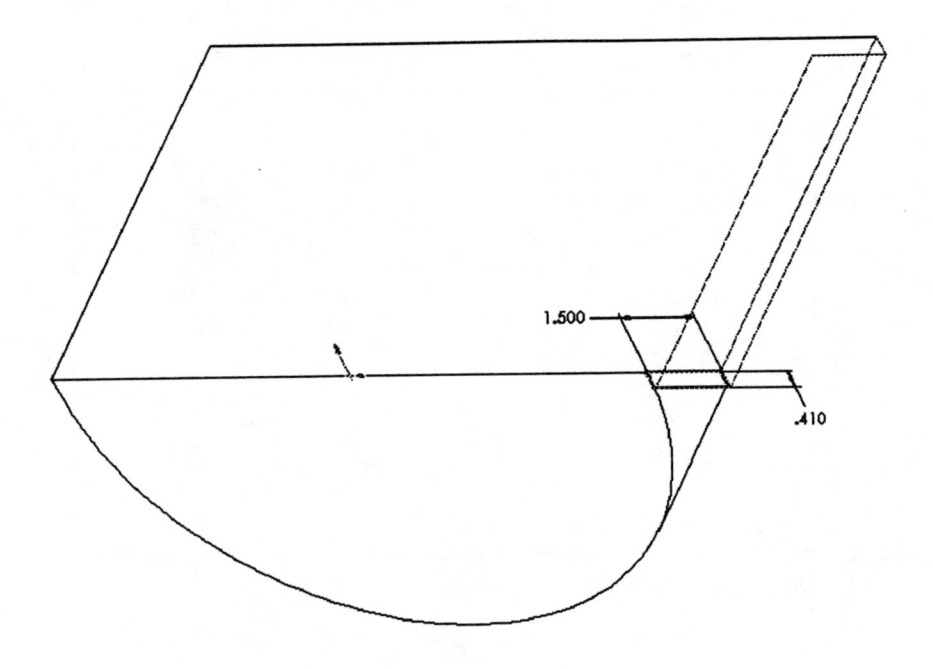

Figure D1C-2

Step 4: Add the base support feature to the model referring to Figures D1C-3 and D1C-4. Use *MidPlane* as the type of extrusion.

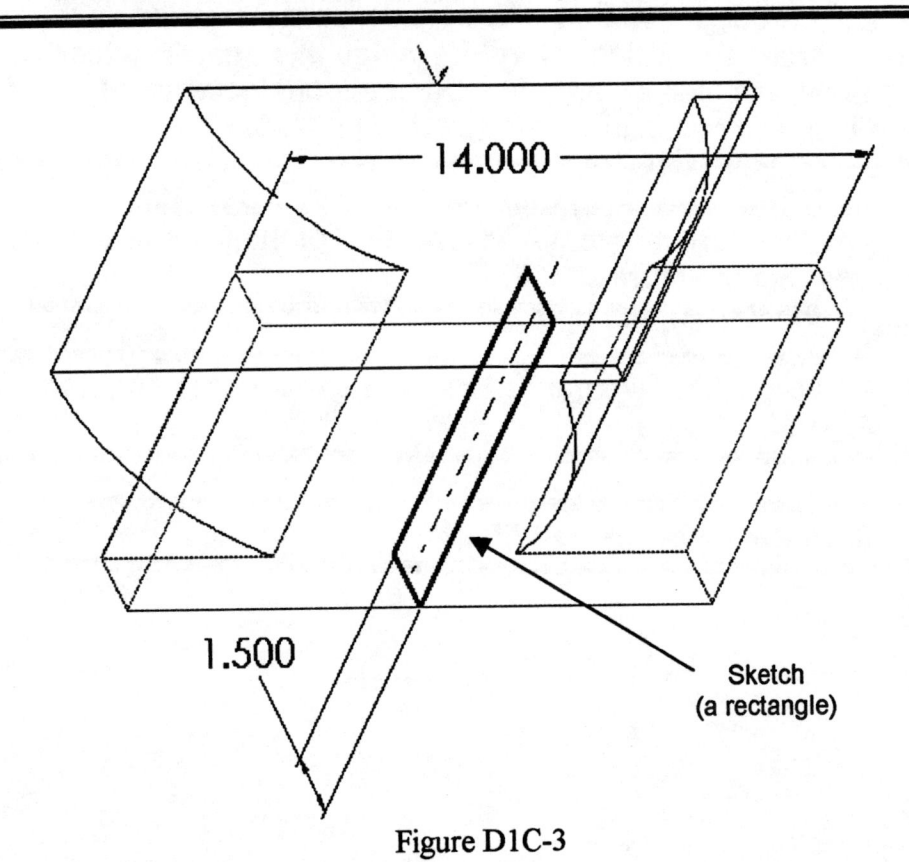

Figure D1C-3

D1-5

DESIGN PROJECT TUTORIAL

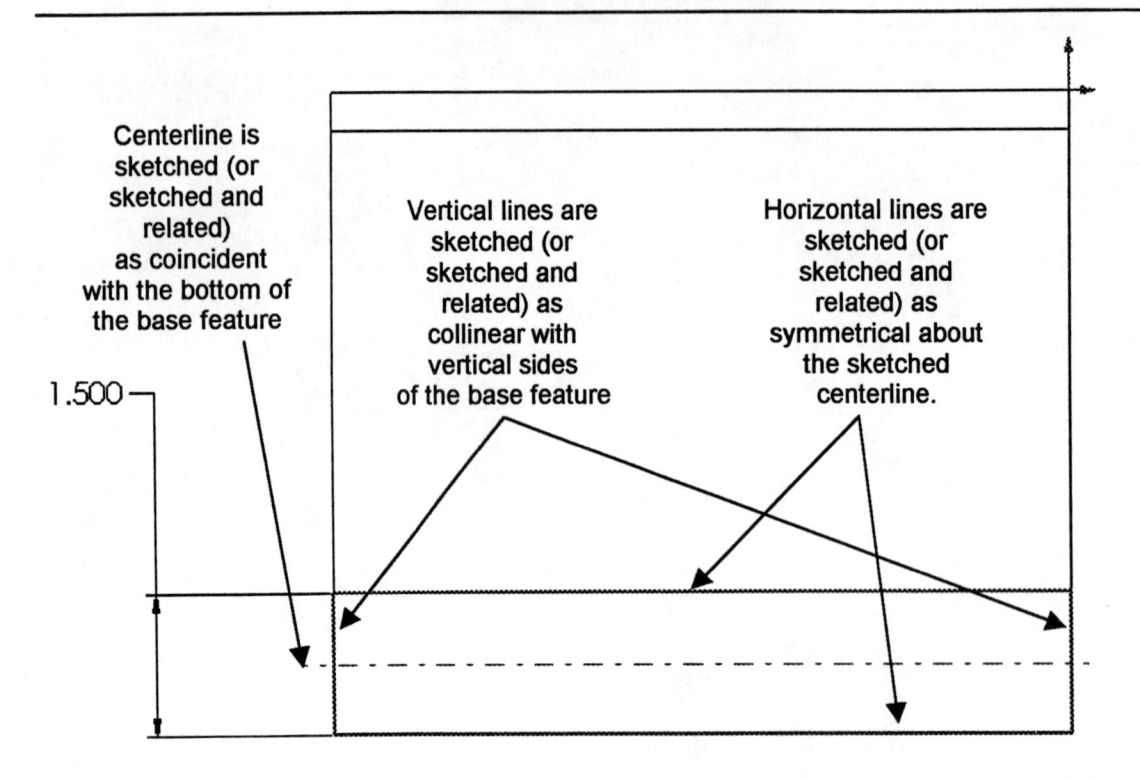

Centerline is sketched (or sketched and related) as coincident with the bottom of the base feature

Vertical lines are sketched (or sketched and related) as collinear with vertical sides of the base feature

Horizontal lines are sketched (or sketched and related) as symmetrical about the sketched centerline.

1.500

Figure D1C-4

Step 5:	Hollow out the interior of the model as a clearance volume for a separate part which will rotate inside this one. The feature can be either revolved or extruded, but it should leave an all-around wall thickness of 0.25in. Refer to Figure D1C-5.
Step 6:	Add a feature that removes a portion of the front of the housing, referring to Figure D1C-6.
Step 7:	Add a Ø 3.00in. clearance hole to the rear of the housing. Refer to Figure D1C-1.
Step 8:	Save and close the part file.

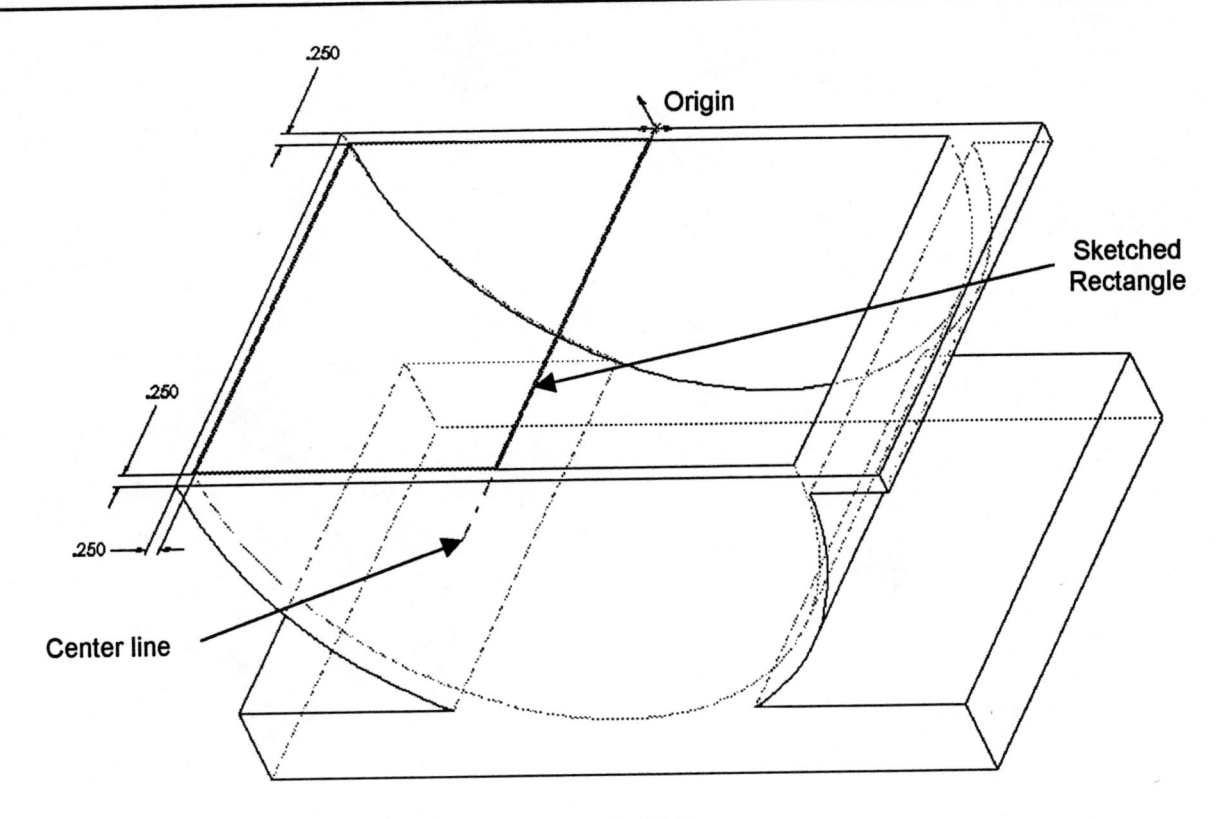

DESIGN PROJECT TUTORIAL

.250

Origin

Sketched Rectangle

.250

.250

Center line

Figure D1C-5

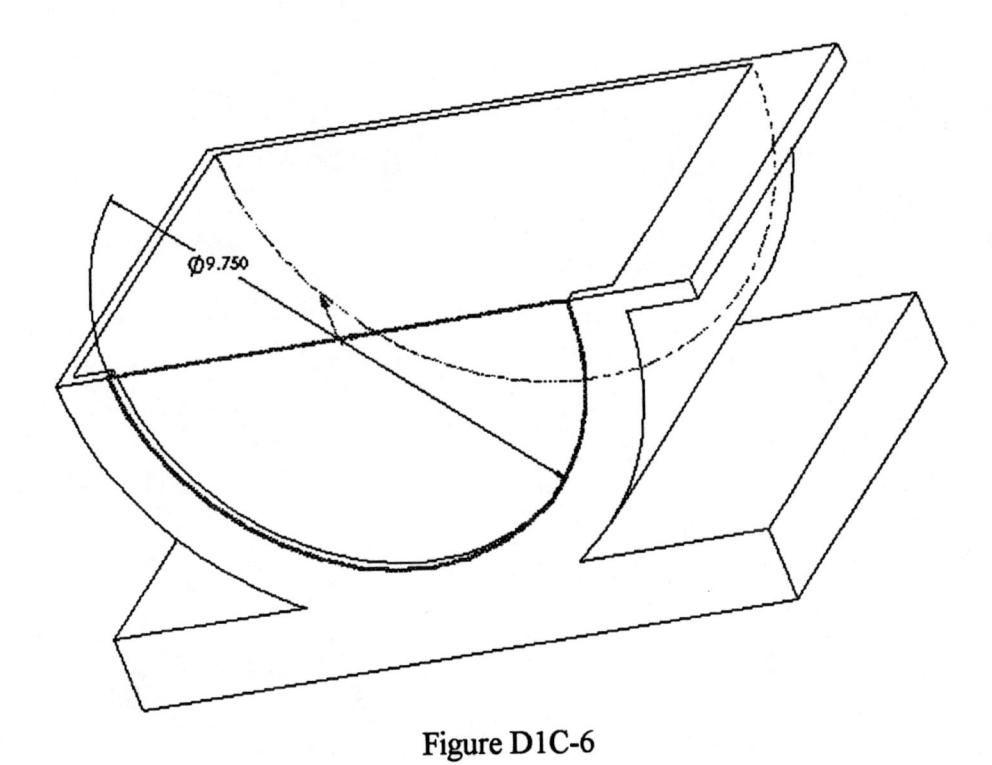

⌀9.750

Figure D1C-6

D1-7

End of Design Project Assignment 1

DESIGN PROJECT TUTORIAL

Exercise 8: Library Feature Creation

A *Library Feature* can contain one or more extruded bosses or cuts, ribs, fillets, drafts, holes, domes, cosmetic threads, reference planes or axes, or sketches. They are easily used over and over again in different part files since their purpose is to avoid duplications of effort.

Complicated features or sketches are likely candidates to become *Library Features*, especially when their re-use at least once in the future is very probable. Frequently used features or sketches are also good candidates, regardless of their complexity.

In this exercise you will practice creating a complicated sketch and save it as a *Library Feature*.

Step 1:   **Open a new part with *inches* as the units.**

Step 2:   **Sketch three circles, dimension the diameters, dimension the locations of the centerpoints, add one relation between the centerpoints, and change the properties of the dimensions.**

A. **Sketch** three circles and **Dimension** them as shown on Figure X8-1:

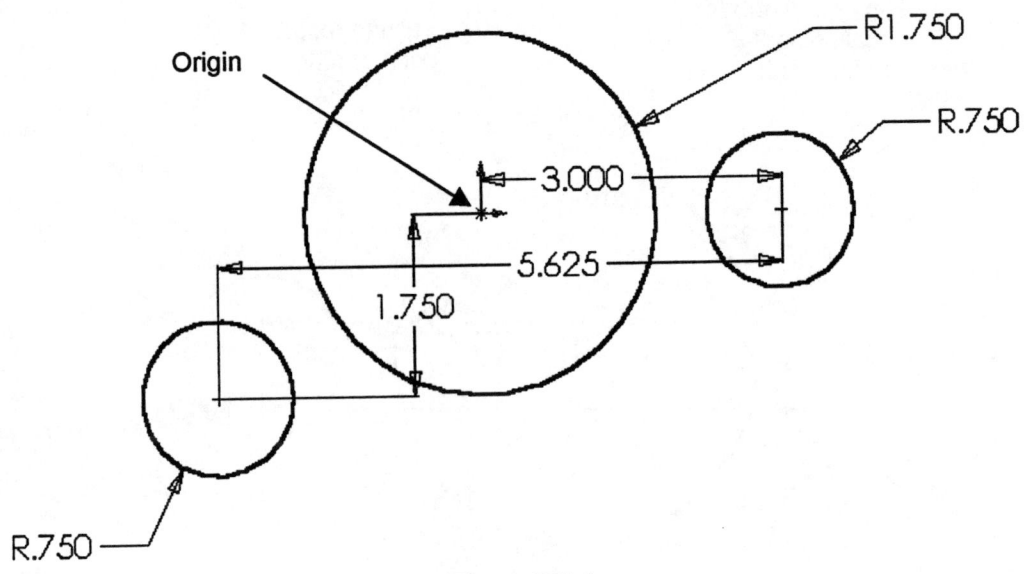

Figure X8-1

Your dimensions will show up by default as diameter dimensions.

B. Add a *Horizontal* relation between the center<u>points</u> of the large circle and the right circle.

8-1

DESIGN PROJECT TUTORIAL

C. Since we will trim away portions of the circles to leave behind only arcs it is best that we convert the diameter dimensions to radius dimensions now. To do this, point at the text of the dimension, right click, select **Properties...** from the popup menu, and uncheck the option **Diameter dimension**. Under the *Arrows* heading select the **Outside** radio button. Press the **Display** button and check the **Display with broken leaders** radio button:

To activate these changes press **OK, Apply,** and **OK** again. Repeat this for each of the three diameter dimensions.

Step 3: **Sketch a *3 Pt Arc* tangent to the circles.**

The creation of a **3 Pt Arc** requires the identification of three points (naturally). First, a reference line is dragged from one endpoint of the arc to the other endpoint, and then you must lift your finger from the left mouse button at the second endpoint. Next, the curvature of the arc is increased, decreased, or reversed (in direction of concavity) by dragging a special handle on the third point.

A. Click the **3 Pt Arc** tool: on the **Sketch** toolbar and drag from one approximate point of tangency to the other as shown in Figure X8-2:

Grip (green dot) for changing the curvature of the arc

Second (approx.) point of tangency

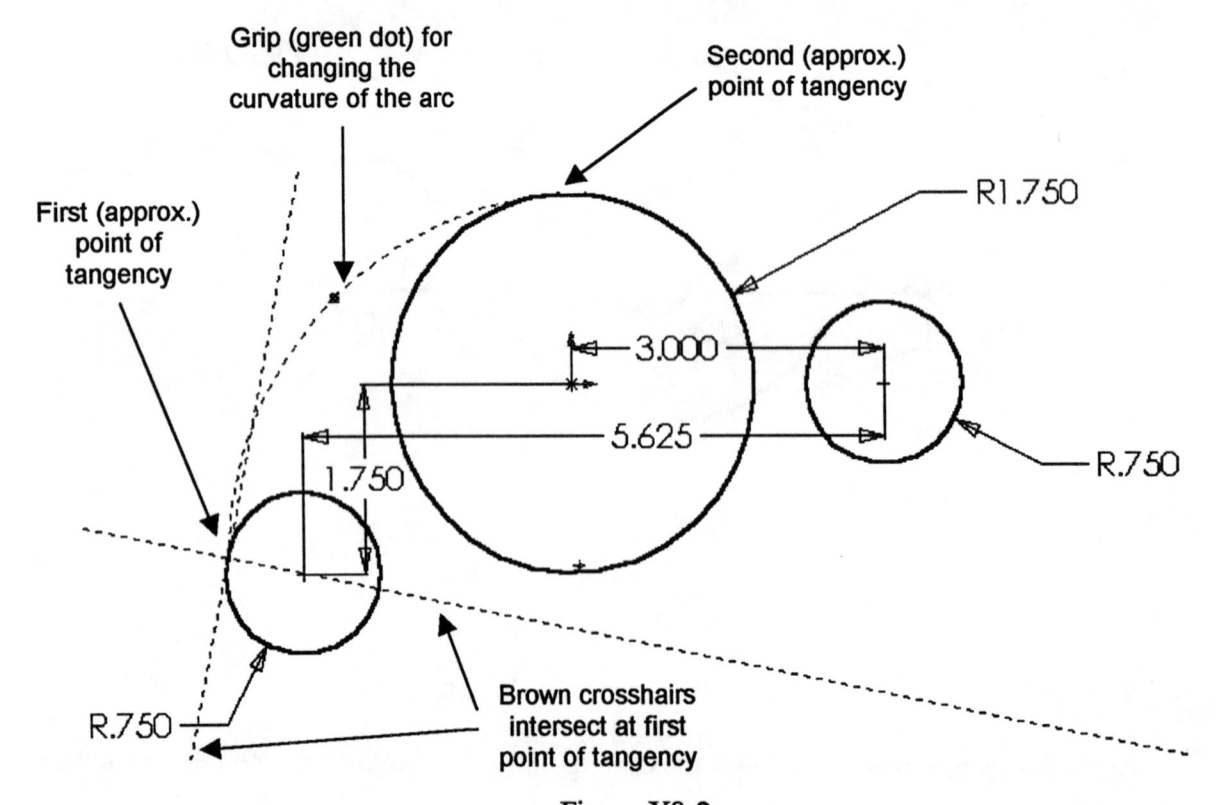

R1.750

First (approx.) point of tangency

3.000

5.625

1.750

R.750

R.750

Brown crosshairs intersect at first point of tangency

Figure X8-2

8-2

DESIGN PROJECT TUTORIAL

Lift up from the left mouse button at the second endpoint

B. If you are dissatisfied with the appearance of the arc then drag the green dot to rearrange it. The two endpoints of the arc also can be dragged to new positions. As a minimum, you must click once on the green dot to finalize the arc.

Step 4: Sketch the second *3 Pt Arc* and *Dimension* both arcs.

A. Check to see if the **3 Pt Arc** tool is still activated. If it isn't then click on it again.

B. Drag a second arc as shown on Figure X8-3:

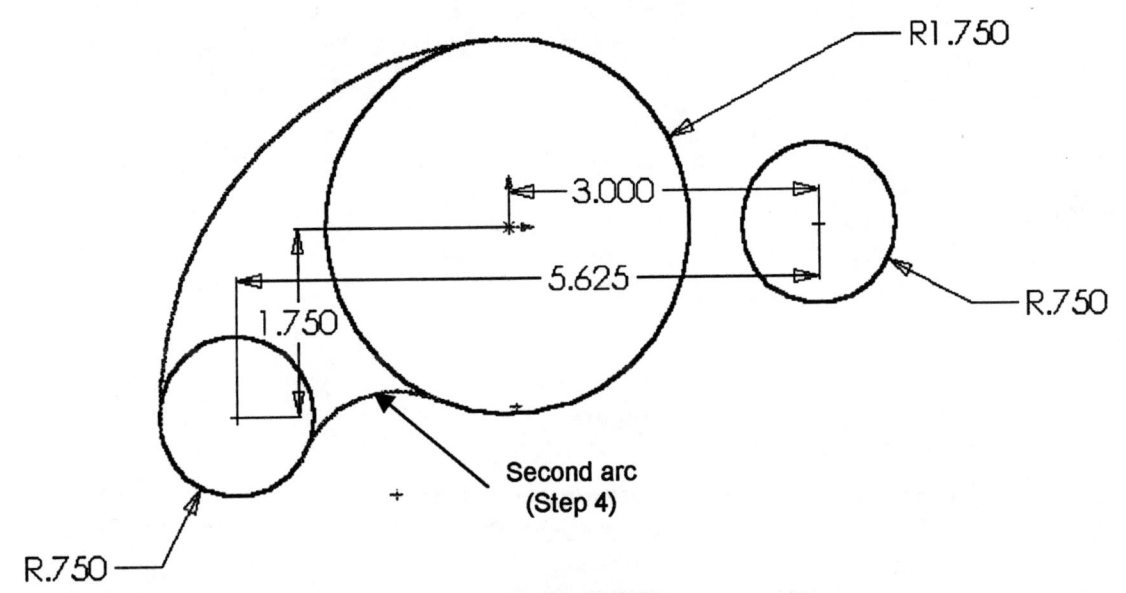

Figure X8-3

C. **Dimension** the radius of each arc. The upper arc has a **5.00in** radius, and the lower arc has a **1.50in** radius.

DESIGN PROJECT TUTORIAL

| Step 5: | Sketch two lines tangent to the center circle and right circle. |

See Figure X8-4 for the appearance of the two new straight lines. Sketch the lines with accurate selection of points of tangency to the best of your ability:

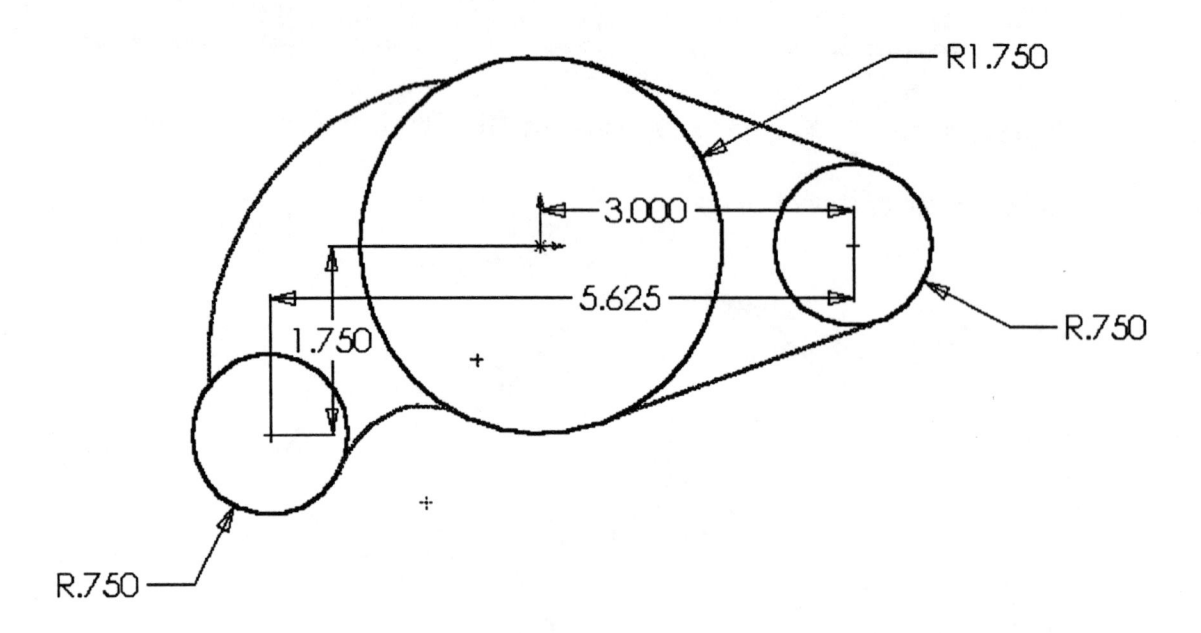

Figure X8-4

| Step 6: | Add *Tangent* geometric relationships between the circles and the arcs and lines. |

A. Select one blue arc and one of the circles (**CTRL** + left click) tangent to it.

B. Click on the **Add Relation** tool: ⊥ to reveal the *Add Geometric Relation* dialog.

C. Two items should appear in the *Items Selected* window. Select the **Tangent** radio button and press the **Apply** button.

DESIGN PROJECT TUTORIAL

D. The **Add Geometric Relations** dialog is "sticky," meaning it won't disappear until you press the **Close** button. Use this to your advantage by picking:

[select arc], [select circle], **Apply**
[select arc], [select circle], **Apply**
[select arc], [select circle], **Apply**
[select line], [select circle], **Apply**
[select line], [select circle], **Apply**
[select line], [select circle], **Apply**
[select line], [select circle], **Apply**

If you select the pairs of one arc and one circle or one line and one circle properly it should not be necessary to add any more than 8 geometric relations. Both arcs and both lines should now be black, indicating that they are fully constrained.

E. Click the **Close** button on the *Add Geometric Relation* dialog.

Step 7: *Trim* away the unneeded portions of the full circles.

A. Select both tangent (sketched 3 point) arcs and both tangent lines using **Ctrl+left pick**. The selected entities will act as boundaries for trimming the circles. Boundaries must always be selected before activating the **Trim** tool. Entities which are selected after the activation of the **Trim** tool will be trimmed!

B. Press the **Trim** tool: and touch the <u>unwanted</u> part of each full circle.

See Figure X8-5 for the desired final configuration:

C. Press **Trim** again.

DESIGN PROJECT TUTORIAL

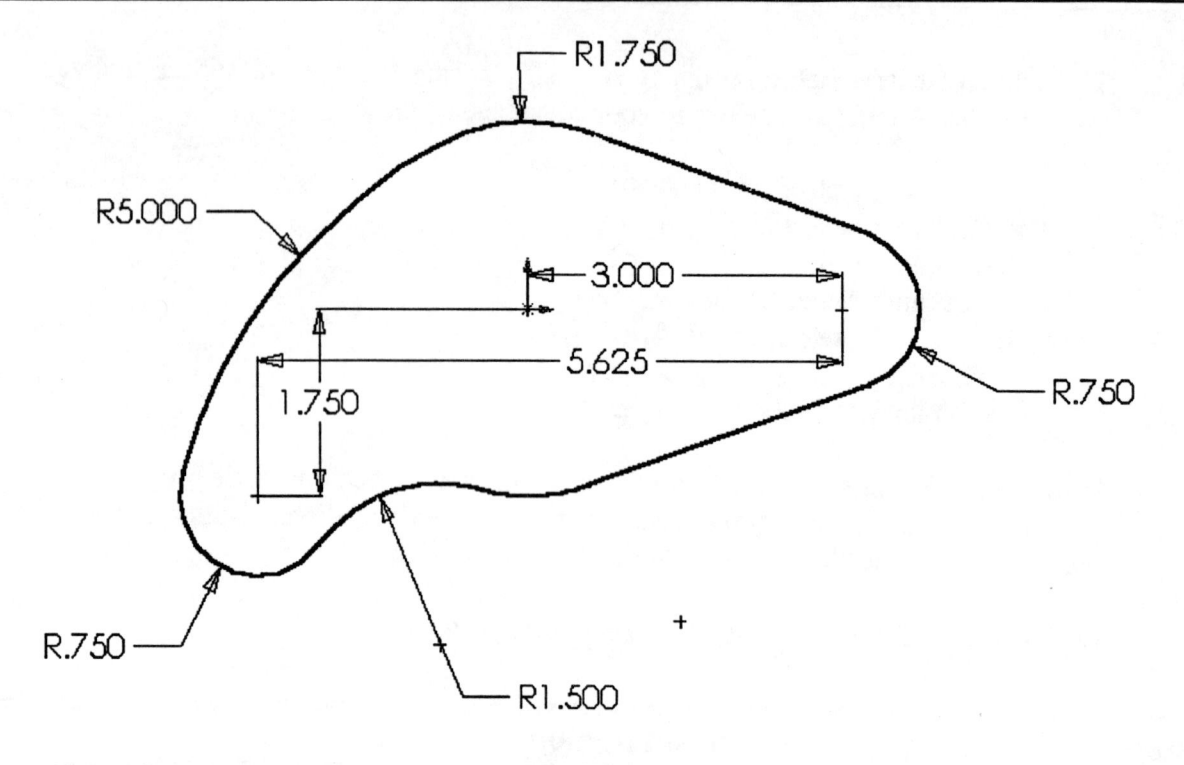

Figure X8-5

Step 8:   **Save the sketch for future use.**

A.   Click the **Sketch** tool to close the sketch.

B.   Select **File ▼ Save As...**

C.   Under the *Save as Type:* flipdown menu select **Lib Feat Part Files (*.sldlfp).** Scroll up and down, as necessary, to find this option within the flipdown list.

D.   Enter the file name as rocker_arm.SLDLFP

E.   Press **Save.**

End of Exercise 8.

DESIGN PROJECT TUTORIAL

Exercise 9: Library Feature Application

In this exercise an extrusion will be added to a shaft to represent the hex head of a bolt. The hex shape is a standard sketch configuration that comes with SolidWorks®.

| Step 1: | Open a new part named HEX_BOLT with *inches* as the units. |

| Step 2: | Create the base feature. |

A.   Sketch a Ø **1.50in** circle on the **Front** plane. The center of the circle should be drawn on the origin or related as *Coincident* with the origin.

B.   Extrude it by a **Blind** depth of **4.50in.**

| Step 3: | Insert the sketch of a hexagon. |

A.   Because the hexagonal sketch from the *Feature Palette* must be dragged and dropped directly onto the end of the bolt change to a **Back** viewing direction:

B.   Select **Tools ▼ Feature Palette...**

C.   Double click on the *Palette Features* tool:

D.   Note the five folders of features: *holes, machined, shaft, shapes,* and *sheetmetal.* Double click on one of these five folders to reveal its contents. Click the **Back** arrow on the toolbar to return to a view of all *Palette Features* folders. Could any of the features in the *Shaft* folder been used to your advantage during the creation of a snap ring groove?

E.   Double click on the **shapes** folder and drag and drop the **Hexagon** out of the *Feature Palette* and onto the end of the shaft. The *Feature Palette* will disappear and the *Edit This Sketch* dialog will appear automatically. Drag and drop the *Title Bar* of the dialog box, as necessary, to obtain a clear view of the graphics window.

F. Select **Tools ▼ Sketch Tools ▶ Modify...** and the *Modify Sketch* dialog will appear, along with two different drag handles on the sketch.

G. Drag and drop the corner point of the black "L" shaped tool (Figure X9-1) to the part origin. Watch for the white circle on the mouse pointer to change to an orange square and then release the left mouse button.

H. Drag and drop the blue crosshair on the red sketch origin tool (Figure X9-2) to the part origin. Watch for the white circle on the mouse pointer to change to an orange square and then release the left mouse button. You will likely receive a question prompt: *New relation will allow only Rotate operations. Would you like to keep this relation?* In response press the **Yes** button.

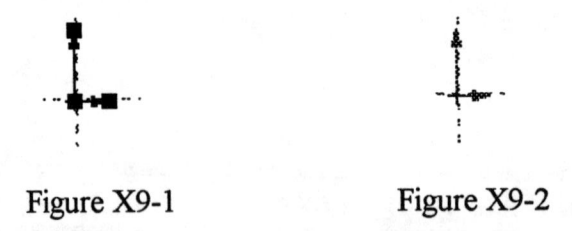

Figure X9-1   Figure X9-2

I. Select **Close** on the *Modify Sketch* dialog. It will disappear. Click **Zoom to Fit**, as necessary, to see the full hexagon.

J. Add a *Horizontal* relation to one of the sides of the hexagon. This should fully define the sketch.

K. Press the **Next** button on the *Edit This Sketch* dialog.

L. Click on **Outside Diameter** in the **Name** column of the *Change Dimensions* dialog.

M. Double click on the default dimension value and change it to **3.000in.**

N. Press the **Finish** button on the *Change Dimensions* dialog.

O. Close the *Feature Palette*.

P. Change to an **Isometric** view of the part.

Q. Select **hexagon1** in the *FeatureManager* design tree and press the **Extruded Base/Boss** tool.

DESIGN PROJECT TUTORIAL

R. On the *End Condition* tab select the *Type:* as **Blind** and the *Depth:* of **1.50in.** and finish the feature. The direction of the *Boss* should be *away* from the *Base feature*, and the final result should look like Figure X9-3:

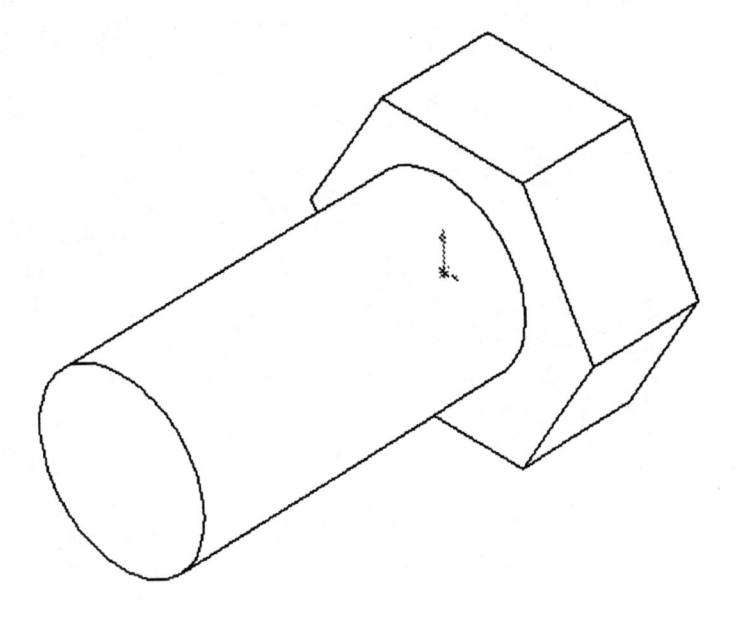

Figure X9-3

Step 4: **Save the part as HEX_BOLT and close the file.**

End of Exercise 9.

Exercise 10: Geometric Relations in Sketches

A *Geometric Relation* is equivalent to, and can substitute for, one or more dimensions in a sketch. Frequently, they are inferred by SolidWorks, and often undesired inferences are made. In this exercise we will fully constrain a complex sketch using only one dimension along with numerous intentional *Geometric Relations*.

Step 1: Open GEO_RELATIONS.SLDPRT and add geometric relations.

A. Open `geo_relations.SLDPRT`. The file will open into *Sketch* mode with Figure X10-1 active.

B. Convert **Sketch1** in this file, shown as Figure X10-1 on page 10-3, into the configuration shown as Figure X10-2 on page 10-4 only by adding *geometric relations* to the sketch. Record the relations as you add them to the sketch on page 10-2. A sample relation is written on the chart to explain how to fill it in.

The following chart of possible relations for lines may be useful:

To add this relation	Select:	Result:
Horizontal or Vertical	One or more lines, or two or more points	The lines become horizontal or vertical (as) defined by the current sketch space). Points are aligned horizontally or vertically.
Collinear	Two or more lines	The items lie on the same infinite line.
Perpendicular	Two lines	The two items are perpendicular to each other.
Parallel	Two or more lines	The items remain parallel.
Equal	Two or more lines, or two or more arcs	The lines lengths or arc radii remain equal.

The only firm rule is that **no dimensions can be added to the sketch!** There are a number of different ways of successfully completing this exercise. It is a very good idea to perform this exercise with another person or compare notes with several other people after you have completed it.

List the *Relations* that will convert *Sketch1* of file `geo_relations.SLDPRT` to a fully defined sketch like Figure X10-2. If, at any time, your sketch turns red use *Undo* to remove the most recent relationship that was added, and try something different. Refer to the alphabetic labels on page 10-3 (A, B, C, etc.) when entering descriptions in the *Entities Related* column:

Type of Relationship	Entities Related	Type of Relationship	Entities Related
B, F	Collinear		

DESIGN PROJECT TUTORIAL

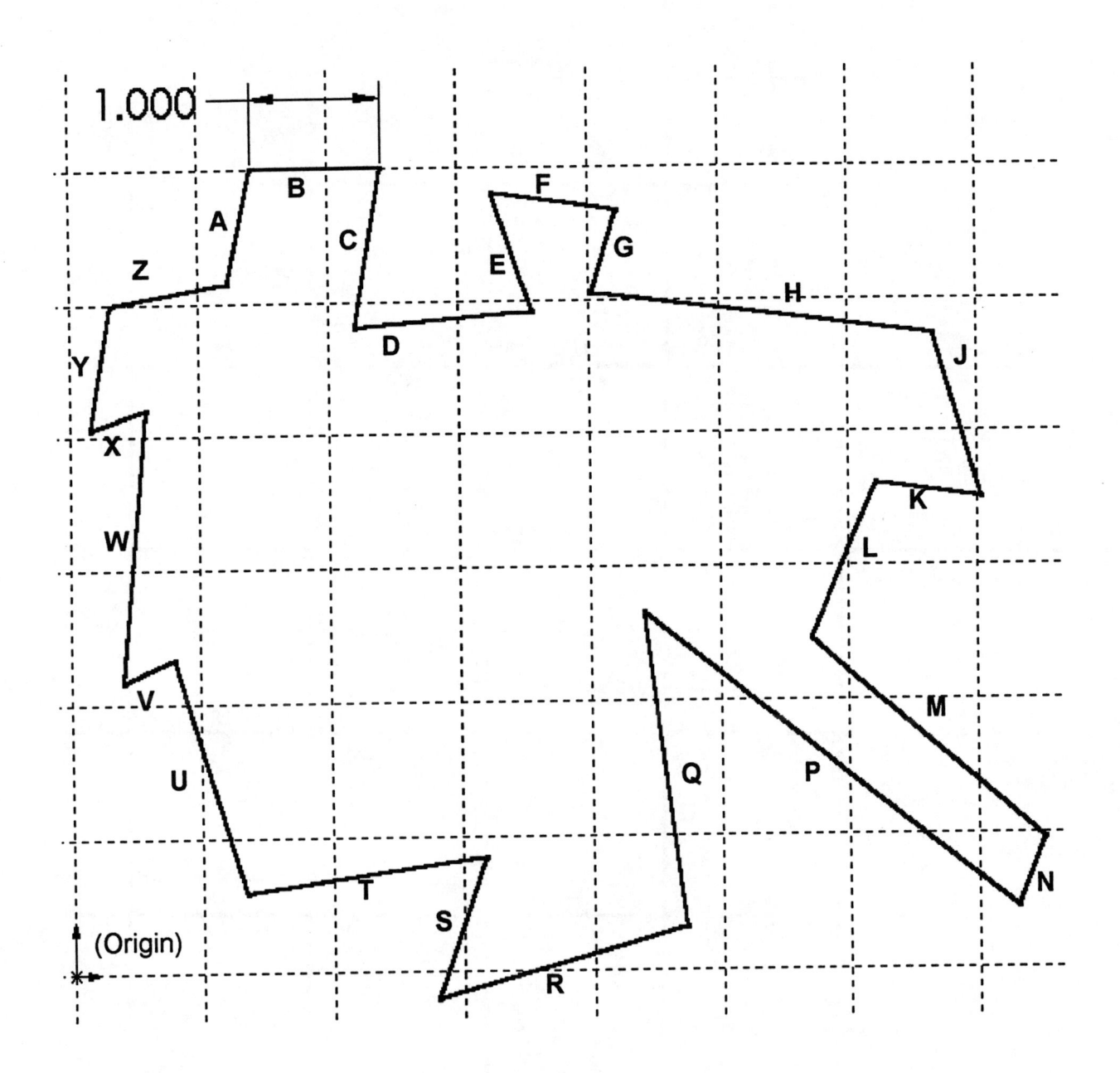

Figure X10-1

DESIGN PROJECT TUTORIAL

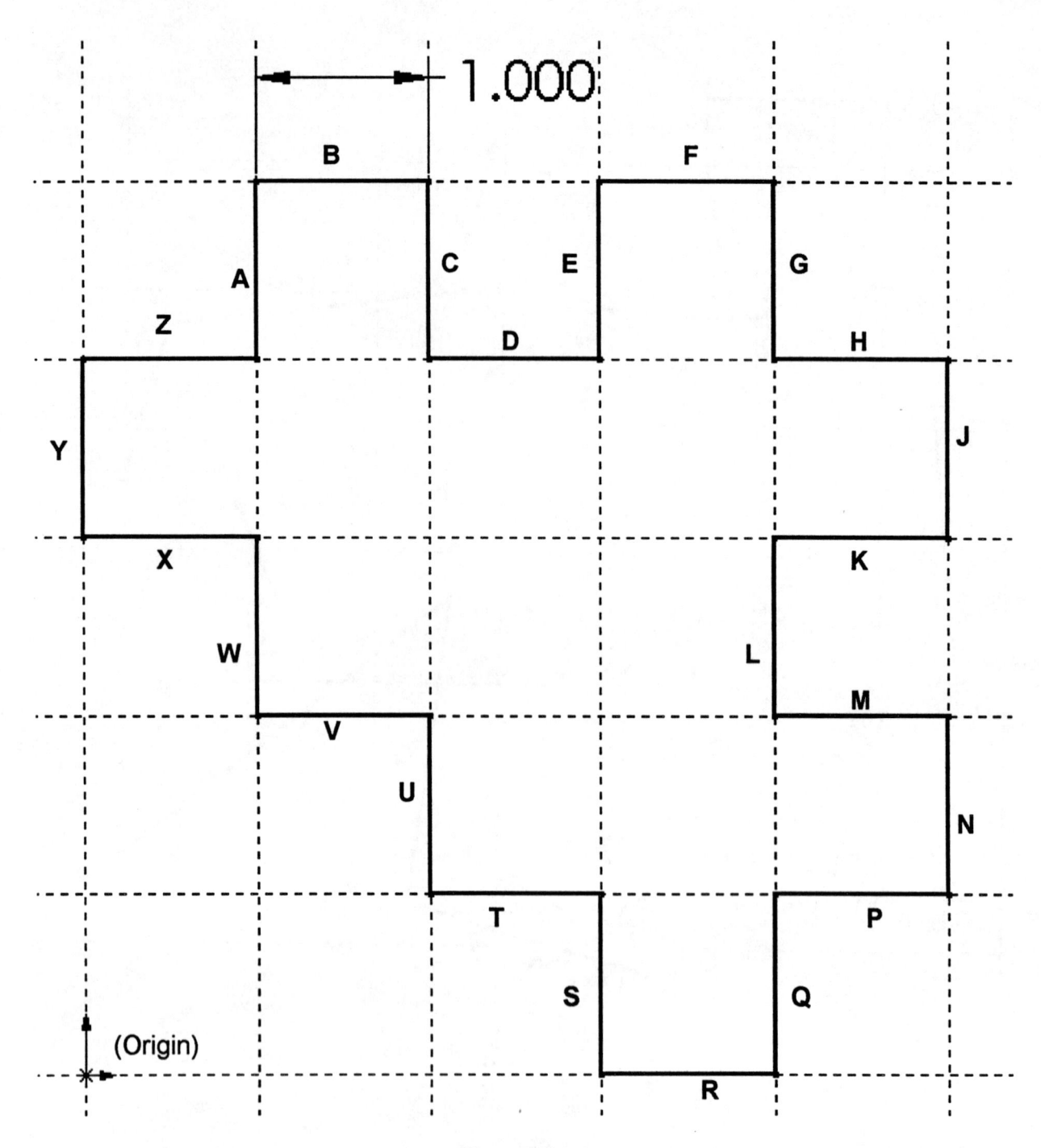

Figure X10-2

End of Exercise 10.

DESIGN PROJECT TUTORIAL

Exercise 11: Feature Suppression, Reorder, and Insertion with Rollback

In this exercise you will be introduced to techniques for simplifying the model without removing information, for rearranging the order of feature creation after-the-fact, and for returning to an earlier point in model construction. The starting configuration of the part for the exercise is shown as Figure X11-1, and the final configuration is shown as Figure X11-6.

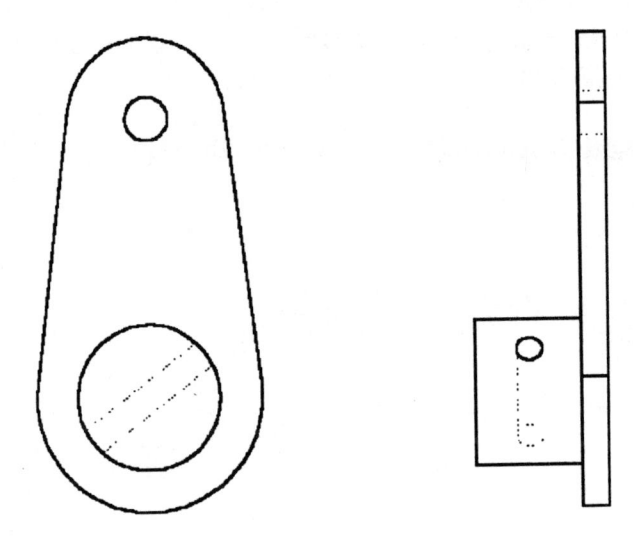

Exercise X11-1

Step 1: **Open CRANK.SLDPRT and simplify the display in preparation for redefining the *Boss*.**

A. Use **File▼ Open...** (or press the **Open** icon) to access `crank.SLDPRT`.

B. To understand the features of the model select a **Shaded** view and use **Rotate View** to spin the model. Return to an **Isometric** view orientation and a **Hidden in Gray** view display.

C. Select **Plane4** in the *FeatureManager* design tree and then select **Edit▼ Suppress**. Notice that both Plane4 and the Cross-hole are grayed out in the *FeatureManager* design tree. The Cross_hole is suppressed because it is a *Child* of Plane4. Note that the model resembles an earlier stage of creation.

DESIGN PROJECT TUTORIAL

Step 2:   **Redefine the *Boss* to extend symmetrically in both directions.**

A.   Select **Boss-Extrude1** in the *FeatureManager* design tree, right click, and select **Edit Definition** from the popup menu.

B.   Check **Both Directions**, select **Direction2** under the *Settings for:* flipdown menu, and set the *Depth:* to **30.00mm**. Press **OK**.

C.   Change to a **Right** view orientation to observe the symmetry of the *boss* as shown on Figure X11-2:

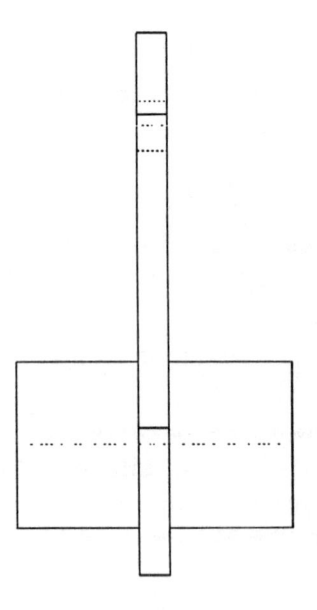

Figure X11-2

D.   Return to an **Isometric** view.

Step 3:   ***Unsuppress* the *Cross_hole*.**

Select the **Cross_hole** on the *FeatureManager* design tree and then select **Edit ▼ Unsuppress**. Notice that *Plane4* was also unsuppressed because it is the *Parent* of the *Cross_hole*.

DESIGN PROJECT TUTORIAL

Step 4: *Rollback* the part to its condition before the creation of *Plane4* and the *Cross_hole* and create a hole through the center of the *Boss*.

It is always advisable to have the order of feature creation in the *FeatureManager* design tree reflect the order of feature creation during manufacturing. A concentric hole is intended to pass completely through the *boss*, and it will be bored before the *Cross_hole* during the manufacturing of the *Crank*. To reflect the order of manufacturing in the design tree we will *Rollback* the part to its condition just before the creation of *Plane4*.

A. Drag and drop the *Rollback Bar* in the *FeatureManager* to a position above *Plane 4*. The 'before' and 'after' positions of the *Rollback Bar* are shown in Figure X11-3 and Figure X11-4, respectively:

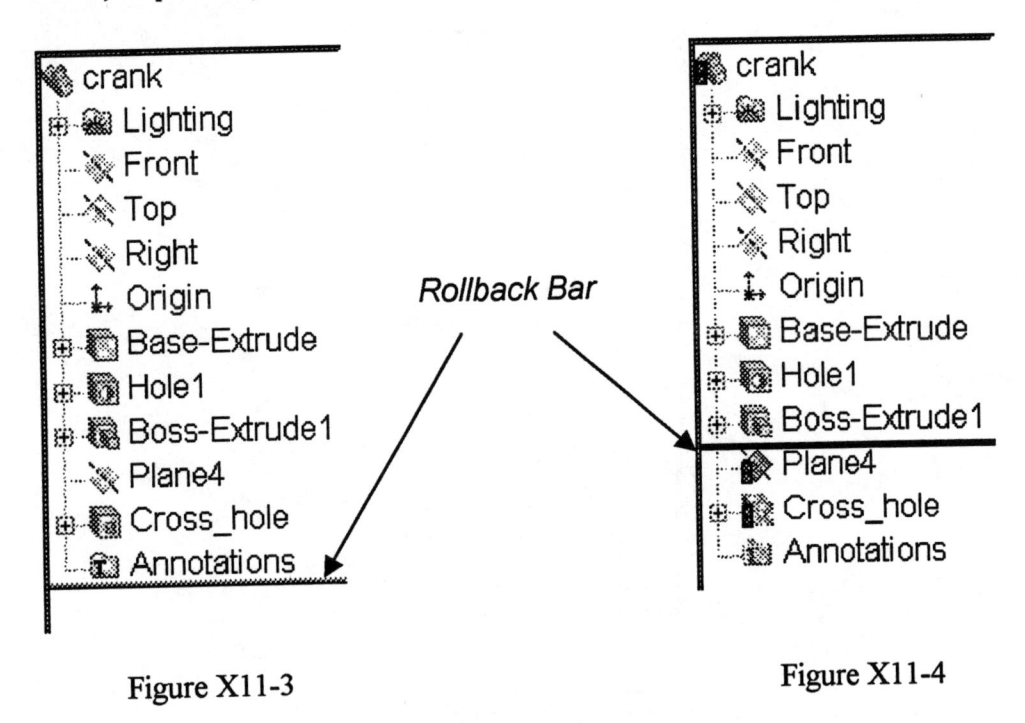

Figure X11-3

Figure X11-4

B. Select the frontmost face of the *boss* and **Sketch** a **Circle** on it.

C. **Dimension** the circle and **Modify** the diameter to a value of **19.00mm.**

D. Click the **Extruded Cut** feature tool and select **Through All** as the *Type*. **OK** feature creation.

E. Notice that new *Cut-Extrude1* has been inserted between *Boss-Extrude1* and *Plane4* in the *FeatureManager*.

Step 5: Restore *Plane4* and the *Cross_hole* in the model display.

Drag and drop the *Rollback Bar* in the *FeatureManager* to its 'normal' position below the *Annotations* folder.

Step 6: Rearrange *Hole1* in the *FeatureManager*.

Drag and drop *Hole1* into a position just below *Boss-Extrude1* in the *FeatureManager* design tree. The result will look like Figure X11-5:

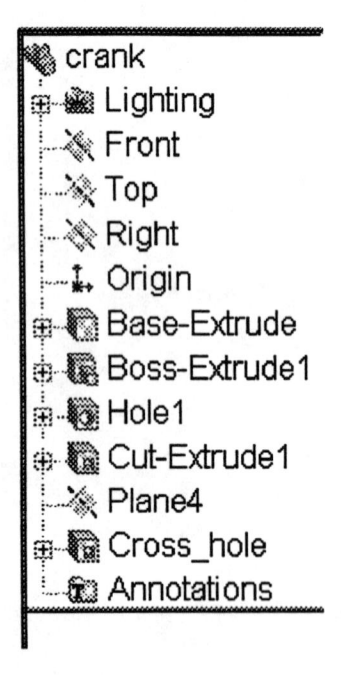

```
crank
   Lighting
   Front
   Top
   Right
   Origin
   Base-Extrude
   Boss-Extrude1
   Hole1
   Cut-Extrude1
   Plane4
   Cross_hole
   Annotations
```

Figure X11-5

This method of reordering features is very fast and easy, but it will not always work as simply as it did in this case. A feature cannot be reordered downward to a position below its *Children* or upward to a position above its *Parents*.

The final display of the part model in the graphics window will look like Figure X11-6:

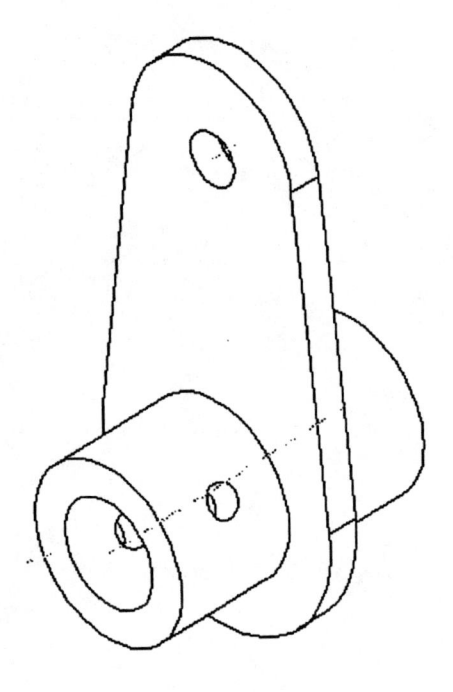

Figure X11-6

End of Exercise 11.

Exercise 12: Sketch and Feature Editing

Parametric solid models always reveal the order in which features were created. Usually, features that are created later are related to, and dependent upon, features that are created earlier. In this sense earlier features are generally more important than later features.

The time sequence of feature creation is reflected intrinsically in the *FeatureManager* design tree. Features that are higher in the design tree, meaning closer to the default features (Origin and primary reference planes), were created earliest. Features that are lower in the design tree, meaning closer to the Annotations folder, were created latest.

It is possible to drastically alter a model with Sketch and Feature editing. In this exercise we will prove this by converting the model of Figure X12-1, which almost resembles gothic art, into the desired model of Figure X12-2 while learning highly important editing skills for the future:

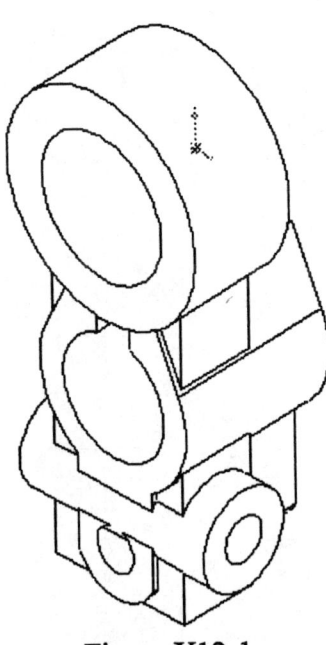

Figure X12-1 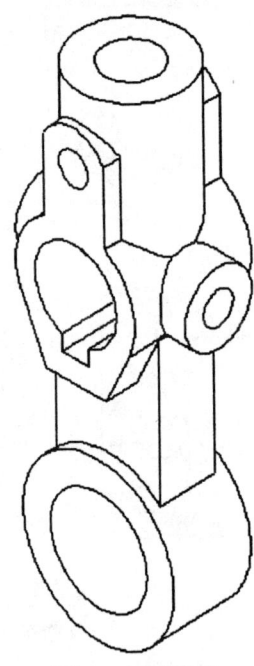   Figure X12-2

Step 1: **Open IDLER_ARM.SLDPRT and simplify the model in preparation for feature redefinition.**

A. Open the file `idler_arm.SLDPRT`.

B. Change to an **Isometric** view. Examine the model against Figures X12-2 and X12-3 for feature content.

DESIGN PROJECT TUTORIAL

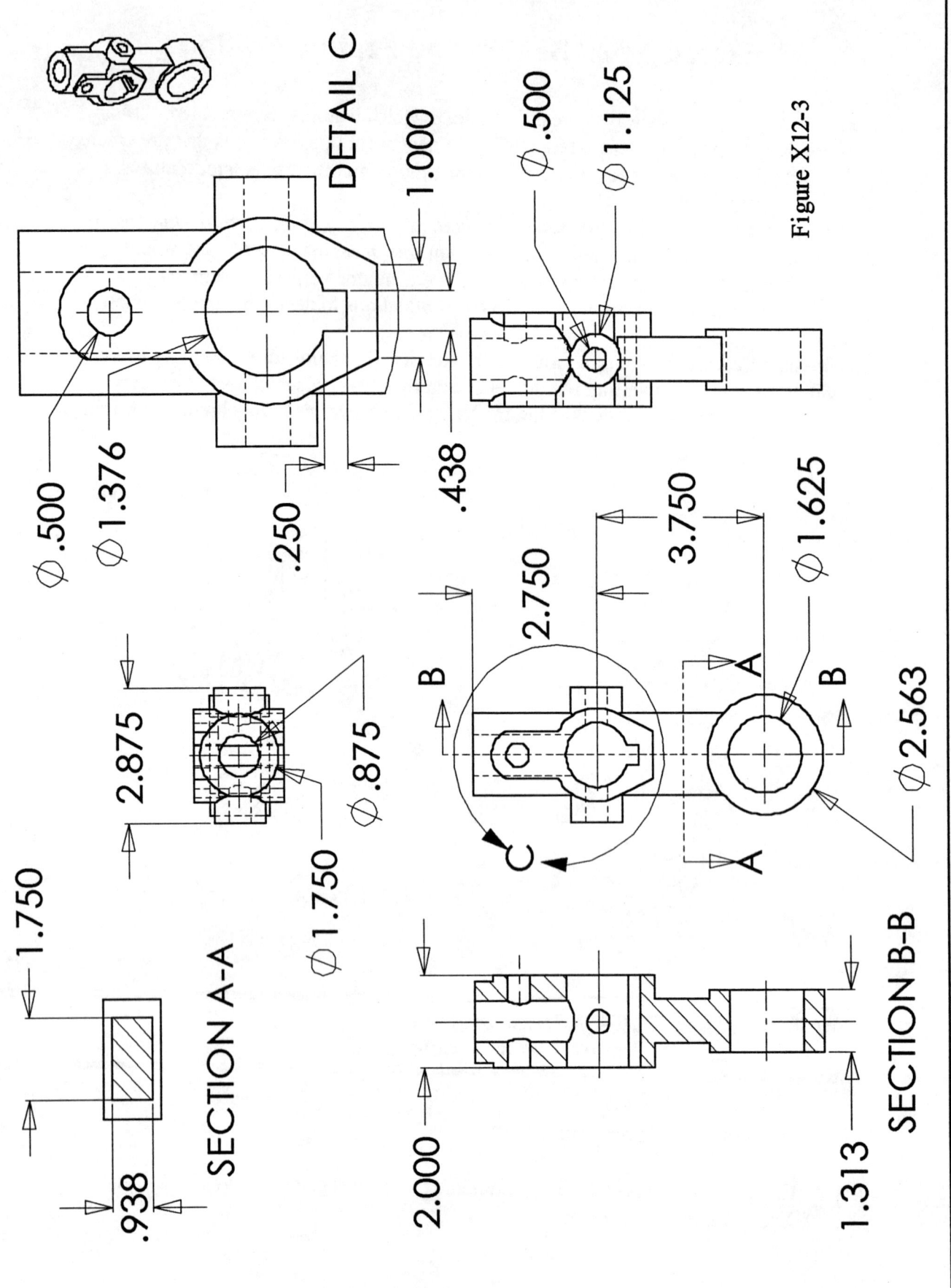

DETAIL C

⌀.500
⌀1.125

1.000

.438

.250

⌀.500
⌀1.376

2.875

⌀.875
⌀1.750

1.750

.938

SECTION A-A

2.750

3.750

⌀1.625

⌀2.563

2.000

1.313

SECTION B-B

Figure X12-3

DESIGN PROJECT TUTORIAL

All features seem to be there except the Ø1.750in. boss on top and maybe a hole or two. We can't really add these until we understand the relationships of the existing features. The model would be easier to analyze in a configuration with fewer features. This occurred earlier in time during model creation, and we can travel back in time.

A critical objective of our modeling editing, because of the symmetry of the part about the *Front* and *Right* vertical planes, is to sketch as many features as possible on these planes and to use *MidPlane* feature types.

C. Rollback the model until only Base-Extrude is active. Do this by dragging and dropping the **Rollback Bar** from the original position to the position shown in Figure X12-5:

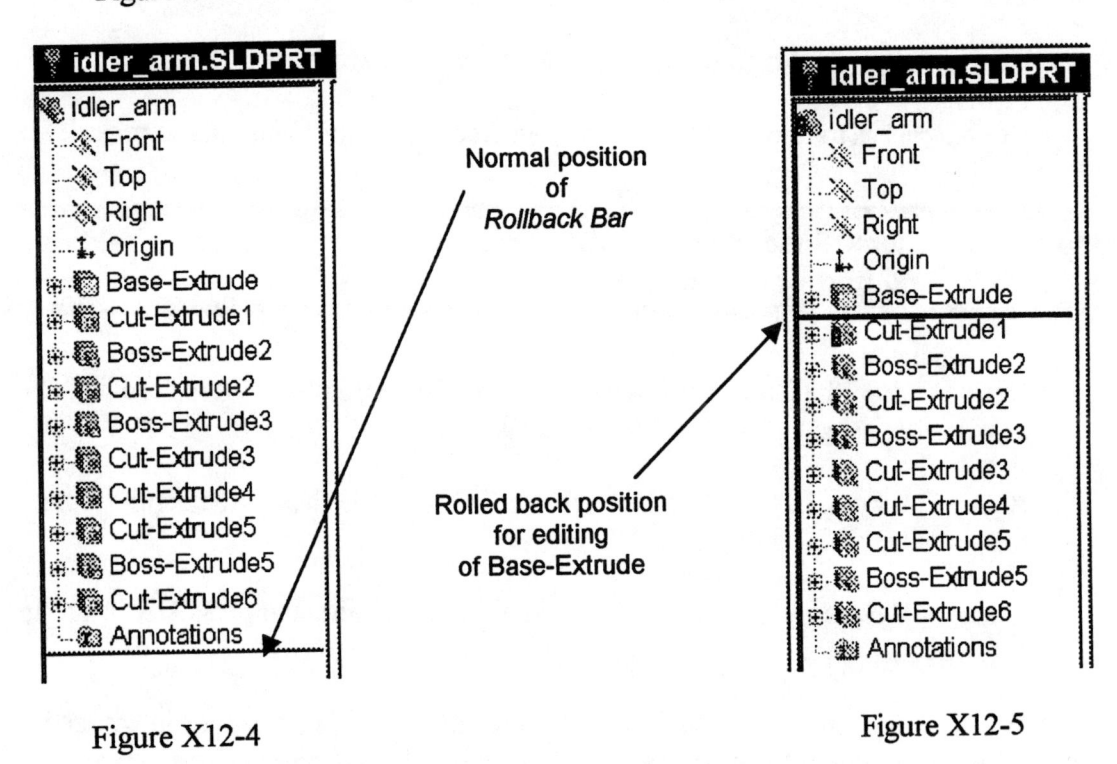

Figure X12-4

Figure X12-5

Step 2: Check *Base-Extrude* dimensions, sketch location, and *End Condition* type.

A. Click the "+" sign beside *Base-Extrude* to expand the *FeatureManager* design tree.

B. Double click on **Sketch1** to check the diameter dimension. Ø2.563in. is correct.

DESIGN PROJECT TUTORIAL

C. Change to a **Right** view and click on the **Front** plane in the *FeatureManager*. The feature is OK as is, but we want to work for front-to-back symmetry wherever possible.

D. Right click on **Base-Extrude**, select **Edit Definition** from the popup menu, select **MidPlane** as the *End Condition Type*, and press **OK** to complete re-definition.

E. Change to an **Isometric** view.

Step 3: Check *Cut-Extrude1* dimensions, sketch location, and *End Condition* type.

A. Drag and drop the **Rollback Bar** to just below Cut-Extrude1.

B. Double click **Cut-Extrude1** to check diameter. Ø1.625in. is correct so press **Esc**.

Step 4: Check *Boss-Extrude2* dimensions, sketch location, *Direction*, and *End Condition* type.

A. Drag and drop the **Rollback Bar** to just below Boss-Extrude2. It is heading downward, instead of upward as we intend.

B. Right click **Boss-Extrude2**, select **Edit Definition**, and change the depth to the proper value of **3.750in**.

C. Uncheck **Reverse Direction** so the feature heads upward, and press **OK** to finish feature redefinition. Click **Zoom to Fit**.

We just added material back into the through hole. This shows poor judgment in the original order of feature creation. It is generally better to create all bosses before creating any cuts. Nonetheless, the model is in a desirable configuration for adding the missing Ø1.750in. by 2.750in. high boss on the top of the part.

DESIGN PROJECT TUTORIAL

Step 5: Add a Ø1.750in. x 2.750in. high boss on top of *Boss-Extrude2*.

A. Select the top surface of *Boss-Extrude2* as a sketching surface and begin sketching. See Figure X12-6.

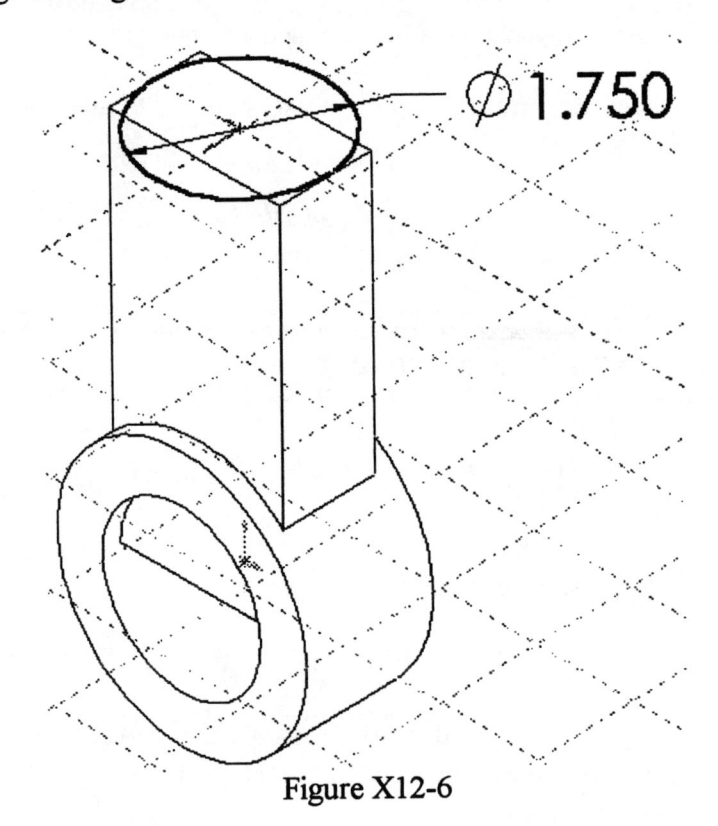

Figure X12-6

B. Sketch a circle with **Ø1.750in.** and it center *Coincident* with the part's *Origin*.

C. Extrude a *boss* upward with a height of **2.750in.** Click **Zoom to fit**.

Step 6: Roll forward and evaluate *Cut-Extrude2*.

A. Drag and drop the **Rollback Bar** to just below *Cut-Extrude2*.

B. *Cut-Extrude2* removes the material that we put in the hole with *Boss-Extrude2*, but why have two features with the same sketch and definition? For model simplicity it is a good idea to remove one or the other from the model. *Cut-Extrude2* is more desirable because it comes after *Boss-Extrude2* and can do the work of both cuts.

C. Click on **Cut-Extrude1** in the *FeatureManager,* press the **Delete** key, confirm the deletion by pressing **Yes**, and read the *idler_arm-Rebuild Errors* dialog which says:

Sketch4: Warning: This sketch contains dimensions or relations to model geometry which no longer exists. Consider :
    o Deleting the dangling sketch entities (shown dashed and in dangling color).
    o Editing the model to restore the missing model geometry.

It appears that we have created a problem with *Sketch4* of another feature. **Close** the *Rebuild Errors* dialog.

D. Delete **Sketch2**. **Close** the *idler_arm-Rebuild Errors* dialog when it appears again since it will say the same thing as before.

Step 7:   Evaluate the error in *Sketch4*.

A. Drag and drop the **Rollback Bar** to just below *Boss-Extrude2*. **Close** the *Rebuild Errors* dialog.

B. Click the "+" sign beside *Boss-Extrude2* to expand the design tree.

C. Right click **Sketch4** and select **Edit Sketch**. Change to a **Top** view.

D. The olive color of the *0.188in.* dimensions shows that it was related to the deleted feature in some way, and its reference no longer exists in the model. This condition is called a *dangling* dimension. This word was used in the error dialog. Deletion is the best way to handle a dangling dimension.

E. Delete the **0.188in.** dimension. Notice that the sketch becomes underconstrained, as indicated by the blue color of the horizontal lines.

DESIGN PROJECT TUTORIAL

F. Sketch a horizontal centerline through origin. Add a **Symmetric** type of *Geometric Relation* between the new centerline and the horizontal lines and **Apply** it.

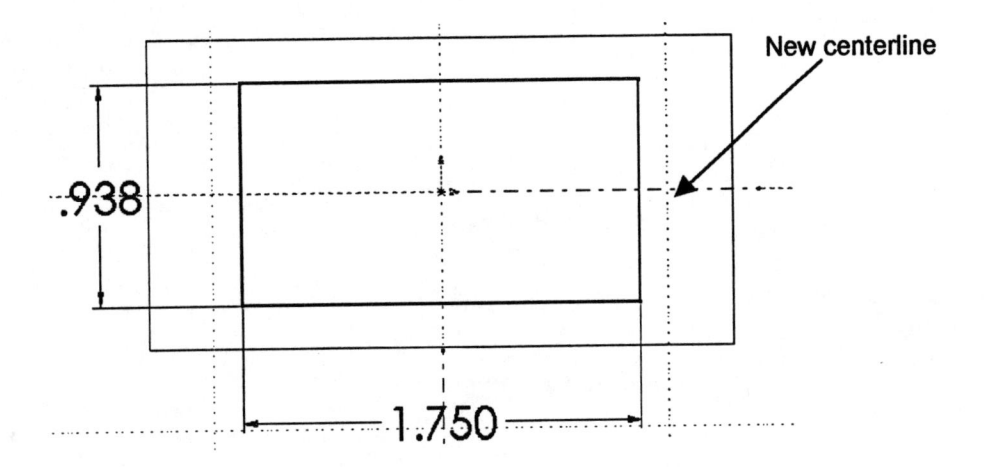

Figure X12-7

G. Close the *Add Geometric Relations* dialog, close the sketch by clicking the **Sketch** icon, note that the rebuild error no longer exists, and change to an **Isometric** view.

Step 8: Roll forward and evaluate the error in *Boss-Extrude3*.

A. Drag and drop the **Rollback Bar** to just below *Boss-Extrude3*. Click **Zoom to Fit**

B. Click the "+" sign beside *Boss-Extrude3* to expand the design tree.

C. Right click **Sketch6** and select **Edit Sketch**. Change to a **Front** view.

D. Draw a horizontal center line through origin as shown on Figure X12-8:

DESIGN PROJECT TUTORIAL

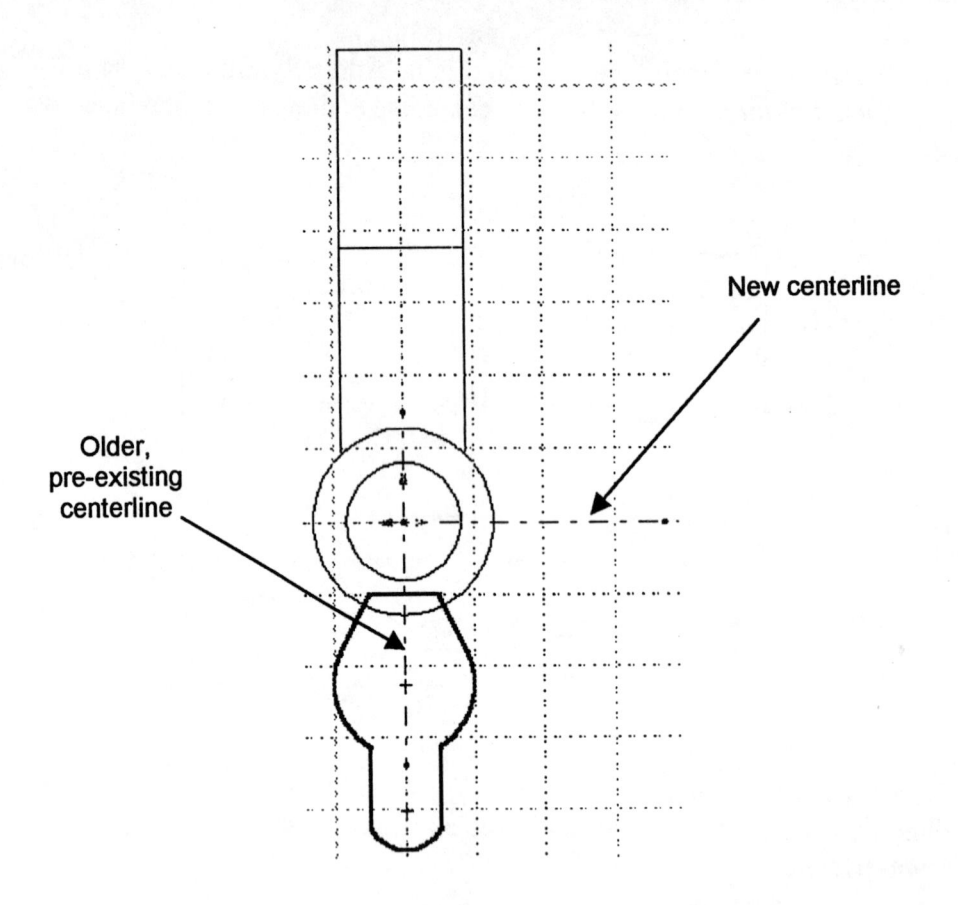

Figure X12-8

E. Select all sketch entities except vertical centerline using **Ctrl+pick**. Make sure horizontal centerline is selected and the vertical centerline is not selected.

F. Press the **Mirror** tool on the *Sketch Tools* toolbar.

G. Select and delete all sketched lines and arcs which lie below the horizontal centerline. Do not delete either centerline.

H. Add the five dimensions as shown on Figure X12-9:

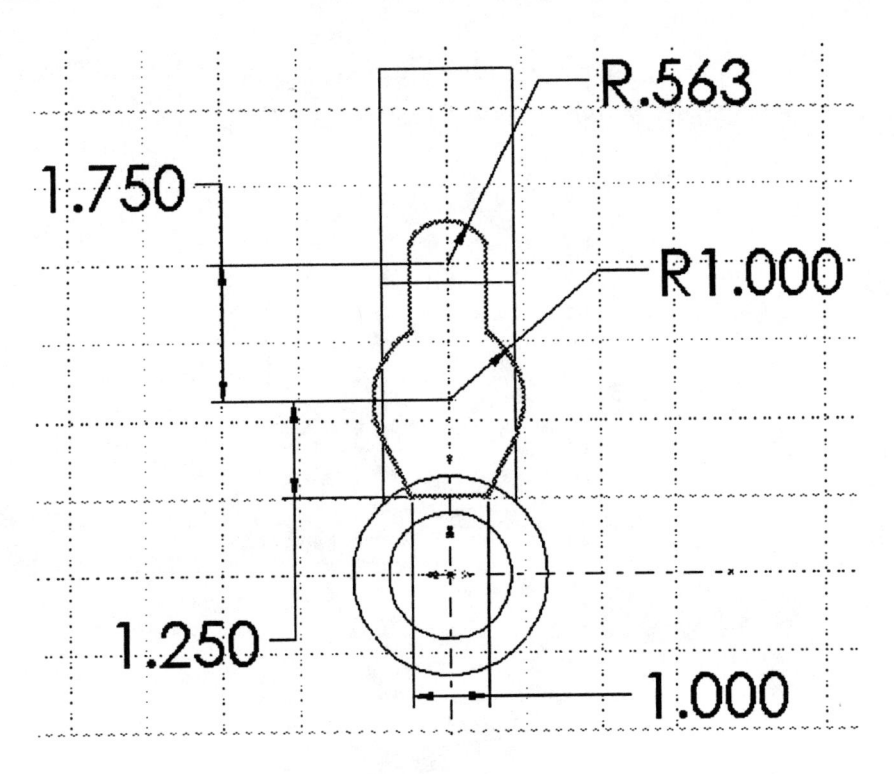

Figure X12-9

I. Add a *Tangent* relation between each of the short vertical lines and the small arc, and **Apply** the relation. Note how the 1.750in. dimension moved away from vertical.

J. Add a *Coincident* between the upper centerpoint and the vertical centerline and **Apply** the relation. Note that the 1.750in. dimension is still not vertical.

K. Add a *Coincident* relation between the lower centerpoint and the vertical centerline and **Apply** the relation.

L. Add a *Coincident* relation between the lower centerpoint to top edge of *Boss-Extrude2* and **Apply** the relation. See Figure X12-10:

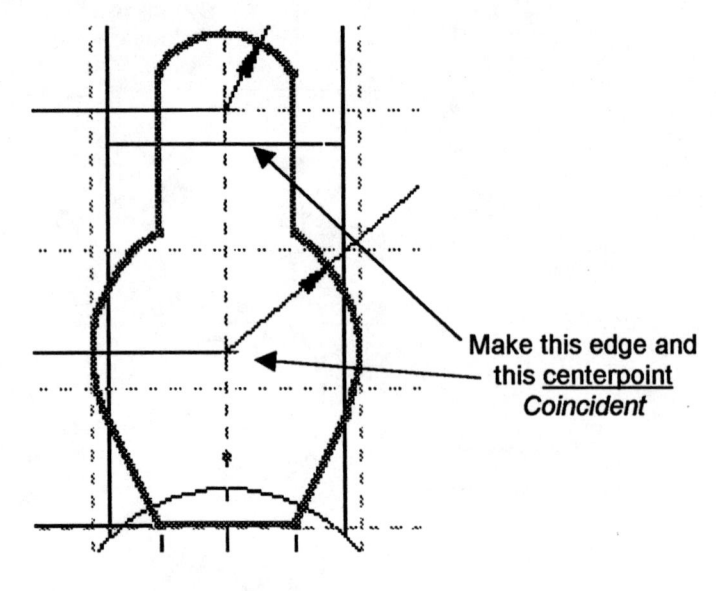

Figure X12-10

M. Add a *Symmetric* relation between the two large arcs (one now blue, one now black) and the vertical centerline. **Apply** it.

N. Add a *Symmetric* relation between the two, short vertical sketched lines and the vertical centerline. **Apply** it.

O. Add a *Vertical* relation to one of the two short vertical lines. It is not necessary to do both because they are already symmetrical. **Apply.**

P. Add a *Horizontal* relation to the short horizontal sketched line and **Apply** it.

Q. Add a *Symmetrical* relation between the two diagonal lines and the vertical centerline and **Apply** it.

R. Add a *Tangent* relation between either large radius arc and its adjacent diagonal line and **Apply** it. The sketch should be fully defined.

S. Close the *Add Geometric Relations* dialog. Close the sketch by clicking the **Sketch** icon. Change to an **Isometric** view.

DESIGN PROJECT TUTORIAL

Step 9: Check the sketching plane and direction for *Boss-Extrude3*.

A. Change to a **Right** view. For the sake of understanding the relationship between these two entities, double click on **Sketch6** and click once on the **Front** plane in the *FeatureManager*. You can see that the feature is not symmetrical with the *Front* plane.

B. Right click on **Sketch6** and select **Edit Sketch Plane.**

C. Select the **Front** plane in *FeatureManager* and press the **Apply** button in the *Sketching Plane* dialog. Change to a **Isometric** view.

D. To clean up the graphics window press the **Esc** key twice and click on the **Redraw** tool.

Step 10: Roll forward and evaluate the error in *Cut-Extrude3*.

A. Drag and drop the **Rollback Bar** to just below *Cut-Extrude3*. Read and **Close** the error dialog, noting that there is a *dangling* dimension in *Sketch7*:

Sketch7: Warning: This sketch contains dimensions or relations to model geometry which no longer exists. Consider :
    o Deleting the dangling sketch entities (shown dashed and in dangling color).
    o Editing the model to restore the missing model geometry.
Cut-Extrude3: This feature would create a disjoint body.

B. Click the "+" sign beside *Cut-Extrude3* to expand the design tree.

C. Right click **Sketch7** and select **Edit Sketch.** Change to a **Front** view. Use **Zoom to Area** to close in on the sketched circle. Since the diameter of the circle is dimensioned only the locating dimensions or relations for the center point can be dangling.

D. Right click on centerpoint of circle and select **Display/Delete Relations...**

E. Immediately, a *Coincident* relation that is *Dangling* is identified. Press the **Delete** button and the **Close** button in the dialog. Notice that the circle is now blue, indicating that it is underconstrained.

F. Change to an **Isometric** view. Select **View ▼ Temporary Axes** to show them.

12-11

DESIGN PROJECT TUTORIAL

G. Add a *Coincident* relation between the lower centerline of *Boss-Extrude3* and the centerpoint of the sketched circle. **Apply** the relation and **Close** the dialog. See Figure X12-11:

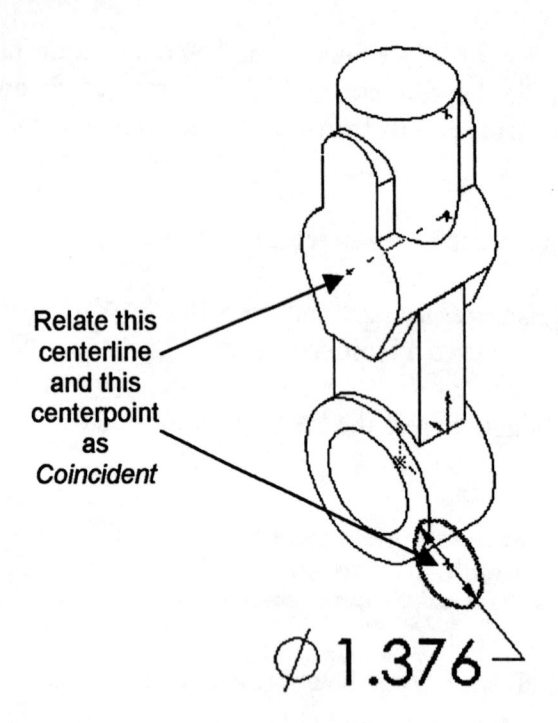

Relate this centerline and this centerpoint as *Coincident*

⌀ 1.376

Figure X12-11

H. Click on the **Sketch** tool to close the sketch.

Step 11: Evaluate the sketching plane and direction of *Cut-Extrude3*.

A. Double click on **Sketch 7** in the *FeatureManager*. Change to a **Right** view. We would prefer features which are symmetrical about the *Front* plane so the Cut definition now needs changed.

B. Right click on **Sketch7**, select **Edit Sketch Plane** from the popup menu, select the **Front** reference plane in the *FeatureManager* and press the **Apply** button in the *Sketching Plane* dialog.

C. Right click over **Cut-Extrude3**, select **Edit Definition** from the popup menu, check the **Both Directions** option, select **Direction2** from the *Settings for:* flipdown menu, select **Through All** as the *End Condition Type* for *Direction2*, and press the **OK** button in the *Extrude Cut Feature* dialog.

D. Change to an **Isometric** view.

DESIGN PROJECT TUTORIAL

Step 12: Roll forward and revise the sketch for *Cut-Extrude4*.

A. Drag and drop the **Rollback Bar** to just below *Cut-Extrude4*.

B. Click the "+" sign beside *Cut-Extrude4* to expand the design tree.

C. Click once on **Sketch9** and change to a **Right** view. The sketch location should be changed to the *Front* plane.

D. Right click over **Sketch9**, select **Edit Sketch Plane** from the popup menu, select **Front** plane in *FeatureManager*, and press **Apply**. The cut does not now extend completely through the part.

E. Right click over **Cut-Extrude4**, select **Edit Definition** from the popup menu, check the **Both Directions** option, select **Through All** as the *Type* for Direction1, select **Direction 2** from the *Settings for* flipdown window, select **Through All** as the *Type* for Direction2, and press **OK**.

F. Change to an **Isometric** view. Alternately, double click **Sketch7** and double click **Sketch9** to understand that they both remove the same material from the same hole. Sketch 9 will be edited to simplify it, to cut the keyway on the bottom of the Ø1.376 hole, and to only cut out the keyway.

G. Right click **Sketch9**, select **Edit Sketch**, and change to a **Front** view.

H. Change to a **Front** view. Delete all sketch entities. Use **Zoom to Area** to obtain close view of the construction area for the keyway.

I. Sketch as shown on Figure X12-12. Close the sketch and change to an **Isometric** view.

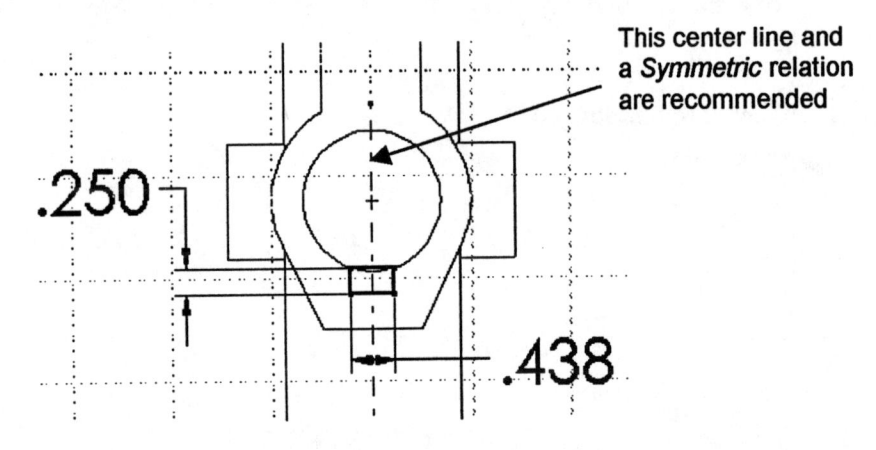

Figure X12-12

12-13

Step 13: Roll forward and evaluate the error in *Cut-Extrude5*.

A. Drag and drop the **Rollback Bar** to just below *Cut-Extrude5*. Read and **Close** the *Rebuild Errors* dialog:

Sketch10: Warning: This sketch contains dimensions or relations to model geometry which no longer exists. Consider :
    o Deleting the dangling sketch entities (shown dashed and in dangling color).
    o Editing the model to restore the missing model geometry.

B. Click the "+" sign beside *Cut-Extrude5* to expand the design tree.

C. Double click **Sketch10**, change to a **Right** view, click **Zoom to Fit**, and note that the sketch is on the back face of the part, rather than on the *Front* plane where we desire.

D. Right click **Sketch10**, select **Edit Sketch Plane**, select the **Front** plane in the *FeatureManager*, press **Apply**, and **Close** the *Rebuild Errors* dialog. Press **Esc** and click **Redraw** to "clean up" the display.

E. Right click **Sketch10** and select **Edit Sketch.** Change to a **Front** view. Since the sketched circle is dimensioned and we know from the error message that there is a dangling dimension somewhere, the center<u>point</u> must have a dangling *relation.*

F. Use **Zoom to Area** to obtain a close up view of the sketched circle. Deactivate **Zoom to Area.**

G. Right click on circle's center<u>point</u> and select **Display/Delete Relations...**

H. Immediately, Relation1 is shown to be a *Coincident* type with *Dangling* status. Press the **Delete** button and then the **Close** button. Note that the circle is now blue.

I. Change to an **Isometric** view.

J. Add a *Coincident* relation between the centerpoint of the circle and the upper axis of Boss-Extrude3. See Figure X12-13. **Apply** the relation, **Close** the dialog, and close the sketch by clicking on the **Sketch** tool.

Relate centerpoint of sketched circle to this axis of Boss-Extrude3

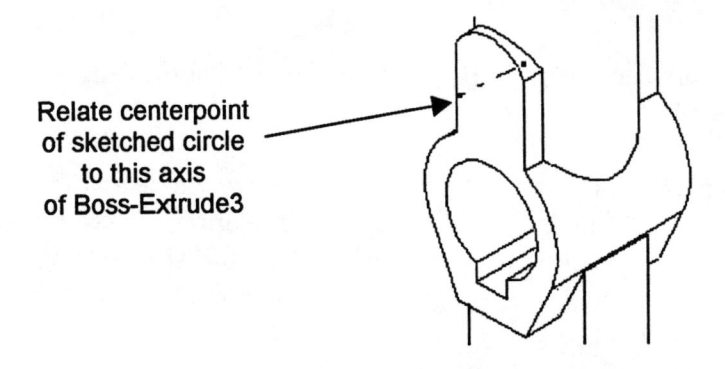

Figure X12-13

K. Right click on **Cut-Extrude5**, select **Edit Definition**, check the **Both Directions** option, select **Through All** as the *Type* for Direction1, select **Direction2** from the *Settings for* flipdown menu, select **Through All** as the *Type* for Direction2, and **OK** the redefinition.

Step 14: Roll forward, evaluate, and repair the error in *Boss-Extrude5*.

A. Drag and drop the **Rollback Bar** to just below *Boss-Extrude5*. Read and **Close** the *Rebuild Errors* dialog:

> This feature would create a disjoint body.

This meaning of this error message is relatively plain. Extruding the sketch will not create a solid feature that connects with the remainder of the part model. This can be repaired rather easily. We'll perform the more difficult editing operation first.

Since Boss-Extrude5 will add material back to the inside of Cut-Extrude3 it is a very good idea to move Boss-Extrude5 to a position above Cut-Extrude3 in the design tree, either by dragging and dropping it there or by deleting it and recreating it in a rolled back position above Cut-Extrude3.

B. Drag and drop Boss-Extrude5 to above Cut-Extrude3 in the *FeatureManager* design tree. The head on the elbowed arrow should be below Boss-Extrude3 and above Cut-Extrude3 when you lift your finger from the left mouse button.

C. Respond with **OK** to the message "This feature would create a disjoint body," and **Close** the *Rebuild Errors* dialog.

DESIGN PROJECT TUTORIAL

D. Click "+" next to Boss-Extrude5 to expand the design tree and show Sketch12.

E. Right click on **Sketch12** and select **Edit Sketch** from the popup menu. Use **Zoom to Fit** to see all of the sketch, as necessary.

F. Add a *Coincident* relation between the centerpoint of the sketched circle center and the **Front** plane, and apply it.

G. Add a *Coincident* relation between the centerpoint of the sketched circle and the lower axis of Boss-Extrude3 (see Figure X12-14), **Apply** the relation, **Close** the *Add Geometric Relation* dialog, and close the sketch by clicking the **Sketch** tool.

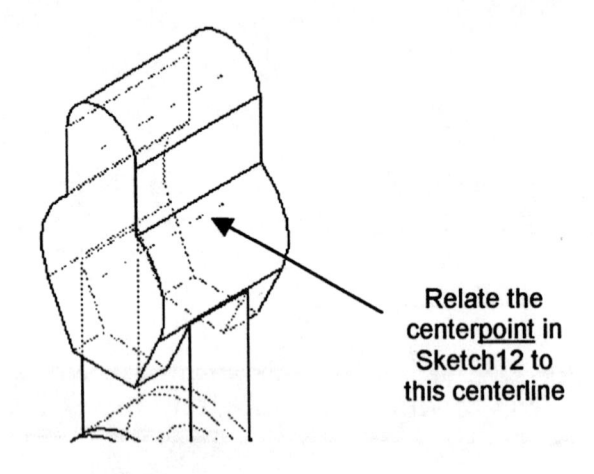

Relate the centerpoint in Sketch12 to this centerline

Figure X12-14

H. Right click on **Boss-Extrude5**, select **Edit Definition**, change the *Depth:* to **2.875in.**, the correct dimension from the part drawing.

Step 15: Roll fully forward and change the definition of *Cut-Extrude6*.

A. Drag and drop the **Rollback Bar** to its normal position below the *Annotations* folder.

B. Right click on **Cut-Extrude6**, select **Edit Definition**, select **Through All** as the *Type*, check the **Both Directions** option, select **Direction2** from the *Settings for* flipdown window, select **Through All** again, and press **OK**.

DESIGN PROJECT TUTORIAL

Step 16: Add the missing cut to the top of the part.

A. Select **View ▼ Temporary Axes** to hide them.

B. Select the top surface of the part, enter **Sketch** mode, sketch a circle with its center at the origin, dimension the circle with a **Ø0.875in**.

C. Extrude the cut downward with the *Type* as **Up to Next**. Shade and spin the model to make sure that there is not any material in any of the holes

Step 17: Save and close the model.

Please note that the techniques which have been employed during this exercise are good practices to employ during model editing. The techniques have not been explained during each step of the Exercise for brevity.

Essentially, the model is checked and verified by one feature at a time, removing all errors and re-referencing the sketch plane and sketch entities as you proceed. During this Exercise, very few new sketches and sketch entities were introduced-- this is a very important facet of editing efficiency.

It would be a good idea to re-perform this Exercise until the "why" of each Step in the editing process begins to dawn. The extent of editing during this Exercise is incredible and will rarely be encountered during gainful modeling, but the *techniques*, and the thought processes underlying them, are extremely valuable to know and to understand.

End of Exercise 12.

Exercise 13: Feature Conflicts and Conflict Resolution

Rollback is useful for model editing, but unintended conflicts between features can arise after the entire model is restored. In common practice feature conflicts usually come as a surprise and are challenging to resolve.

In this exercise a feature will be created with a *Rollback* in effect in such a way that a simple feature conflict is created. The conflict will then be resolved quickly and logically. Normally, you would never intentionally create a feature conflict, but this practice is useful in this exercise for learning about them.

Step 1:   Open the file WIDGET_X13.SLDPRT and use *Rollback* to return to an earlier part configuration.

A.   Open the file `widget_x13.SLDPRT`.

B.   Drag and drop the **Rollback Bar** (see Figure X12-3) to a position just below *Base-Loft*.

Step 2:   Add rounds to the part using the *Fillet* command.

A.   Select the four bottom edges of *Base-Loft* as shown on Figure X13-1:

Select these four edges

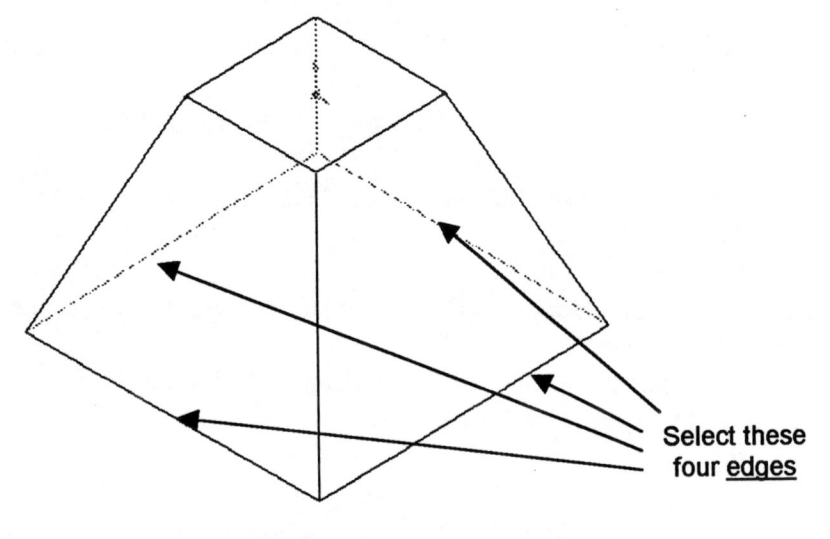

Figure X13-1

B.   Press the **Fillet** tool, select **Constant Radius** as the *Fillet Type*, and enter a *Radius* of **2.00in.**, and create the feature.

Step 3: Roll the model status fully forward.

A. Drag and drop the *Rollback Bar* into its 'normal' position below the *Annotations* folder.

B. A *Rebuild Errors* message window will appear with the following message:

> Chamfer2: Some chamfered items are no longer in the model. You can reselect the items using the Edit Definition in the FeatureManager design tree.

C. **Close** the *Rebuild Errors* message window.

Step 4: Resolve the feature conflict.

A. Observe the red arrow at the top of the *FeatureManager* design tree and the red exclamation point at the feature *Chamfer2*. Do you understand how the conflict was created and what the error message meant? *Chamfer2* was created by selecting the same sharp corners as were used to create *Fillet1*. It isn't logical to desire two different features on the same sharp corner at the same time.

B. Select **Chamfer2** in the *FeatureManager* and then select **Edit ▼ Suppress**. What has happened to the error indications?

C. Select the **Fillet1** in the *FeatureManager* and then select **Edit ▼ Suppress**.

D. Select **Chamfer2** in the *FeatureManager* and then select **Edit ▼ Unsuppress**.

This is one way to store multiple part configurations in the same file. It is not the best method because the feature conflict will return anytime that you attempt to **Unsuppress** both corner treatments at the same time. To change from one corner treatment to the other you must first **Suppress** them both (so that there is no conflict) and then **Unsuppress** only one.
   The decision whether or not to keep both features in the model depends upon the function and use of the part. If both will be used in the future then it makes sense to keep both in the model.

E. If you learned that *Chamfer2* would never again be used on the part what would be the logical change to make to the model and how would you do it? Perform that operation.

End of Exercise 13.

DESIGN PROJECT TUTORIAL

Exercise 14: Linear Pattern in One Direction

Parts often contain multiple features that share identical geometry and a common function. Patterning is a powerful technique for creating many related features in a single command.

In this exercise one feature will be patterned in one direction. Features can also be patterned in two directions, as in a rectangular array, and in a circular or radial pattern. These two more complex operations will be investigated in Exercises 15 and 20.

| Step 1: | Open the file PATTERN1.SLDPRT and pattern the cut. |

A. Open pattern1.SLDPRT.

B. Select **Cut-Extrude1** in the *FeatureManager* design tree.

C. Select **Insert ▼ Pattern/Mirror ▶ Linear Pattern...** or click the tool on the *Features* toolbar:

All of the defining dimensions of the cut will appear.

D. Select the **1.250** dimension and notice the direction of the pattern.

E. Check **Reverse Direction** if the pattern is heading away from the part.

F. Enter the **Spacing** as **0.400in** and the **Total Instances** to **12**. Note that the original feature is included in the total number of instances.

G. **OK** the creation of the *Linear Pattern*.

| Step 2: | Modify the original cut. |

A. **Right click** over **Plane4** and select **Edit Definition.**

B. Set the **Angle** to **65deg.**

C. **Finish** the redefinition.

Your part should now look like Figure X14-1:

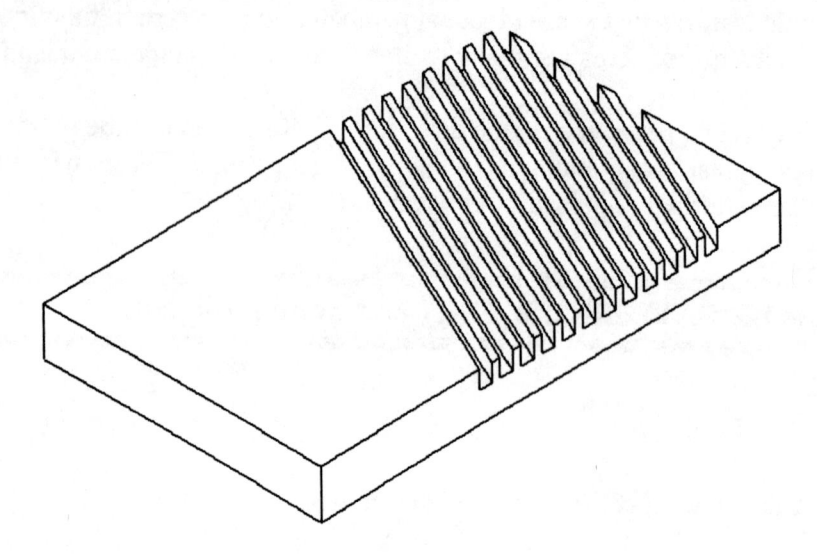

Figure X14-1

End of Exercise 14.

Exercise 15: Linear Pattern in Two Directions and Pattern Redefinition

In this exercise a feature will be patterned in two directions and redefined.

Step 1:	Open the file PATTERN2.SLDPRT and pattern the hole.

A. Open `pattern2.SLDPRT`.

B. Select **Hole1** in the *FeatureManager* design tree.

C. Select **Insert ▼ Pattern/Mirror ▶ Linear Pattern...** or click the tool on the *Features* toolbar:

All of the defining dimensions of the cut will appear.

D. Select the **1.250** hole location dimension and notice the direction of the pattern.

E. Check **Reverse Direction** if the pattern is heading away from the part.

F. Enter the *Spacing*: as **2.500in** and the *Total Instances*: to **2**. Note that the original feature is included in the total number of instances.

G. Select **Second Direction** in the flipdown menu, select the **2.000** hole location dimension, check **Reverse Direction** as necessary, enter the *Spacing*: as **3.000in.** and the *Total Instances:* to **3**.

DESIGN PROJECT TUTORIAL

H. Preview and **OK** the creation of the *Linear Pattern*. Figure X15-1 shows the result:

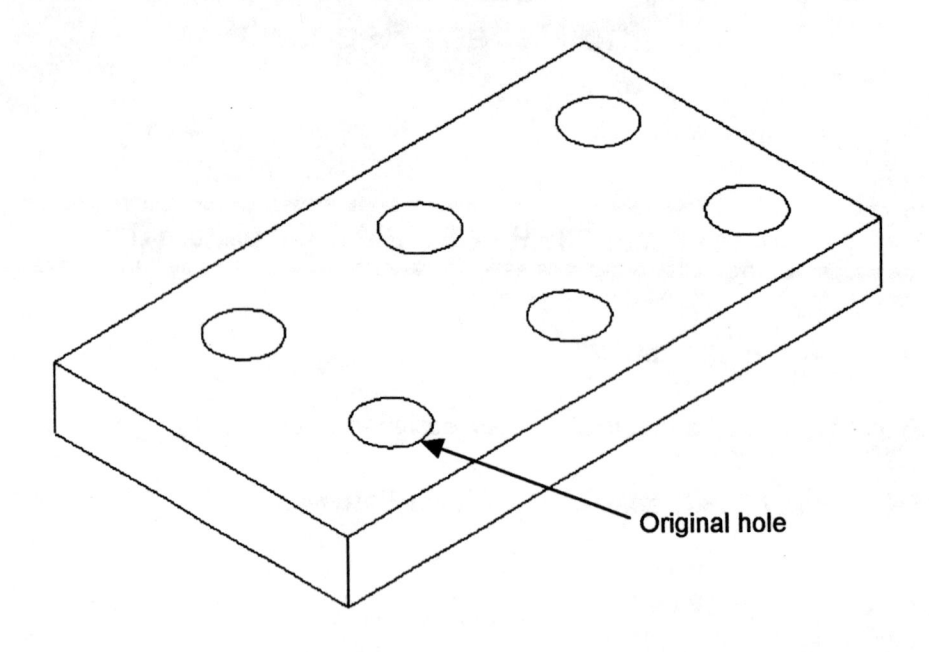

Figure X15-1

Step 2: Add a cut to the original hole.

A. Select the topmost surface of the *Base* feature.

B. Before you begin sketching become **absolutely certain** about which of the six holes on the part was the parent of the pattern. The new sketch **must be** sketched over this hole. See Figure X15-1. In situations like this it is a good idea to sketch a few entities while in an *Isometric* view.

C. Begin a **Sketch**, draw two centerlines (one horizontal and one vertical) over the axis of the first hole, draw a **Rectangle**, turn off **Rectangle**, and **Dimension** one side of the rectangle and **Modify** the dimension to **1.500in**. If you can't recall which hole is the first hole use *Rollback* to identify it.

D. Select the four sides of the rectangle, click **Add Relation**, select the **Equal** radio button, and press **Apply.**

E. Select one centerline and the two sides of the rectangle which are parallel to it, select the **Symmetric** radio button, and press **Apply.**

DESIGN PROJECT TUTORIAL

F. Select *the other* centerline and the two sides of the rectangle which are parallel to it, select the **Symmetric** radio button, and press **Apply**. The sketch should be fully defined (all sides black) so press the **Close** button in the *Add Geometric Relations* dialog.

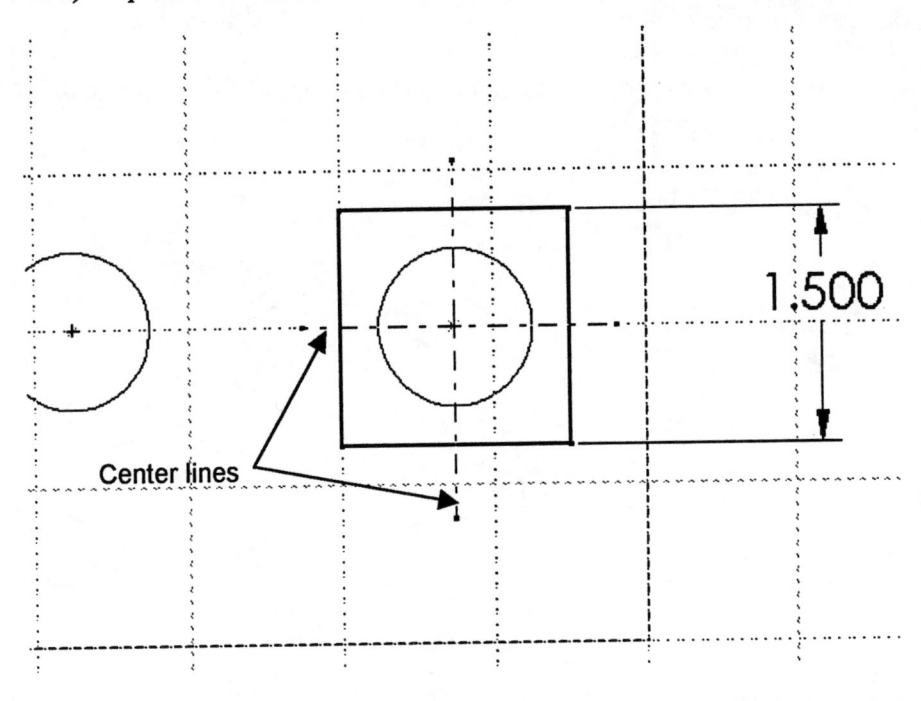

Figure X15-2

G. Press the **Extruded Cut** tool, set the *Type:* as **Blind**, enter a *Depth:* of **0.250in.**, and **OK** the feature creation.

Step 3:	Reorder the rectangular cut.

Drag and drop *Cut-Extrude1* in the *FeatureManager* design tree to a position just above the *LPattern1*.

Step 4: Add the rectangular cut to the pattern definition.

A. Select *LPattern1* in the *FeatureManager* design tree, right click, and select **Edit Definition** from the popup menu.

B. Click inside the *Items to Copy* window and then select **Cut-Extrude1** in the *FeatureManager* design tree.

C. **OK** the redefinition. The final part configuration should look like Figure X15-3:

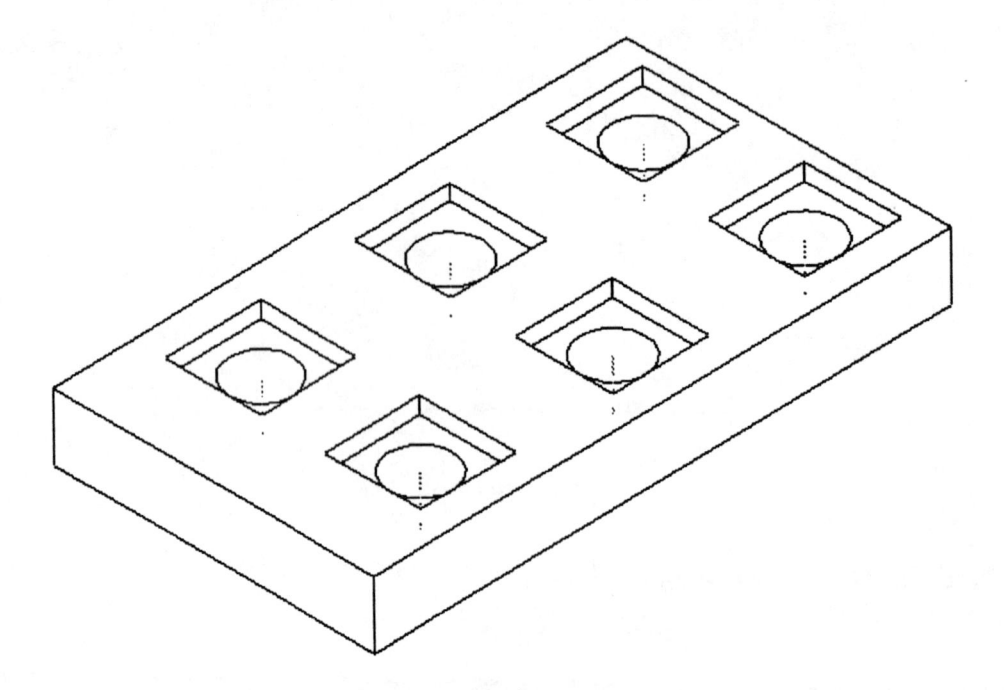

Figure X15-3

End of Exercise 15.

Design Project Assignment 2

Seven different parts will be created and assembled in the nine Design Project Assignments. In this second assignment we will complete two parts:
- A. DRIVE_SHAFT (begun in Assignment 1)
- B. SNAP_RING

Add features to two parts begun in Assignment 1:
- C. MOTOR
- D. LOWER_HOUSING

And begin a new part:
- E. COVER

Assignment 2A: Finish the DRIVE_SHAFT Part

Step 1: Open the DRIVE_SHAFT

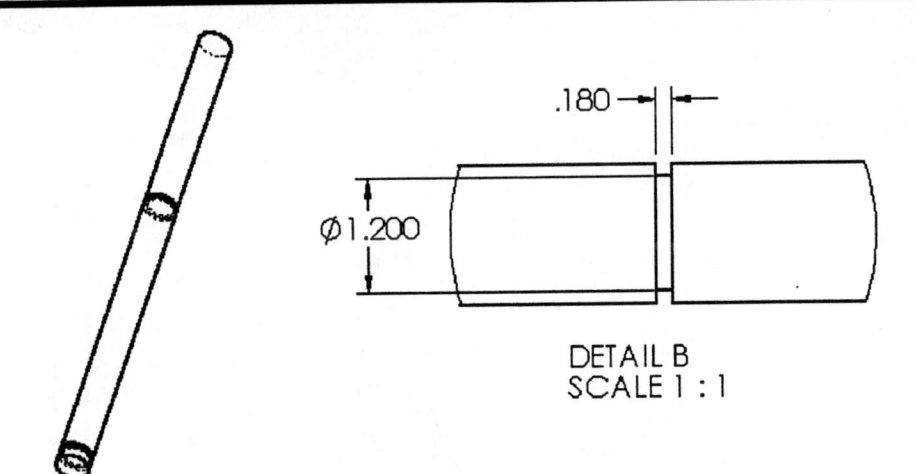

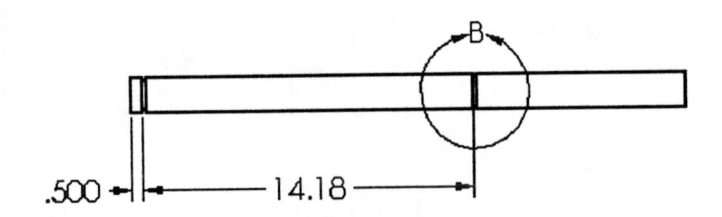

Figure D2A-1

DESIGN PROJECT TUTORIAL

Step 2: Pattern the first snap ring groove to create a second one. Make the new instance 14.18in. from the existing groove as shown in Figure D2A-1.

Step 3: Save the part file.

Assignment 2B: Create the SNAP_RING Part

Step 1: Create a part named SNAP_RING with inches as the units.

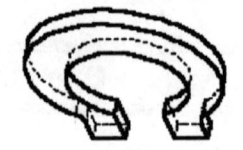

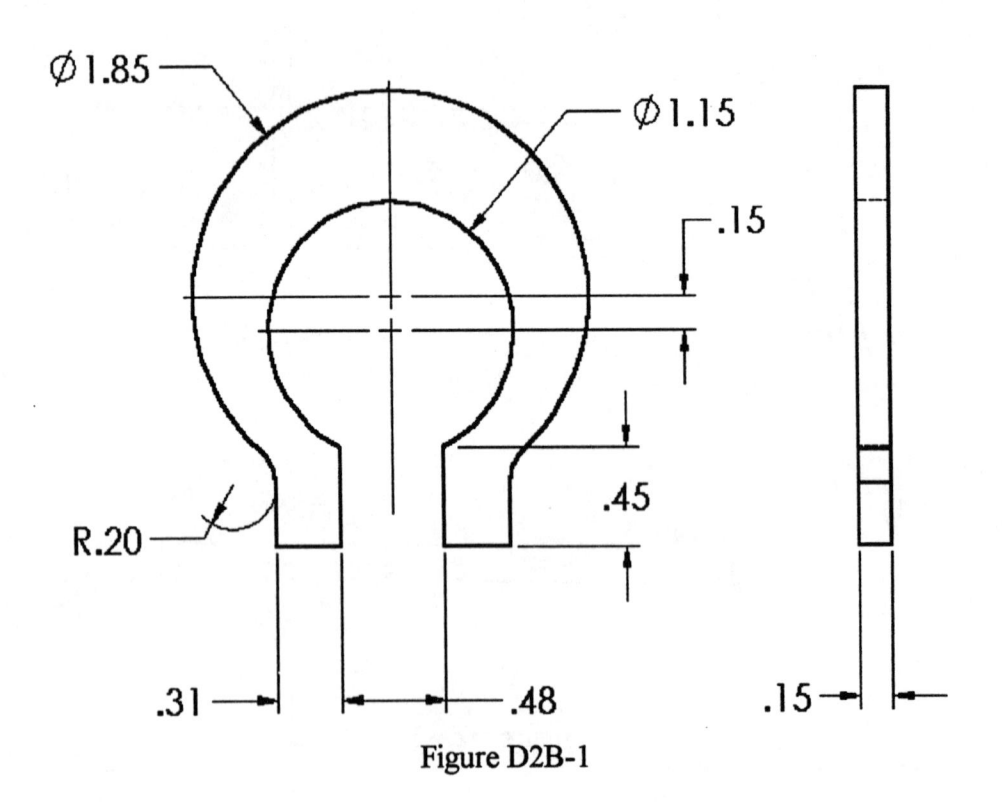

Figure D2B-1

Step 2: Create the *base* feature by extruding the outline of the snap ring. It is not recommended to include the 0.20in. radius in the sketch since this can be added as a fillet. The sketch is shown in Figure D2B-2. Extrude to a depth of 0.15in.

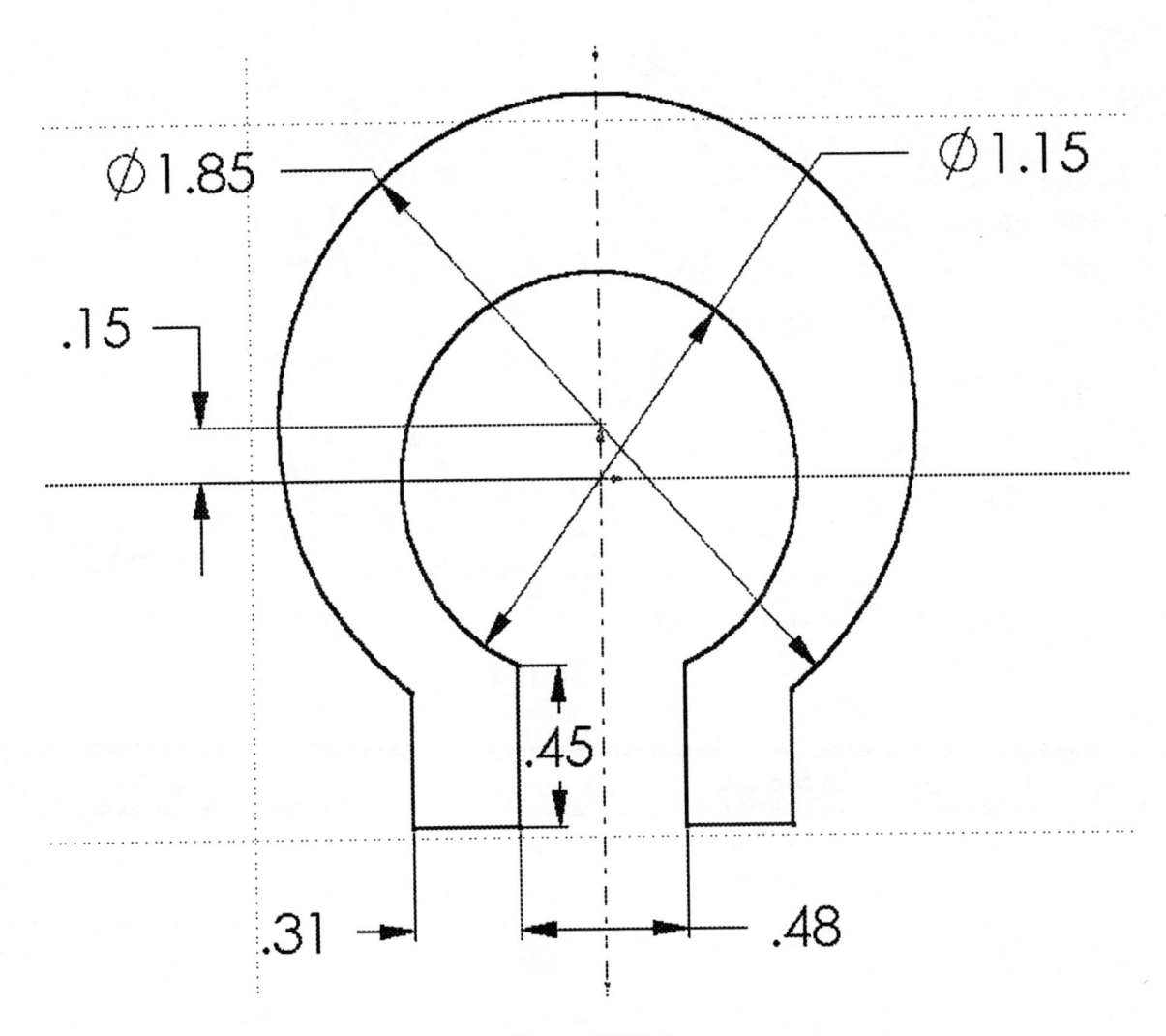

Figure D2B-2

DESIGN PROJECT TUTORIAL

Step 3: Add a 0.20in. radius edge round feature to the two inside corners as indicated in Figure D2B-3.

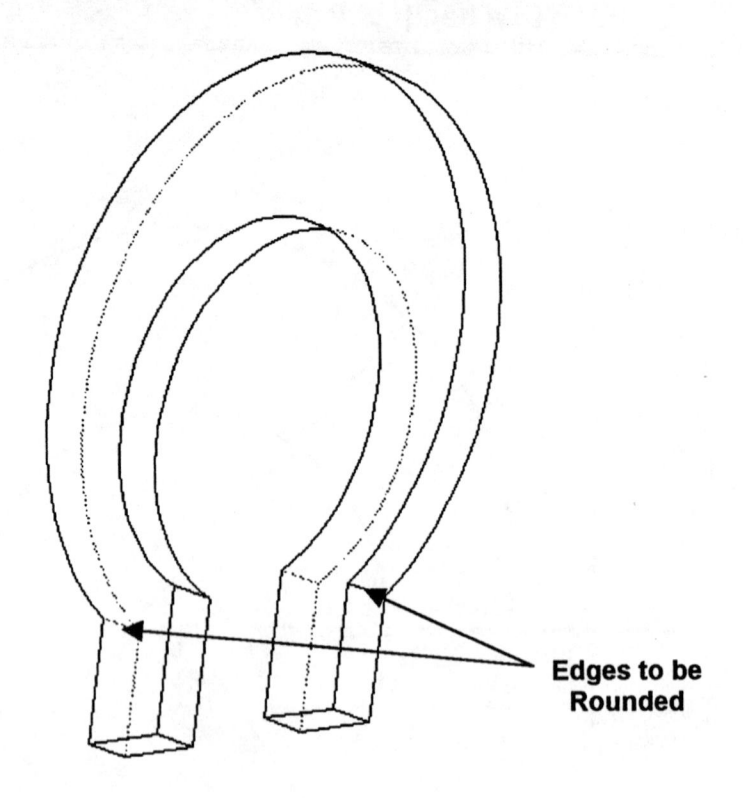

Edges to be Rounded

Figure D2B-3

Step 4: Save the model.

DESIGN PROJECT TUTORIAL

Assignment 2C: Continue the MOTOR Part

Step 1: Open the MOTOR part.

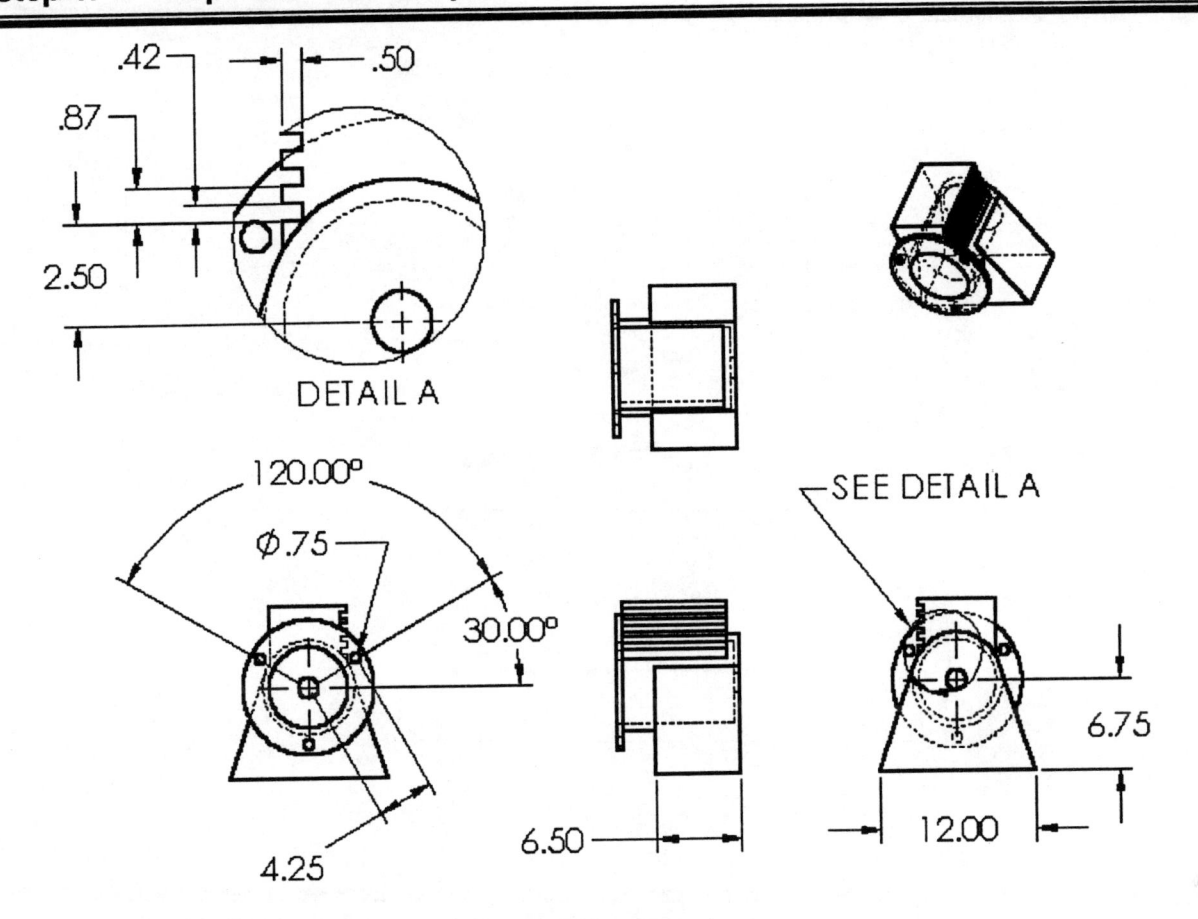

Figure D2C-1

Step 2: *Rollback* the model until only the *base* feature is shown.

DESIGN PROJECT TUTORIAL

Step 3: Add a feature for the motor pedestal as shown on Figure D2C-2. Use geometric relations to control the tangency. Note that the points of tangency are *above* the horizontal center plane of the base feature.

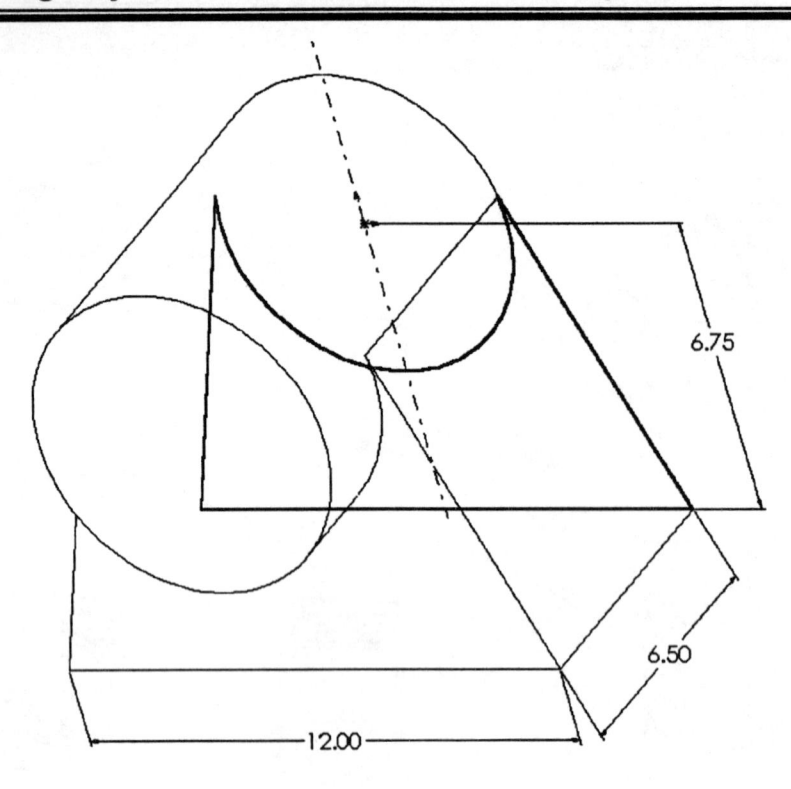

Figure D2C-2

Step 4: Reverse the *Rollback* to restore the display of all model features.

Step 5: Add a Ø0.75in. radial hole on the flange. Use a 4.25in. radius (rather than a diameter) for dimensioning the hole location.

Step 6: Pattern the hole in the flange to create three equally spaced holes.

DESIGN PROJECT TUTORIAL

Step 7: Create a cut on the side of the wiring housing by sketching on its front surface as shown in Detail A of Figure D2C-1 and in Figure D2C-3. Extrude it *Through All* in one direction.

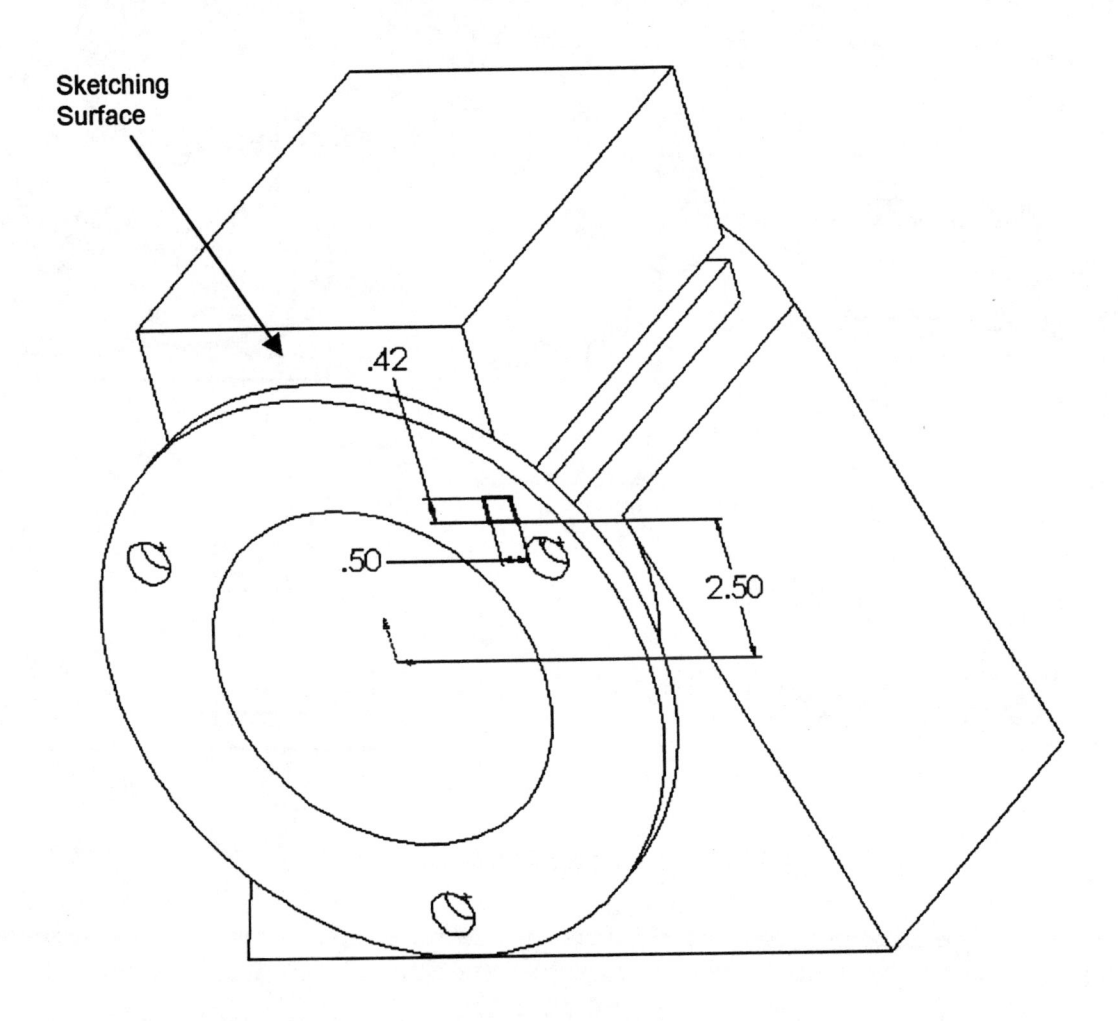

Figure D2C-3

Step 8: Pattern the side cut to create a total of four instances, including the original.

Step 9: Save the model.

DESIGN PROJECT TUTORIAL

Assignment 2D: Continue the LOWER_HOUSING Part

Step 1: Open the LOWER_HOUSING part.

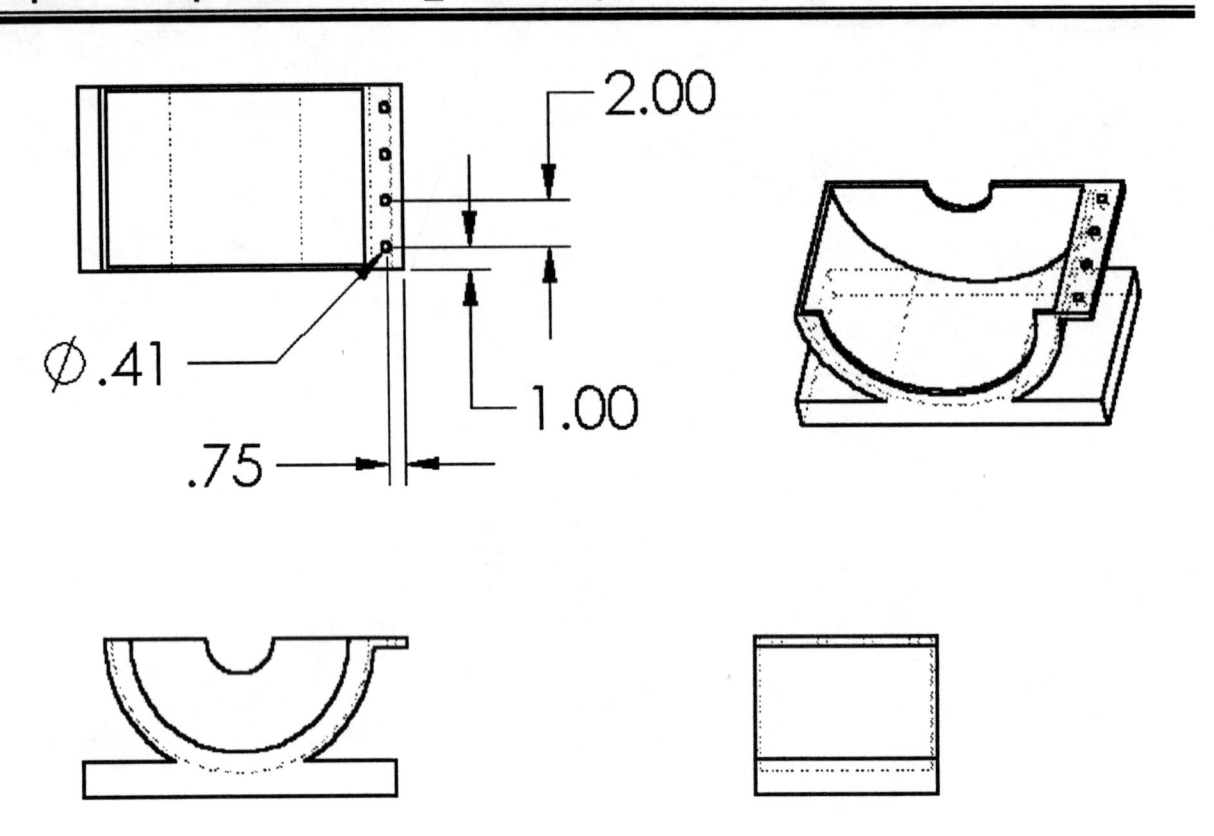

Figure D2D-1

Step 2: Create a straight hole through the flange with the dimensioning scheme shown on Figure D2D-1.

Step 3: Pattern the hole for a total of four instances including the original.

Step 4: Save the model.

Assignment 2E: Start the COVER Part

Step 1: Create a part named COVER with inches as the units. *Show* the default construction planes.

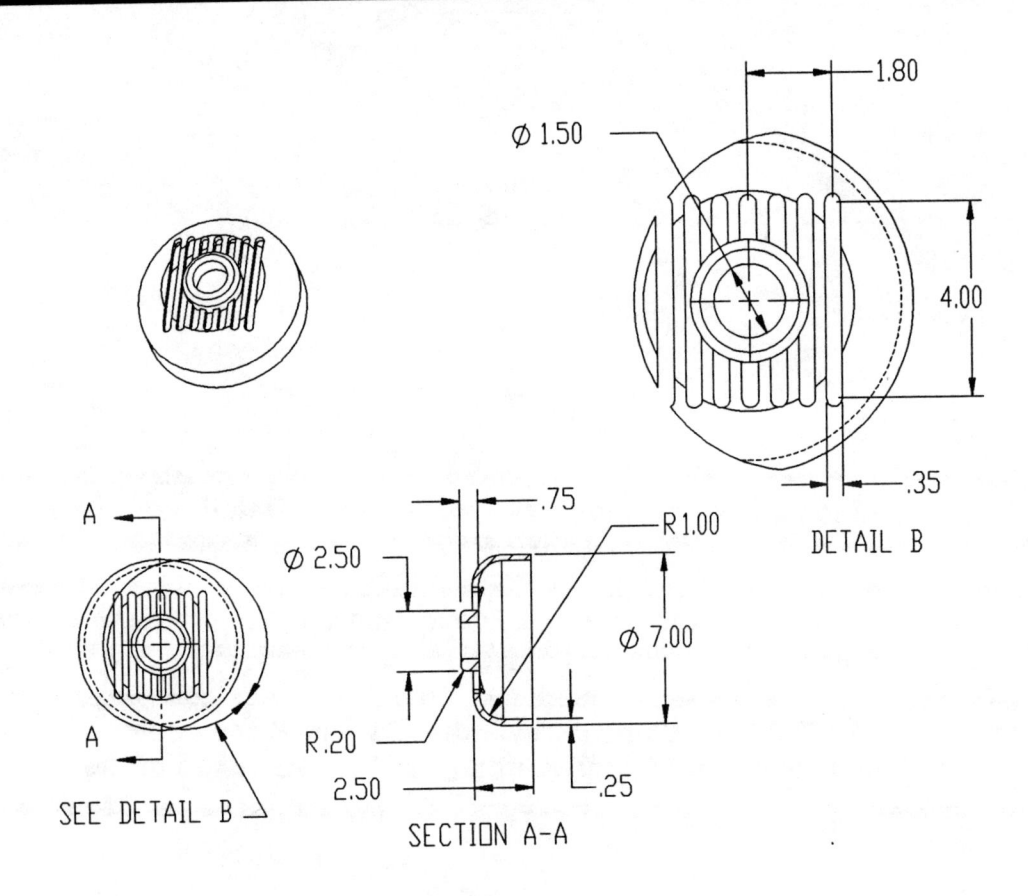

Figure D2E-1

DESIGN PROJECT TUTORIAL

Step 2: Create the base feature as a revolved extrusion with a section and centerline as shown in Figure D2E-2.

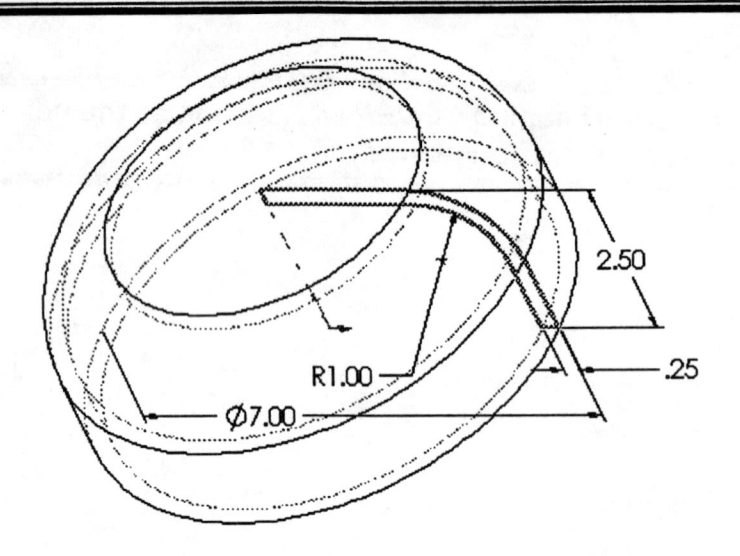

Figure D2E-2

Step 3: Add the first (outermost) slot as shown in Detail B of Figure D2E-1.

Step 4: Pattern the slot for a total of seven instances (including the original).

Step 5: Add a Ø 2.50in. diameter cylindrical boss at the center of the Cover. The 0.75in. depth is measured from the top inside of the Cover.

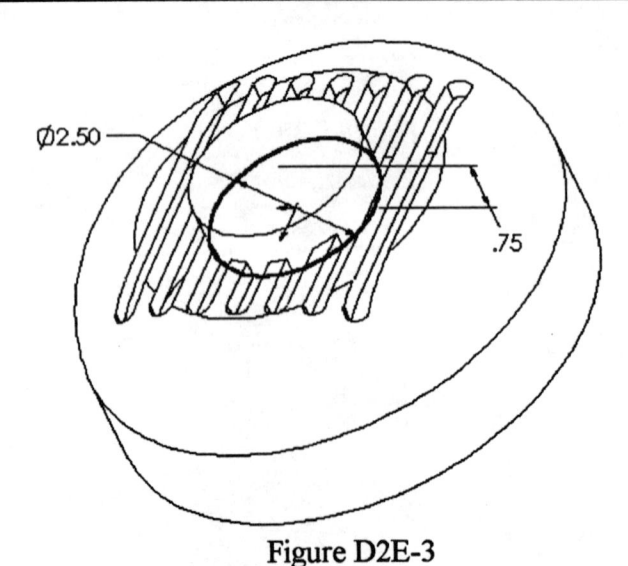

Figure D2E-3

DESIGN PROJECT TUTORIAL

Step 6: Add a Ø 1.50in. hole through the center of the boss.

Step 7: Add a 0.20in radius edge round to the top outside edge of the boss as shown of Figure D2E-4.

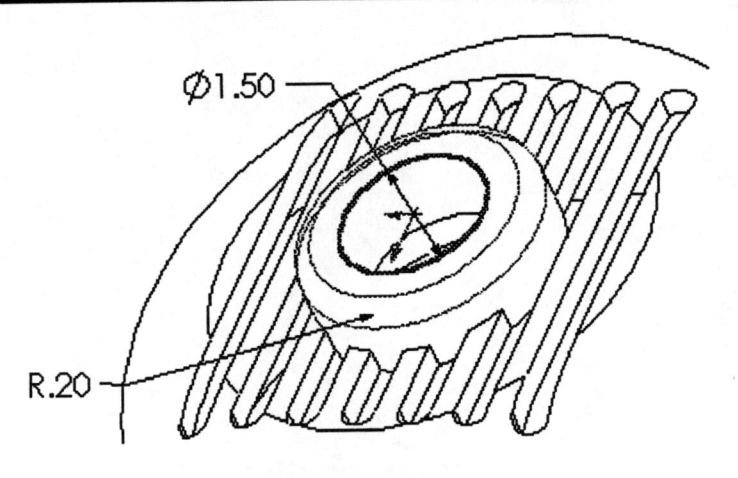

Figure D2E-4

Step 8: Save the model.

End of Design Project Assignment 2.

DESIGN PROJECT TUTORIAL

Exercise 16: Creating a Base Sweep

The features of "real world" parts can most often be modeled with extrusions and revolutions. Extrusion and revolution simulate the action of the most common and, generally for metals, least expensive of the fabrication operations--machining, turning, and rolling.

Sweeps and *Lofts* are powerful commands because of their capability to produce complex part geometry. In this exercise we will create a cotter pin (see Figure X16-1) with a single base feature.

Generally speaking, features which are difficult to model in SolidWorks are difficult and expensive to realize in raw materials. For this reason these operations should be avoided except where the resulting component will be cast (for thick metals), formed (for thin metals), or molded (for plastics).

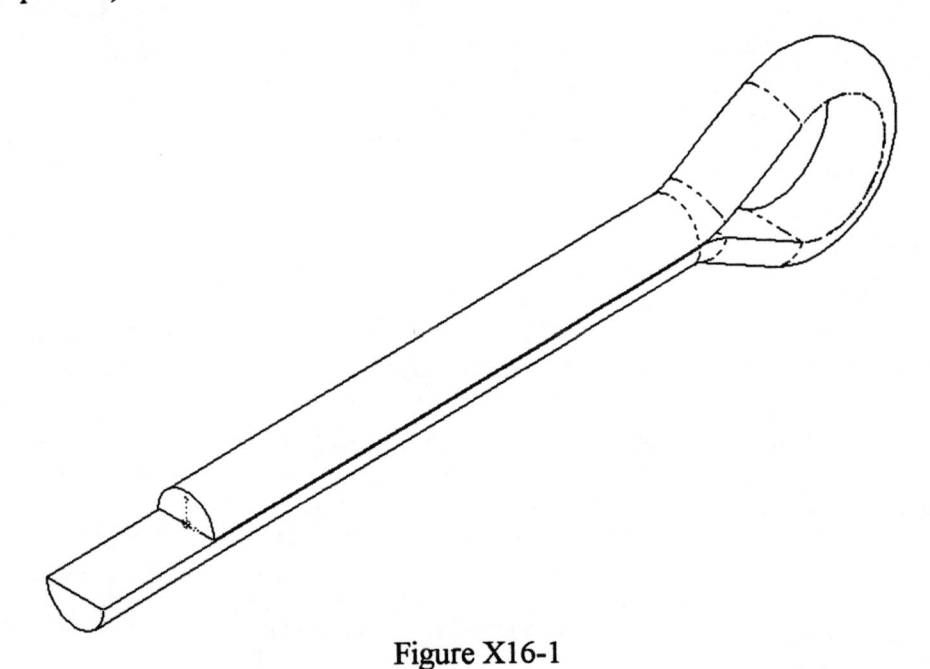

Figure X16-1

Step 1: **Create a new part called COTTER_PIN with *inches* as the units.**

A. Create a new part named `cotter_pin.SLDPRT`.

B. Select **Tools ▼ Options...** and the *Grid/Units* tab. Disable **Snap to Points (or Grid)**. Set the *Length Unit* to **Inches.**

DESIGN PROJECT TUTORIAL

Step 2: Sketch the *Sweep Path* on the *Right* plane. This is one of two sketches required for a *Sweep*--the other is called the *section*.

A. Select the **Right** plane in the *FeatureManager* and begin sketching the four straight lines (two of these are horizontal) and a *Tangent Arcs* as shown in a *Right* view on Figure X16-2. The first horizontal line begins at the origin:

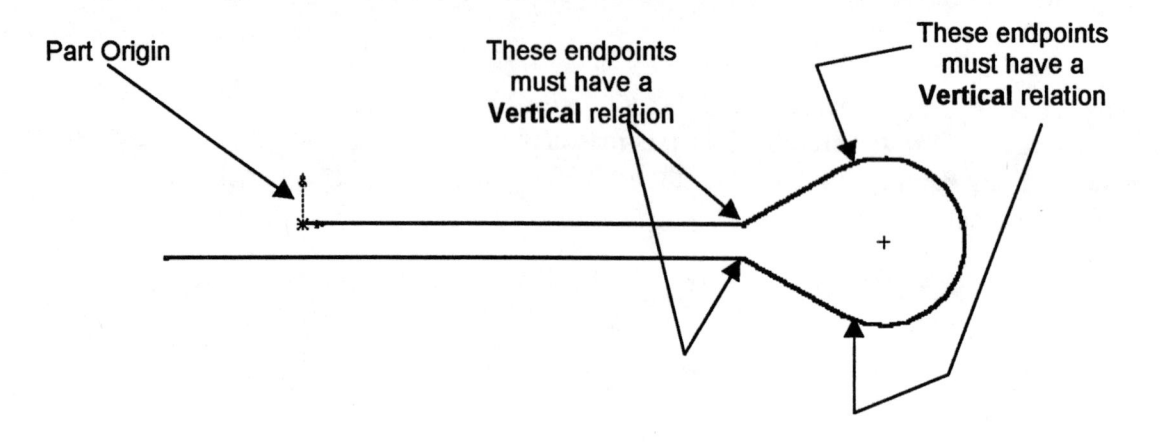

Figure X16-2

B. In addition to the obvious *Tangent* and *Horizontal* relations add *Vertical* geometric relations to the endpoints as shown on Figure X16-2.

C. **Dimension** and **Modify** the sketch as shown on Figure X16-3:

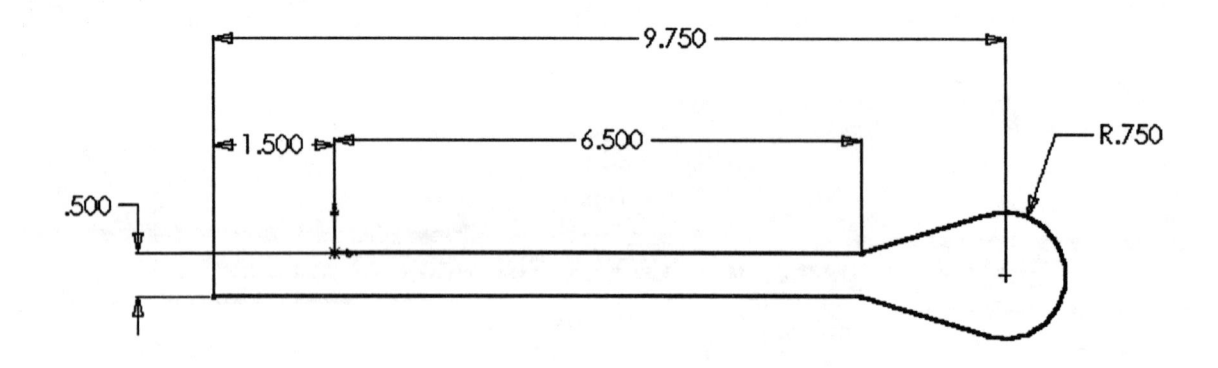

Figure X16-3

16-2

DESIGN PROJECT TUTORIAL

D. Use the **Fillet** tool on the *Sketch Tools* toolbar to add **0.750in** radii at the sharp corners where the straight lines meet. After clicking the tool, you input the radius value and then click on pairs of adjacent straight lines. Press the **Close** button on the *Sketch Fillet* dialog when both corner radii have been added. Dimensions to the sharp corners stay related to the theoretical sharp corners.

E. Finally, **Modify** the 0.500in. vertical dimension to **0.010in.** and close the sketch

Step 3: Create the *section* sketch on the *Front* plane.

A. Select the **Front** plane and sketch the cross-section as shown in a *Front* view on Figure X16-4. Notice the location of the origin--at the center of the semi-circle.

B. **Dimension** and **Modify** the sketch.

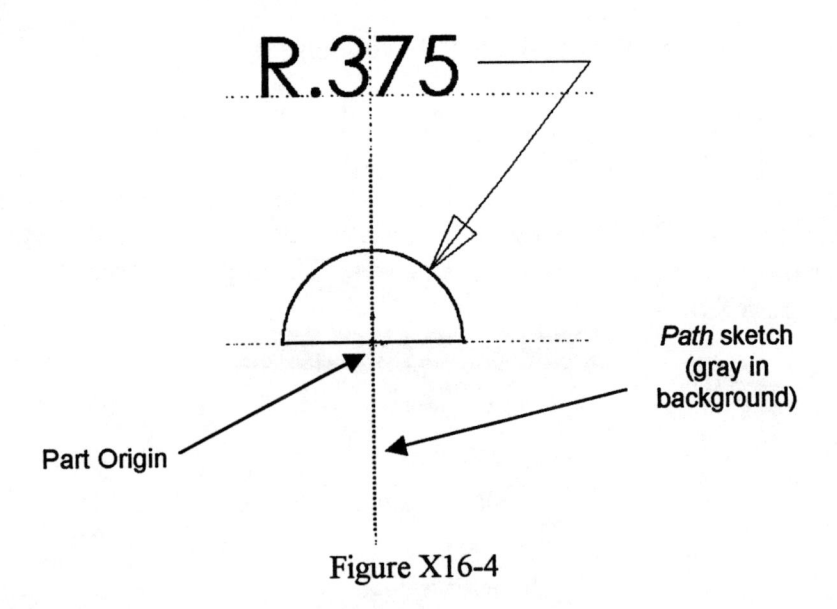

Figure X16-4

C. Change to an *Isometric* view. The two sketches should now look as shown on Figure X16-5.

D. If the sketch of the cross-section is fully defined close the sketch. You may need to add a *Collinear* relation between the *Top* plane and the horizontal line in the sketch.

DESIGN PROJECT TUTORIAL

R.375

Figure X16-5

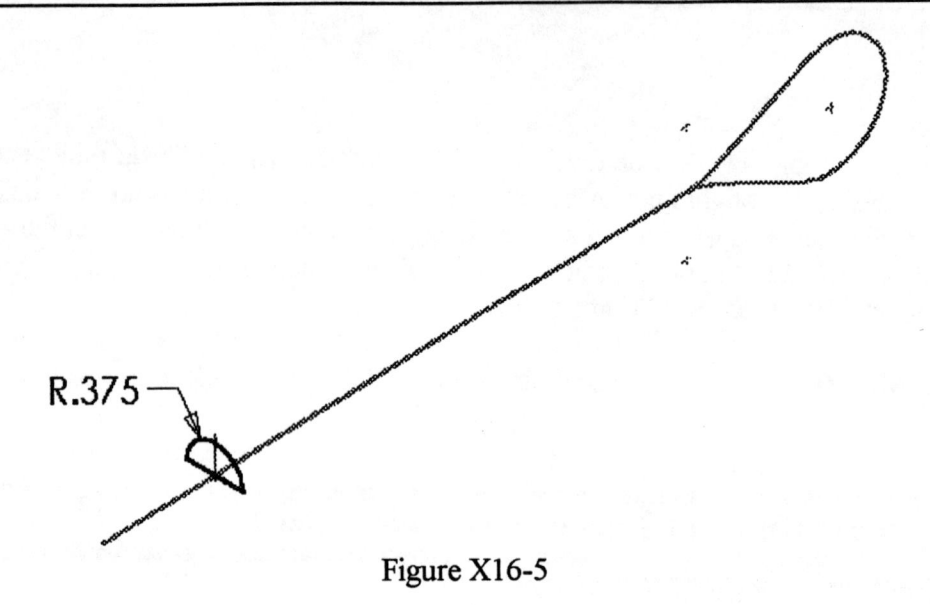

Step 4:   **Create the *Base Sweep*.**

A. Select **Insert ▼ Base ▶ Sweep...** or click the tool on the *Features* toolbar:

B. Pick inside the *Sweep Section* window of the *Sweep* dialog. Then select *Sketch2* (the semi-circular sketch) in the *FeatureManager* design tree.

C. Pick inside the *Sweep Path* window of the *Sweep* dialog and then select *Sketch1* (the open loop sketch) in the *FeatureManager* design tree. The upper left area of the dialog should look like Figure X16-6:

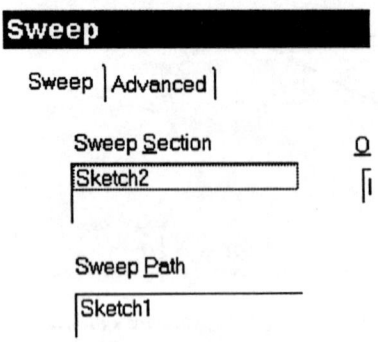

```
Sweep
 Sweep | Advanced |
      Sweep Section         O
      | Sketch2         |   |I

      Sweep Path
      | Sketch1         |
```

Figure X16-6

D. Press **OK** to finalize the creation of the *Sweep*. The final result in an *Isometric* view should look like Figure X16-1.

End of Exercise 16.

DESIGN PROJECT TUTORIAL

Exercise 17: Creating a Revolved Boss Loft

The difference between a sweep and a loft is subtle but very important. Generally, sweeps are used when a constant cross-section is needed, and lofts are used when a variable cross-section is needed. Lofts do not ever used a sketched path, but the *preview line* performs a similar function.

Lofts with parallel sections are most common because they are easiest to visualize, create, and understand. This exercise varies from Chapter 7 in the SolidWorks® Tutorial, *Creating a Loft*, in this principle. The sections in this exercise will revolve through 180°.

This exercise is intended to provide a variation of the skills first practiced during Chapter 7 in the SolidWorks® Tutorial. Normally, the *Tutorial* is available for viewing at

C:\Program Files\SolidWorks\Lang\English\Manuals\Tutorial.pdf

Please perform the exercise of Chapter 7 on pages 7-1 through 7-6 of the SolidWorks® Tutorial, or a similar lofting exercise with parallel sections, before performing this exercise.

This exercise demonstrates the advanced capability of a loft feature to use revolved sections. The part shown in Figure X17-1 will be finalized during this exercise:

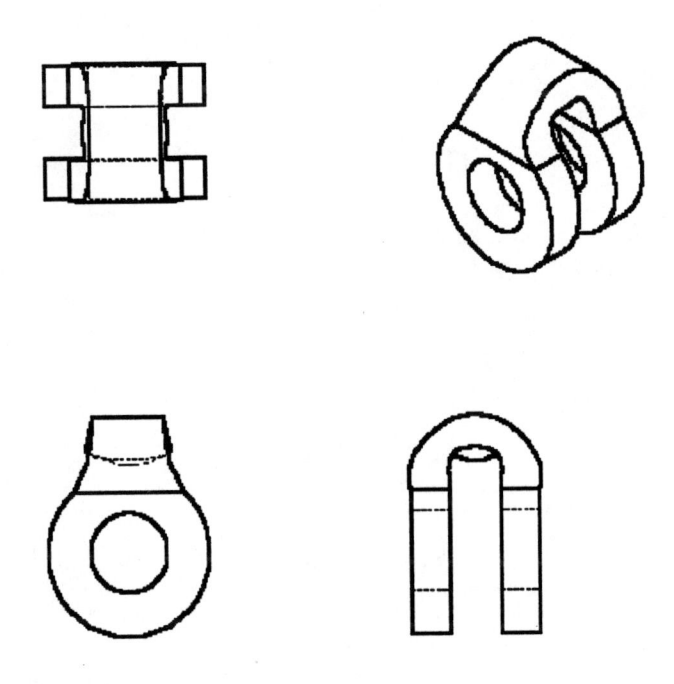

Figure X17-1

| Step 1: | Open the file CLEVIS.SLDPRT. |

17-1

Step 2: Create a *Boss Loft*.

The purpose of this loft feature is to allow the clevis to fit closely with a lifting ring. The inside diameter, outside diameter, and mean diameter of the lifting ring were sketched on the *Front* plane to help understand the purpose of the loft feature:

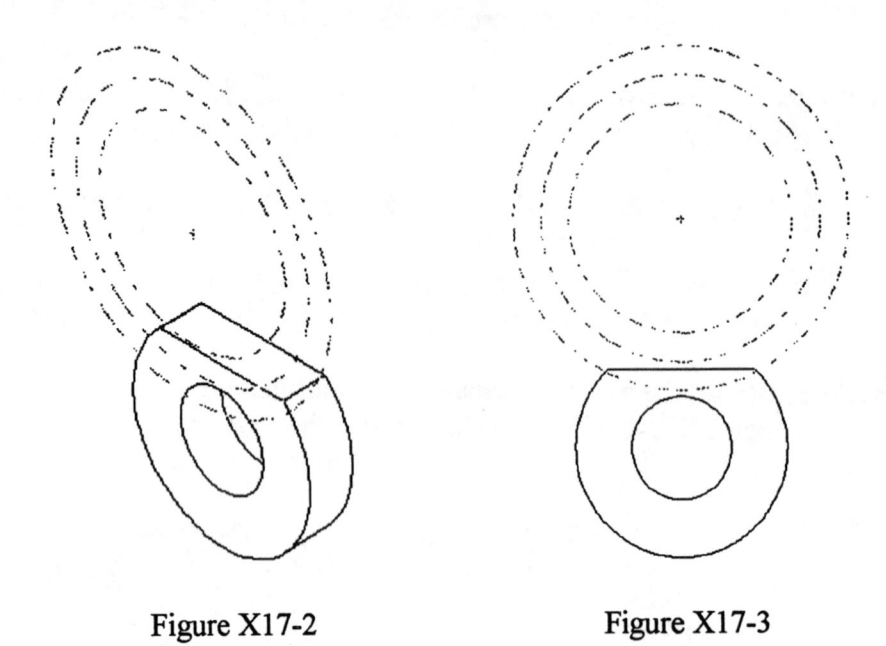

Figure X17-2   Figure X17-3

A. Right click over **Sketch4** and select **Show** from the pop-up menu. Repeat this action to show *Sketch3* through *Sketch7*.

B. Use **Zoom to Fit** to obtain a close-up view of the five section sketches as shown on FigureX17-4:

DESIGN PROJECT TUTORIAL

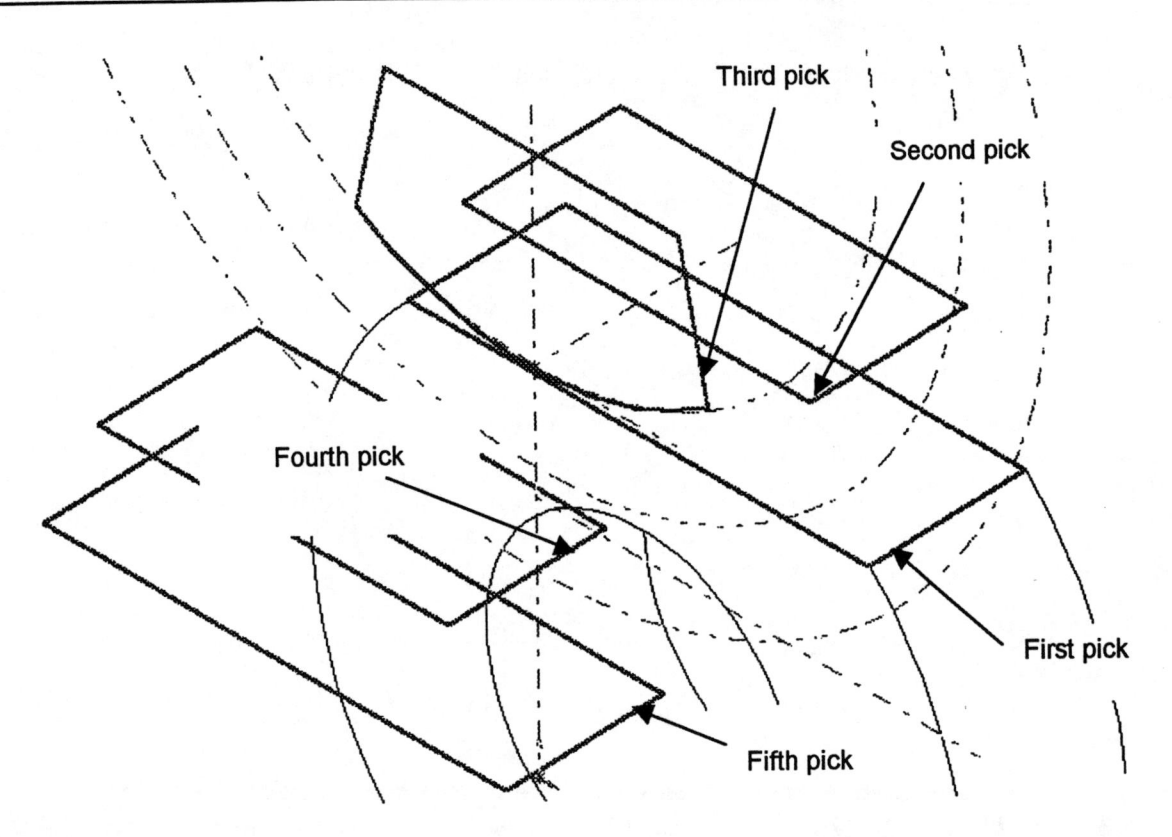

Figure X17-4

B. Select **Insert ▼ Boss ▶ Loft...** or click the tool on the *Features* toolbar:

C. Pick once on each of the sketches as shown on Figure X17-4. The order and location of the picks is critically important. The resulting appearance of the dialog must match Figure X17-5:

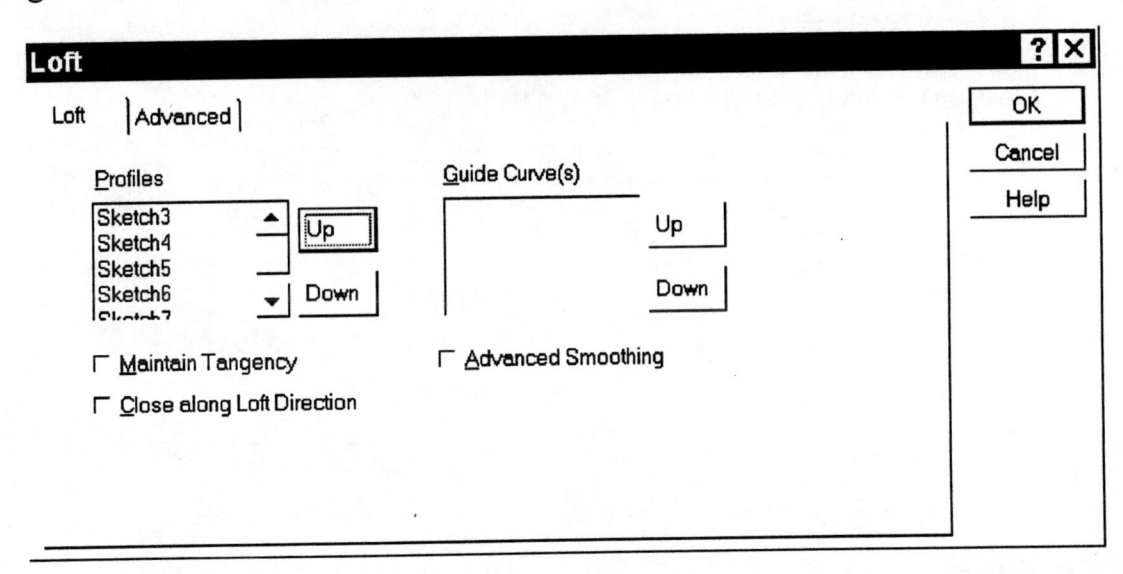

Figure X17-5

17-3

DESIGN PROJECT TUTORIAL

D. Press **OK** to create the *boss loft*. The result will look like Figure X17-6:

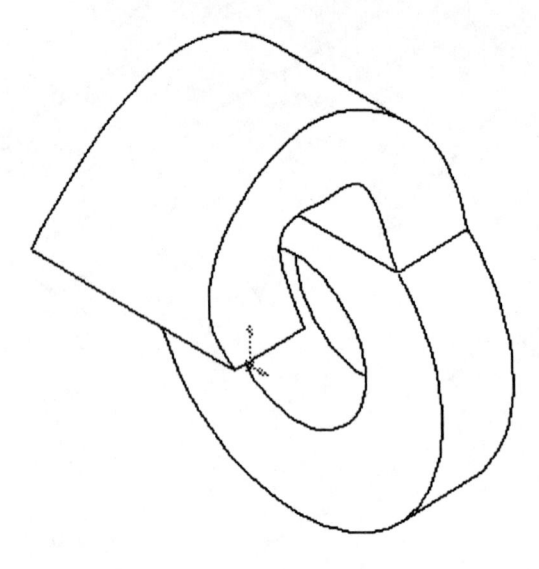

Figure X17-6

Step 3: Use *Mirror Feature* to duplicate the *Base-Extrude* and *Cut-Extrude1* features.

A. Select **Insert** ▼ **Pattern/Mirror** ▶ **Mirror Feature...**

B. The orange color in the *Mirror plane* window indicates that the dialog is ready to receive this information. Select the **Front** plane in the *FeatureManager* design tree.

C. Click inside the *Features to Mirror* window and then select **Base-Extrude** and **Cut-Extrude1** in the *FeatureManager* design tree.

D. The final result of the selections should look like Figure X17-7:

DESIGN PROJECT TUTORIAL

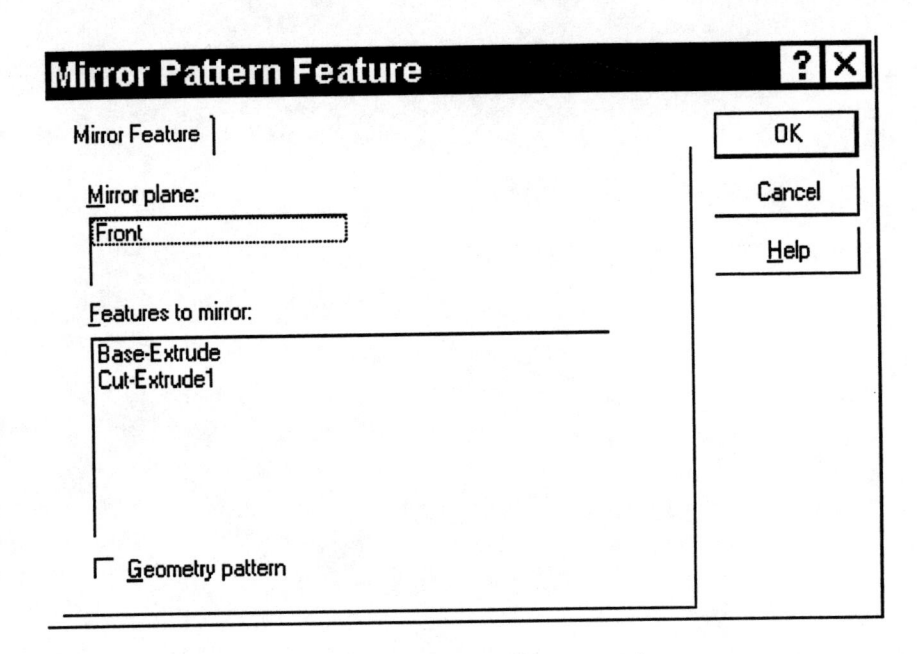

Figure X17-7

E.   Press **OK** to finalize feature creation. The final part will look like Figure X17-8:

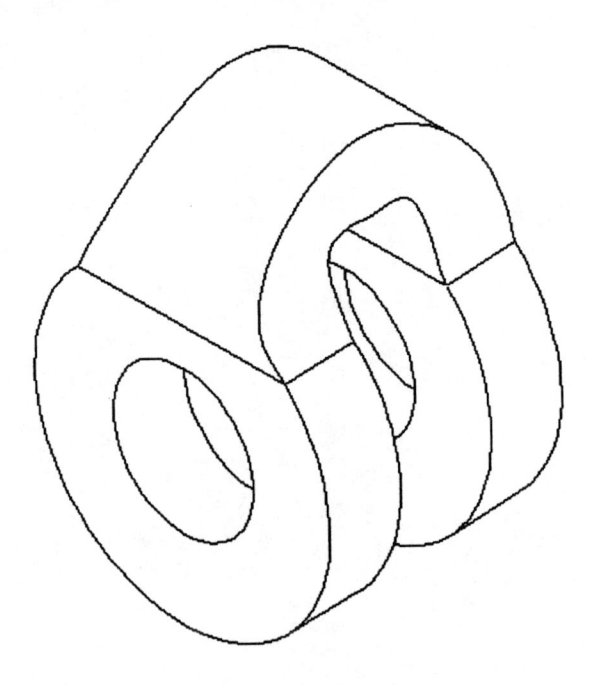

Figure X17-8

A "bulge" was created where the loft will contact the lifting ring because of the radius within *Sketch5*. **Shade** and spin the model to observe the shape of the loft. Save the file if you desire.

End of Exercise 17.

DESIGN PROJECT TUTORIAL

Exercise 18: Creating a Basic Drawing

In this exercise you will create your first drawing which contains top, front, section, and general views of a solid part called **GEAR**. The objective is to create a drawing like Figure X18-1:

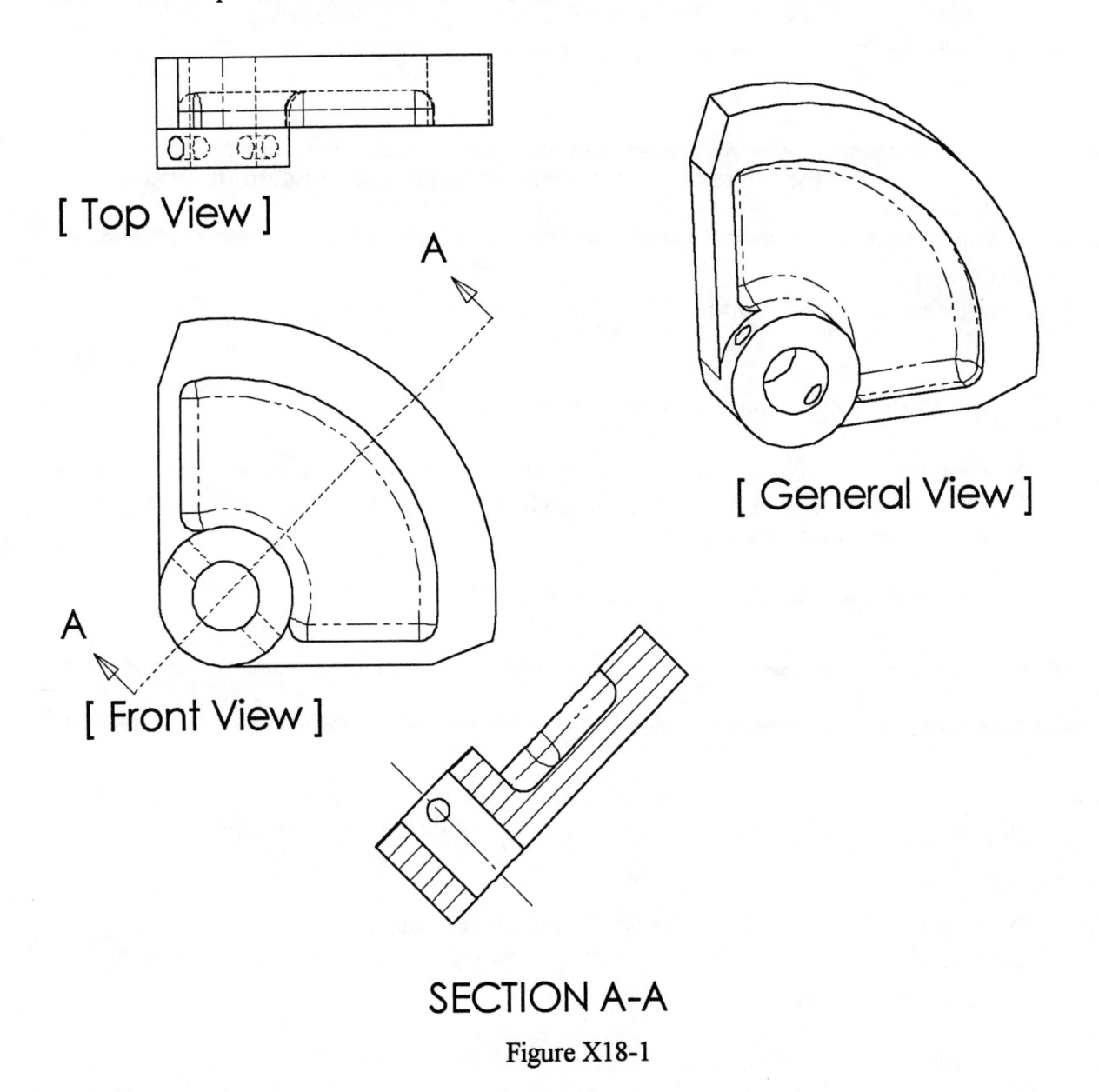

[Top View]

[General View]

A

A

[Front View]

SECTION A-A

Figure X18-1

Step 1: **Open the file Gear.sldprt. Begin a drawing.**

A. Open gear.SLDPRT.

18-1

DESIGN PROJECT TUTORIAL

B. Click the **New** tool, select **Drawing**, and press **OK**.

C. Select the **No Template** radio button, select **A-Landscape** from the *Paper Size:* flipdown menu, and press **OK**.

D. Select **Window ▾ Tile Horizontally** to see the new drawing sheet and the **GEAR** solid part in equally sized windows.

Step 2: **Create the three standard orthographic views and delete the right view.**

A. Select the **Standard 3 View** tool: and pick inside the `gear.sldprt` window.

The views will appear automatically in the drawing.

B. The right side view is unnecessary because it is essentially identical to the top view. Move the mouse pointer near the right view until a gray shadow appears around the view. **Click** on the gray shadow and press the **Delete** button.

C. Press the **Yes** button in the *Confirm Delete* dialog.

Step 3: **Create the general view.**

A. Select the **Named View** tool: and pick inside the `gear.sldprt` window.

The *Drawing View-Named View* dialog will appear. **Doubleclick** on the view called **spun**. Click in the upper right quadrant of the drawing sheet where we want the center of the general view to appear.

B. When you are asked, "Do you want to switch the view to use Isometric (True) dimensions," press **No**.

C. *Maximize* the drawing window.

DESIGN PROJECT TUTORIAL

Step 4: Sketch the section line and create the section view.

A. Use **Zoom to Area** to obtain a close-up of the front drawing view.

B. Press the **Line** tool and draw a line at a diagonal over top of the front view as shown in Figure X18-2. Turn **Line** off.

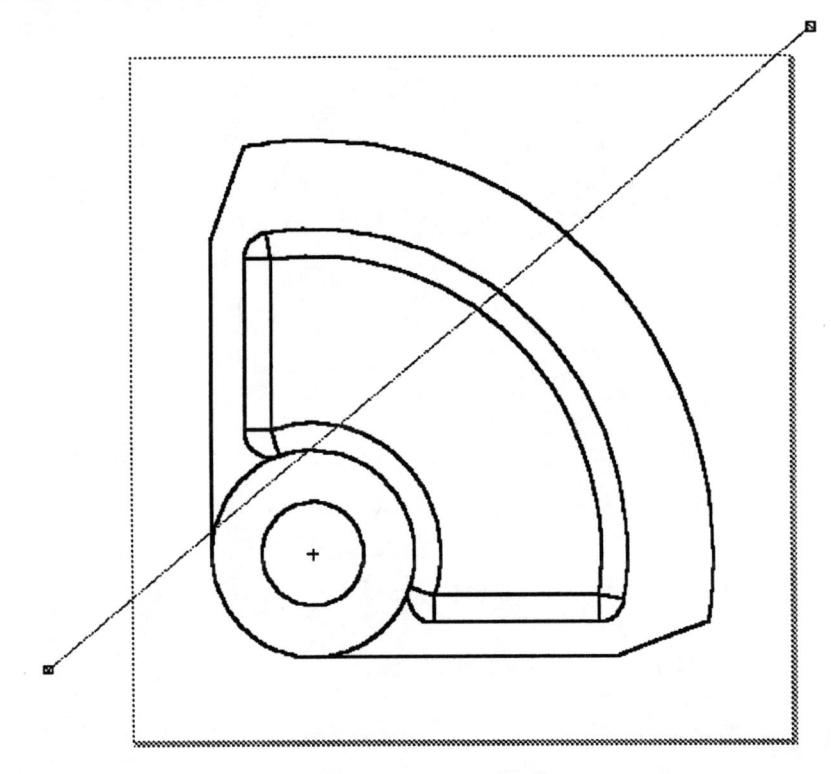

Figure X18-2

C. Look at the **View** pulldown menu. If a check mark does not already appear in front of **Temporary Axes** then click once on **Temporary Axes** to turn them on.

D. With the diagonal line already selected (highlighted in green) press and hold down the **CTRL** button while picking on the center axis of the through hole.

E. Press the *Add Relations* tool, select the *Coincident* radio button, press **Apply**, and press **Close**. The sketched line should move to pass through the center of the hole.

DESIGN PROJECT TUTORIAL

F. Add an angular dimension between the sketched line and any horizontal edge or surface on the part. **Modify** the value to **45deg**. Then delete the dimension. The line should look similar to Figure X18-3 at this point:

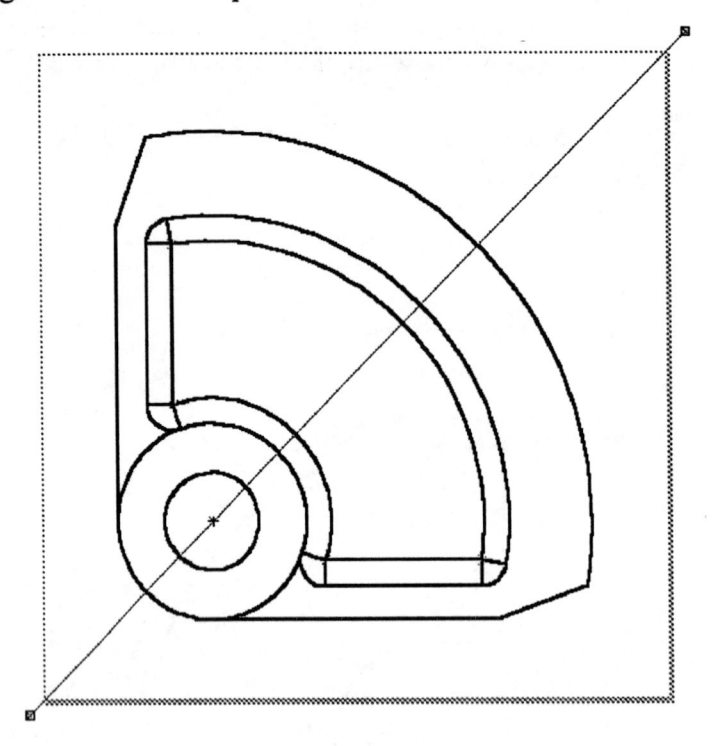

Figure X18-3

G. **Click** on *Zoom to Fit* to see the entire drawing..

H. If it isn't already completely highlighted in green click on the sketched line so that it is highlighted in green and green editing "grips" appear on both ends.

I. **Click** on the **Section View** tool: and then left click below and to the right of the front view to place the section view.

J. **Doubleclick** on the section line to make it point to the upper left corner of the drawing.

K. Press the **Esc** button to unselect the section line.

L. If you see a grey cross-hatch over top of the section view a *Rebuild* is necessary. Press the **Rebuild** tool: to update the section view.

Step 5: Adjust the location of each view, as necessary.

If you are dissatisfied with the location of a particular view click once near the view (inside the grey *drawing view border* but outside of the actual part view) to activate a green outline frame. Move the mouse pointer to the outline of the frame until the pointer turns into a **Move** indicator (it is a four-headed arrow pointing up, down, left and right). Then drag and drop the view where you want it.

Sometimes, projected views will move to maintain the proper alignment of views. Refer to Figure X18-1 for an example of fairly good view positioning.

Step 6: Adjust the hidden line visibility in each view and turn off the *Temporary Axes*.

A. Click near the *Top View* to activate a highlight frame (green) around it. Press the **Hidden in Gray** tool to show all hidden lines.

B. Similarly, show all hidden lines on the *Front View* in gray.

C. Go to the **View** pulldown menu and click once on **Temporary Axes** to turn them all off.

D. Go to **Tools ▼ Options...** and select the *Drawings* tab. Unselect the option *Display drawing view borders*.

Step 7: Change the appearance of the crosshatch pattern on the *section view*.

A. Use *Zoom to Area* to obtain a close-up of the section view.

B. It is <u>very undesirable</u> to have crosshatch lines run parallel or perpendicular to the outline of a section view (such as shown on Figure X18-1), and the initial appearance of the crosshatch lines must be changed. Point at one of the crosshatch lines and right click. Select **Properties...** from the popup menu.

C. Change the *Scale:* to **1.500** and the *Angle* to **135deg.** Select **View** from the *Apply to:* flipdown menu.

DESIGN PROJECT TUTORIAL

D. Press the **OK** button to finalize the crosshatch changes. Press the **Esc** button to remove the blue selection point from the section view.

E. Press *Zoom to Fit* and *Redraw* to finalize the drawing views. The revised crosshatch should look like Figure X18-4. This appearance of the crosshatch lines is much more desirable than the previous appearance.

F. Save the file as `gear.slddrw`.

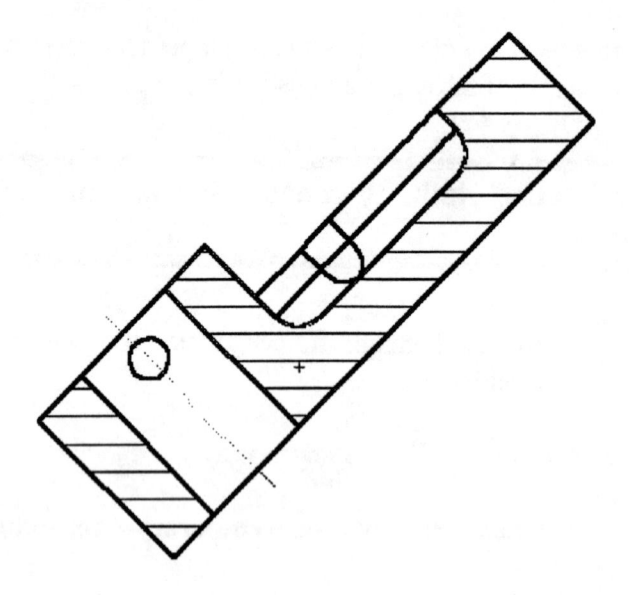

SECTION A-A

Figure X18-4.

End of Exercise 18.

Exercise 19: Detailed Drawing

In this exercise you will fully dimension the **GEAR** drawing. The objective is to create a drawing like Figure X19-1 using semi-automatic dimensioning and manual modifications of the dimensions.

Step 1: Open the file Gear.SLDDRW. Insert semi-automatic dimensions.

A. Open gear.SLDDRW. You may be asked to specify the path for gear.SLDPRT while opening the drawing.

B. Select **Insert ▼ Model Items...** and make sure the **Dimensions** option under the *Annotations* heading is checked and the **Import items into all views** option at the bottom of the dialog are checked. Press **OK** to finalize semi-automatic dimensioning. Press **Esc** to deselect any highlighted views.

Step 2: Add center marks.

A. Select **View ▼ Toolbars ▶ Annotation** to activate this toolbar.

B. Click on the **Center Mark** tool:

C. Click on the circles that represent the holes to add center marks to them.

D. Click on the **Center Mark** tool again to de-activate center marking.

DESIGN PROJECT TUTORIAL

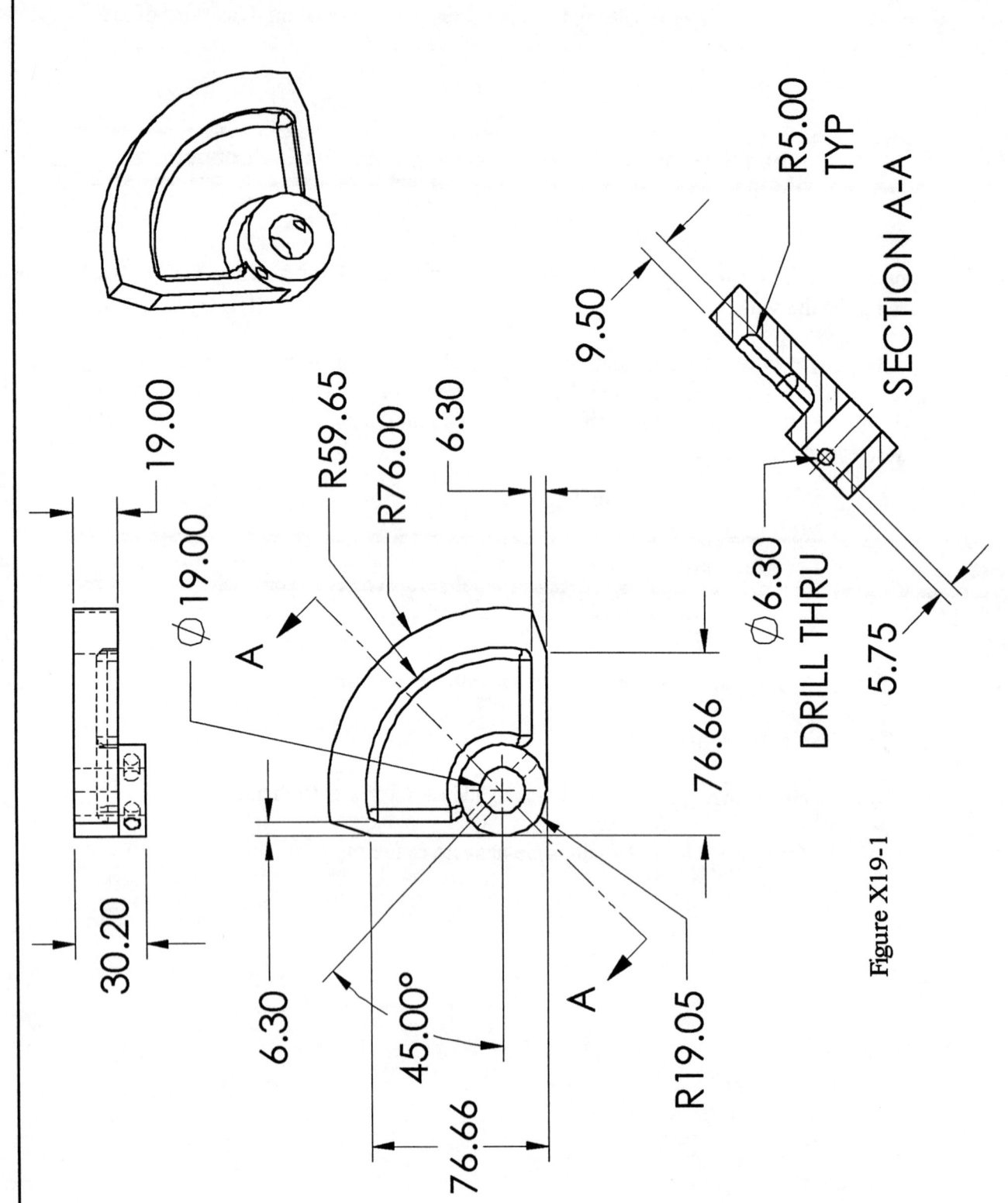

Figure X19-1

DESIGN PROJECT TUTORIAL

Step 3: Clean up the dimensions manually.

The appearance of the semi-automatic dimensions does not conform to the traditional standards of *Engineering Graphics*. The user must employ a combination of options to finalize the drawing details:

- a. Move dimension text.
- b. Delete a dimension
- c. Hide or Show a parametric dimension.
- d. Move a dimension to a different view.
- e. Re-establish missing dimensions.
- f. Modify dimension text.
- g. Move the attachment points of a dimension.
- h. Change a diameter dimension from a *linear* type to a *leader* type.
- i. Change a diameter or radius dimension to a leader type **or**
   Align the text of an angular dimension with its dimension line.
- j. Flip arrows on a dimension from inside to outside.

Option 3a: Move dimension text.

A particular problem with semi-automatic dimensioning is the placement of entire dimensions right on top of the object, hidden, and crosshatch lines. This is highly unacceptable according to standard practices because it obscures the important line work of the orthographic view. To move all dimension text and features to the outside of the view:

A. Drag and drop the text of the dimension. The dimension line, extension lines, and arrows will follow the text. Repeat this option until all dimension text and features are well positioned.

B. If the text of a dimension refuses to move using this method then delete it using Option 3b or hide it using Option 3c and redraw the dimension using Option 3e.

Option 3b: Delete a dimension.

For instance, it is unnecessary to show the R5.00mm in more than one location. A "typical" annotation can be added to the single remaining location. To delete a dimension:

A. Click on the dimension text (a green outline box should appear around the dimension's text, and "grips" should appear on the extension lines). Press **Delete**.

Extreme caution must be exercised when deleting parametric dimensions because bi-directional associativity can be lost. If you have any doubt about the advisability of deleting a parametric dimension it is better to *Hide* the dimension using Option 3c.

Option 3c: *Hide* or *Show* a parametric dimension.

To *Hide* a single parametric dimension, simply **Right click** over the text of that dimension and then select **Hide** from the popup menu. To *Hide* numerous parametric dimensions at the same time, use the following procedure:

A. Select **View ▼ Hide/Show Dimensions...** A *"half moon"* mouse cursor will appear, and all previously hidden dimensions will be shown in gray.

B. **Click** on the offending black dimension to *Hide* it. Temporarily, the dimension will turn gray. In sub-step D all of the gray dimensions will disappear from view.

C. If you wish to *Show* a previously hidden dimension **click** on it, and it will turn from gray to black.

D. Press **Esc** to end the *Hiding* and *Showing* of dimensions. The gray dimensions will disappear at this point.

Option 3d: Move a dimension to a different view.

According to standard rules the dimension for the diameter of a hole should appear in the view where the hole appears as a circle. The Ø6.30 dimension for the cross hole belongs on the section view, along with its locating dimensions. To move a dimension between views:

A. Press and hold down the **Shift** button. Drag the dimension and drop it on the desired view. If you try this twice unsuccessfully with each dimension then try sub-steps B through D.

B. Delete the dimensions that refuse to be moved.

C. Highlight the views one-at-a-time where the deleted dimensions should appear. Select **Insert ▼ Model Items...**, make sure the **Dimensions** option is checked, and press **OK**. The dimensions may or may not appear in the new location. Extraneous dimensions may appear that need to be deleted.

D. If neither method of moving the dimension works then use Option 3e to re-establish missing dimensions.

Option 3e: Re-establish missing dimensions.

This is just like dimensioning a sketched profile.

A. Click on the **Dimension** tool. Click on the entity or vertices to be dimensioned. Click to indicate the desired location for the dimension text. It is better to click once on the middle of an entity than to click on its two endpoints because the endpoints are more easily misinterpreted. Click again on the **Dimension** tool to terminate dimensioning.

B. To remove the parentheses from the dimension Click on the dimension text. Right click and select **Properties...** from the popup menu.

C. Click on the *Display with parentheses* option to unselect it.

D. Press **Apply** and **OK** to enact the parentheses removal.

Option 3f: Modify dimension text.

For instance, we want to add a "TYP" annotation to the R 5.00mm dimension.

A. Click on the dimension text. Right click and select **Properties...** from the popup menu.

B. Press the **Modify Text** button. Modify the text.

For the example of the **R5.00** dimension press **Tab** once to move the cursor to the next window. Type "TYP." Observe how the text in the *Preview* window has changed.

For the example of the Ø6.30 dimension press **Tab** once to move the cursor to the next window and then type "**DRILL THRU ONE PLACE.**"

C. Press **OK** then **Apply** then **OK** again to finalize the changes.

Option 3g: Move the attachment points of a dimension.

Often, extension lines will extend into object lines. A small offset between the object line and the extension line is required. To create the offsets where they are missing:

A. Pick on the dimension text once to activate the green highlights. Drag and drop the green "grip" box at the origin end of the dimension to its new location.

B. Press the **Esc** button on the keyboard to unselect the dimension.

Option 3h: Change a diameter dimension from a linear type to a *leader* type.

A. Click on the dimension text. Right click and select **Properties...** from the popup menu.

B. Click on the *Display as linear dimension* option to unselect it.

C. Click on the **Outside** option in the *Arrows* area of the *Dimension Properties* dialog.

D. Press **Apply** and **OK** to enact the change of dimension type.

DESIGN PROJECT TUTORIAL

Option 3i: Change a diameter or radius dimension from a linear type to a *leader* type or align the text of an angular dimension with its dimension line.

A. Click on the dimension text. Right click and select **Properties...** from the popup menu.

B. Press the **Display** button and select a radiou button other than *Use document's leader display*. Usually, you'll want the *broken leader* type:

C. Press **OK** and **Apply** and **OK** to enact the change of dimension type.

Option 3j: Flip dimension arrows.

A. **Right click** on the dimension text and select **Properties...** from the popup menu.

B. Click on the **Outside** option in the *Arrows* area of the *Dimension Properties* dialog.

C. Press **Apply** and **OK** to enact the change of dimension type.

Step 4: *Preview* and *Print* the drawing.

A. Select **File ▼ Print Preview** to preview the print-out of the drawing.

B. If you are satisfied with what you see then press the **Print** button to print the drawing.

C. If you would like to change something then press the **Close** button to return to drawing editing.

End of Exercise 19.

Exercise 20: Circular Pattern

In this exercise we will design a part named IMPELLER using Circular Patterning. The impeller blades will be patterned radially about the part's central axis.

The first blade will be located by an angular dimension relative to reference geometry, and this angular dimension will be used to create the circular pattern. The IMPELLER part (shown in its final configuration as Figure X20-1) will be used in an assembly later so please be sure to save the part.

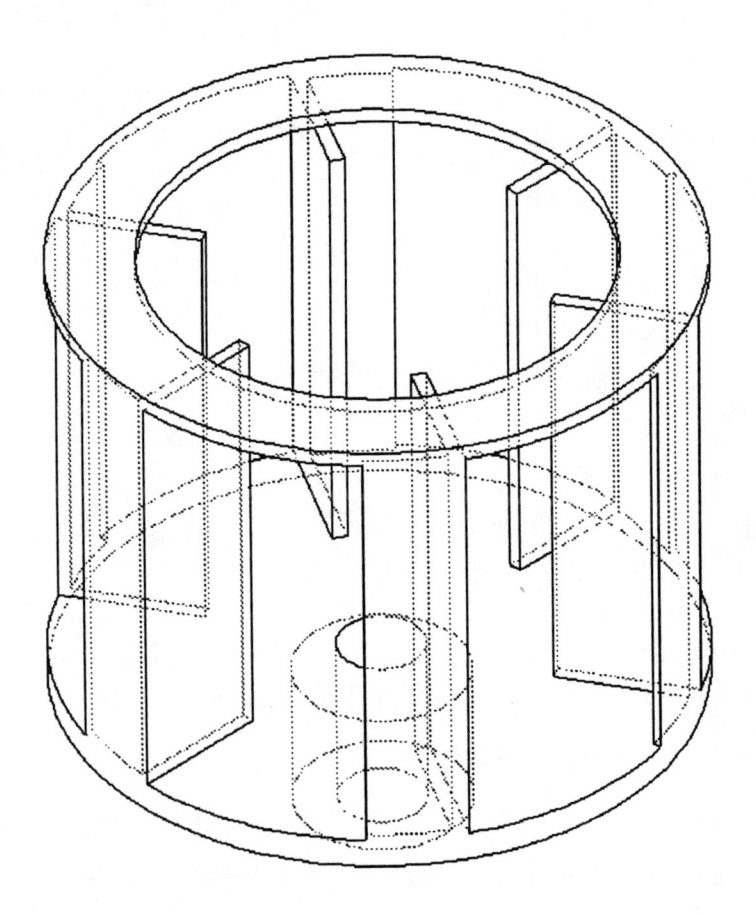

Figure X20-1

Step 1:	**Create a part named IMPELLER. The sketch for the base feature will be a circle and will be extruded.**

Sketch a Ø **11.00in.** circle on the *Top* plane and extrude it upward by a **Blind** depth of **0.50in.,** as shown on Figure X20-2.

DESIGN PROJECT TUTORIAL

Step 2:   **Sketch and extrude the first blade.**

A. Select the top surface of the base (See Figure X20-2) as the sketching surface for the first blade cross-section and begin sketching.

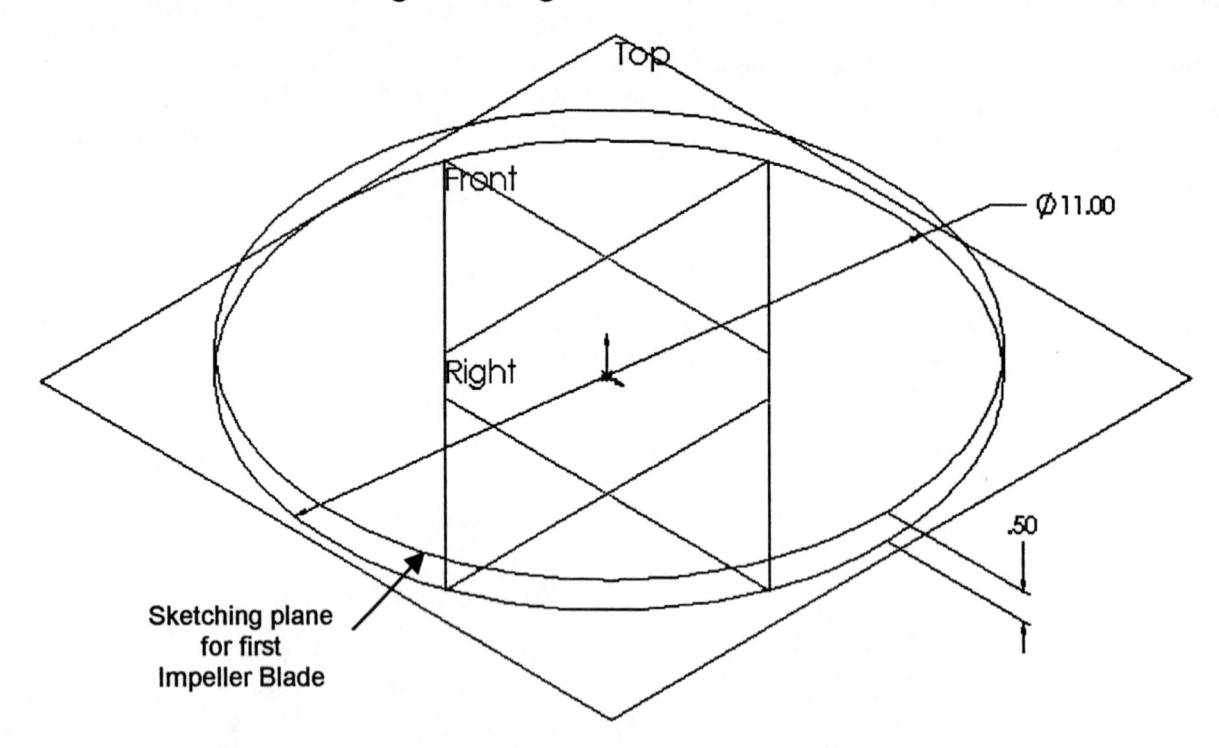

Figure X20-2

B. Select the outside edge of the base and use *Convert Entities* to obtain a sketched circle which is related to the outer diameter of the base.

C. Sketch two radial **Lines,** two additional lines, and one **Centerpoint Arc** as shown on Figure X20-3.

D. Use **Trim** to remove the unneeded portions of the outer arc and radial lines and to obtain the cross-section shown in Figure X20-4.

E. **Dimension** the sketch and **Add Relations** to obtain a state of full definition. Possible relations which might be required:
   a. Arcs as *Concentric*
   b. Radial lines as *Coincident* with the origin
   c. Longest two straight lines of the sketch as *Parallel*
   d. Short (0.25in.) straight line as *Perpendicular* to the two longest straight lines.

F. Extrude the fully defined sketch by a **Blind** depth of **7.35in.**

DESIGN PROJECT TUTORIAL

Figure X20-3

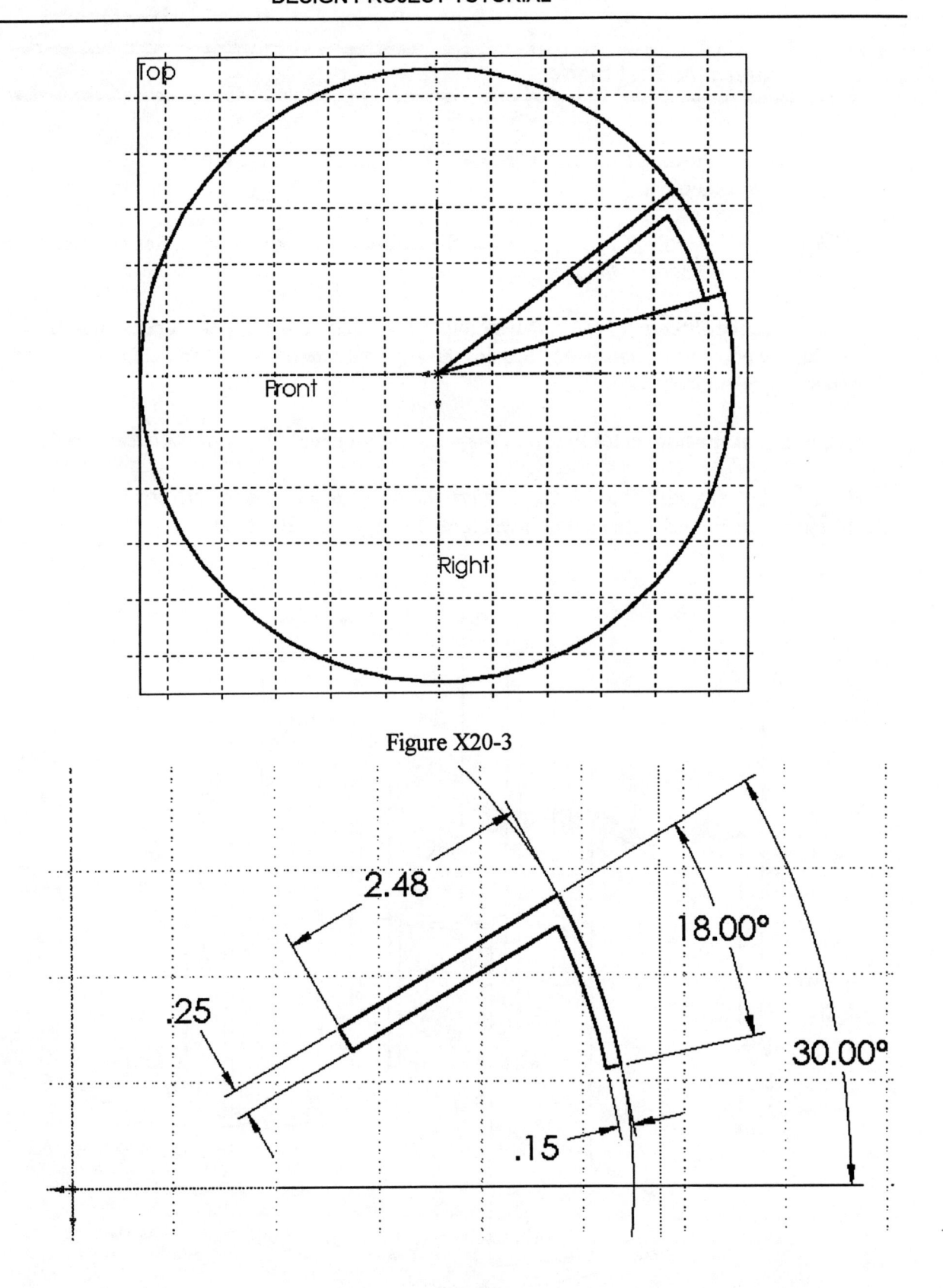

Figure X20-4

20-3

DESIGN PROJECT TUTORIAL

Step 3: Pattern the first blade.

A. Select **Insert ▼ Pattern/Mirror ▶ Circular Pattern...** or click the tool: on the *Features* toolbar.

B. Click inside the *Items to Copy:* window of the *Circular Pattern* dialog. Click on **Boss-Extrude1** in the *FeatureManager* design tree.

C. Click inside the *Direction Selected:* window. Then click on the **30.00°** dimension in the graphics window (this dimension becomes the key characteristic for the circular patterning operation).

D. Check **Equal spacing**, enter the *Total angle:* as **360deg** and the *Total instances:* as **6.**

E. Press the **OK** button in the *Circular Pattern* dialog to finalize the pattern creation. With the circular pattern effected the part will look like Figure X20-5:

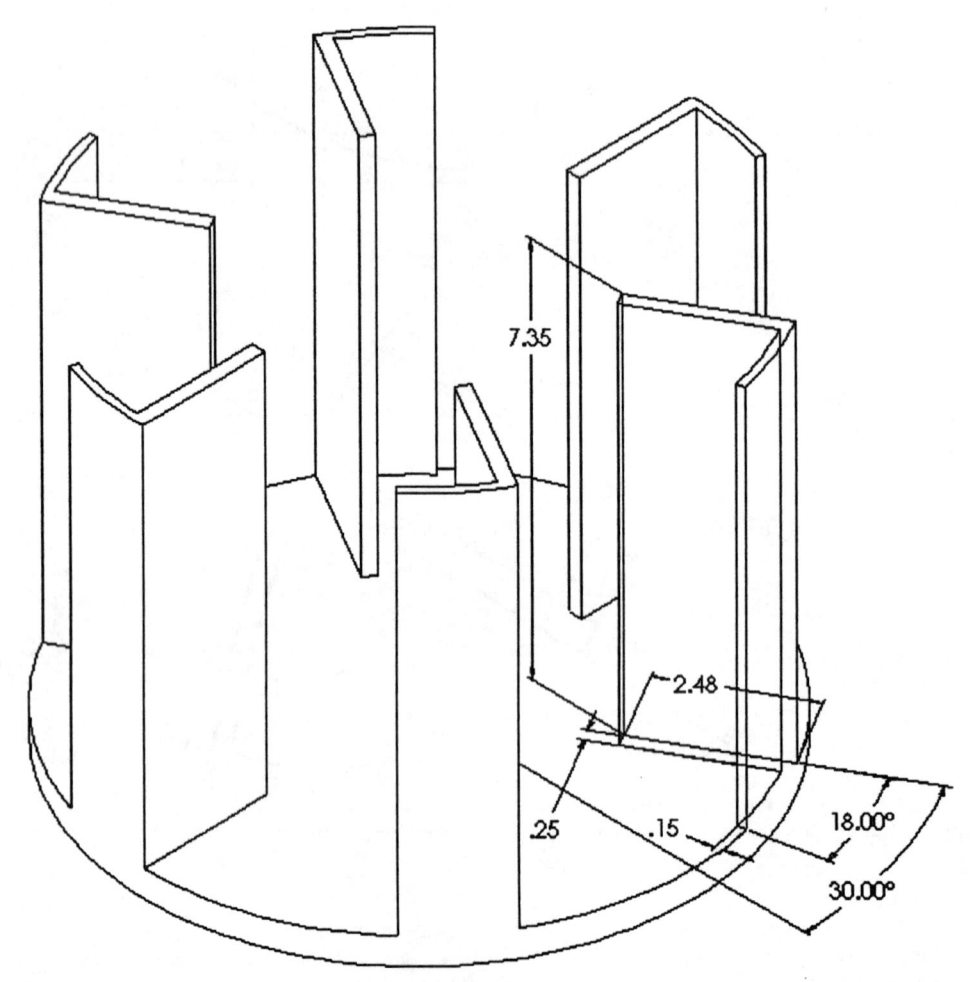

Figure X20-5

DESIGN PROJECT TUTORIAL

Step 4: Create the top of the Impeller as an extruded boss.

A. Select the top surface of *one* of the blades as the sketching surface and begin sketching.

B. Select the edge of the bottom surface of the part (see the call-out on Figure X20-6) and use *Convert Entities* to obtain the complete sketch cross-section.

C. Extrude the sketch upward (away from the blades) by a **Blind** depth of **0.25in.** Refer to Figure X20-6:

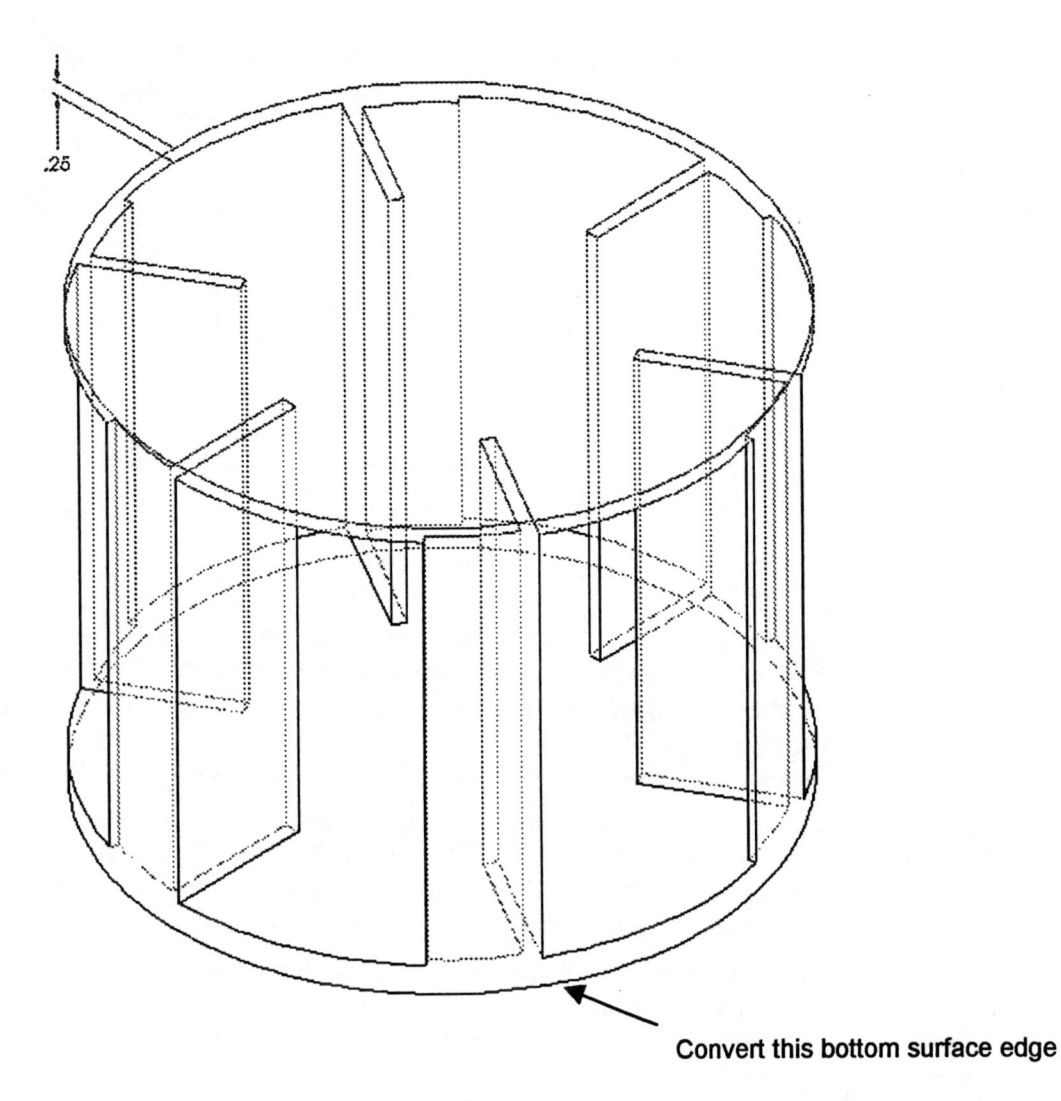

Convert this bottom surface edge

Figure X20-6

DESIGN PROJECT TUTORIAL

Step 5: Create a Ø 8.00in. cut in the previous feature. Sketch on the top of that boss and extrude up to its underside surface.

See Figure X20-7:

Extrude *Up to Surface* (bottom of top boss)

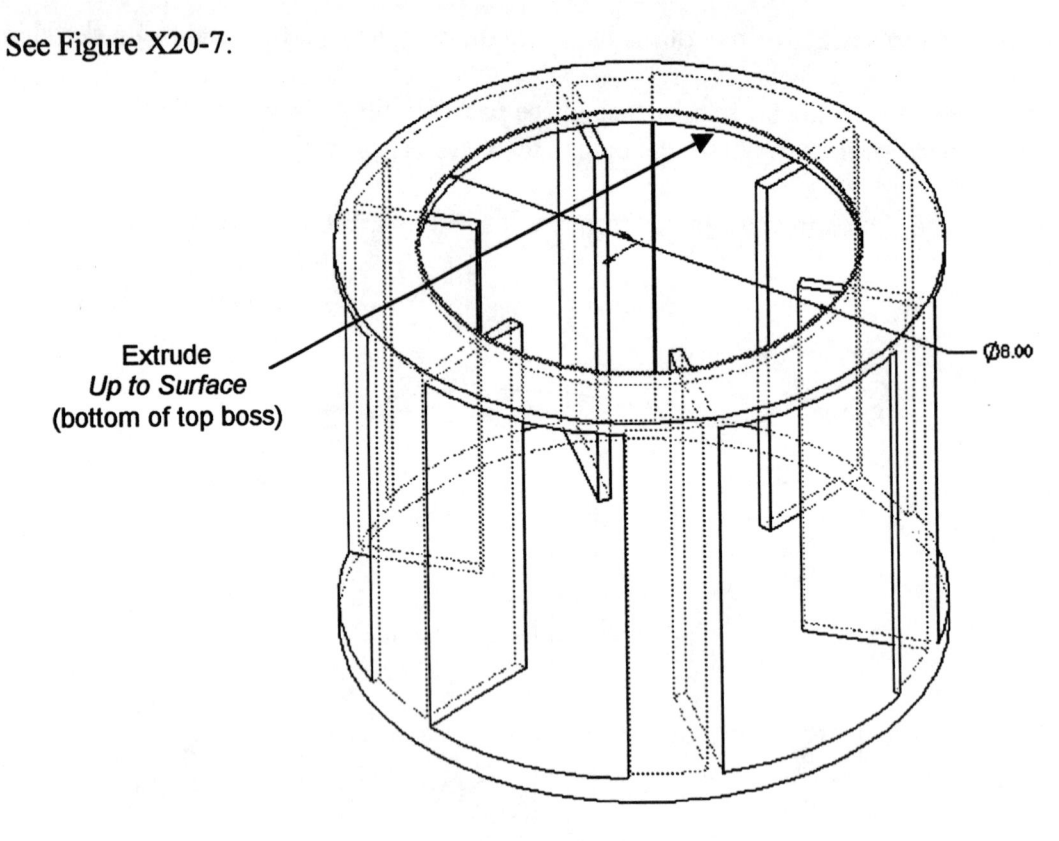

Ø8.00

Figure X20-7

Step 6: Sketch and extrude a concentric circular boss on the bottom surface of the impeller. Give it a Ø 3.00in. and a *Blind* depth of 2.50in. See Figure X20-8.

Step 7: Create a Ø 1.50in. hole *Through All*. Sketch on the bottom surface of the previous boss. See Figure X20-9.

Step 8: Save the model.

Figure X20-8

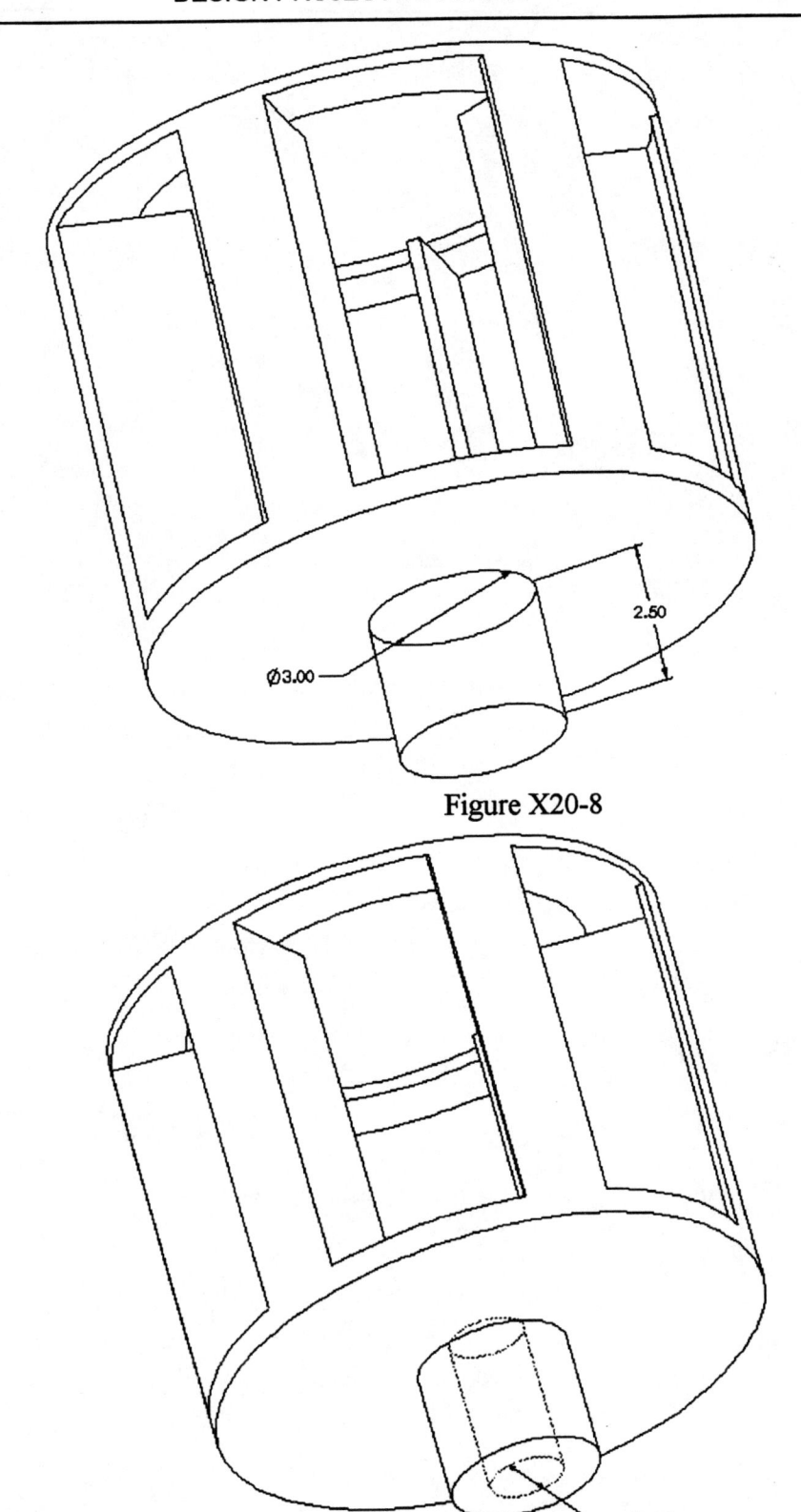

Figure X20-9

End of Exercise 20.

Design Project Assignment 3

Seven different parts will be created and assembled in the nine Design Project Assignments. In this third assignment we will begin a new part:
  A. UPPER_HOUSING
And complete one part:
  B. COVER

Assignment 3A: Begin the UPPER_HOUSING Part

| Step 1: | Create a part named UPPER_HOUSING with inches as units. |

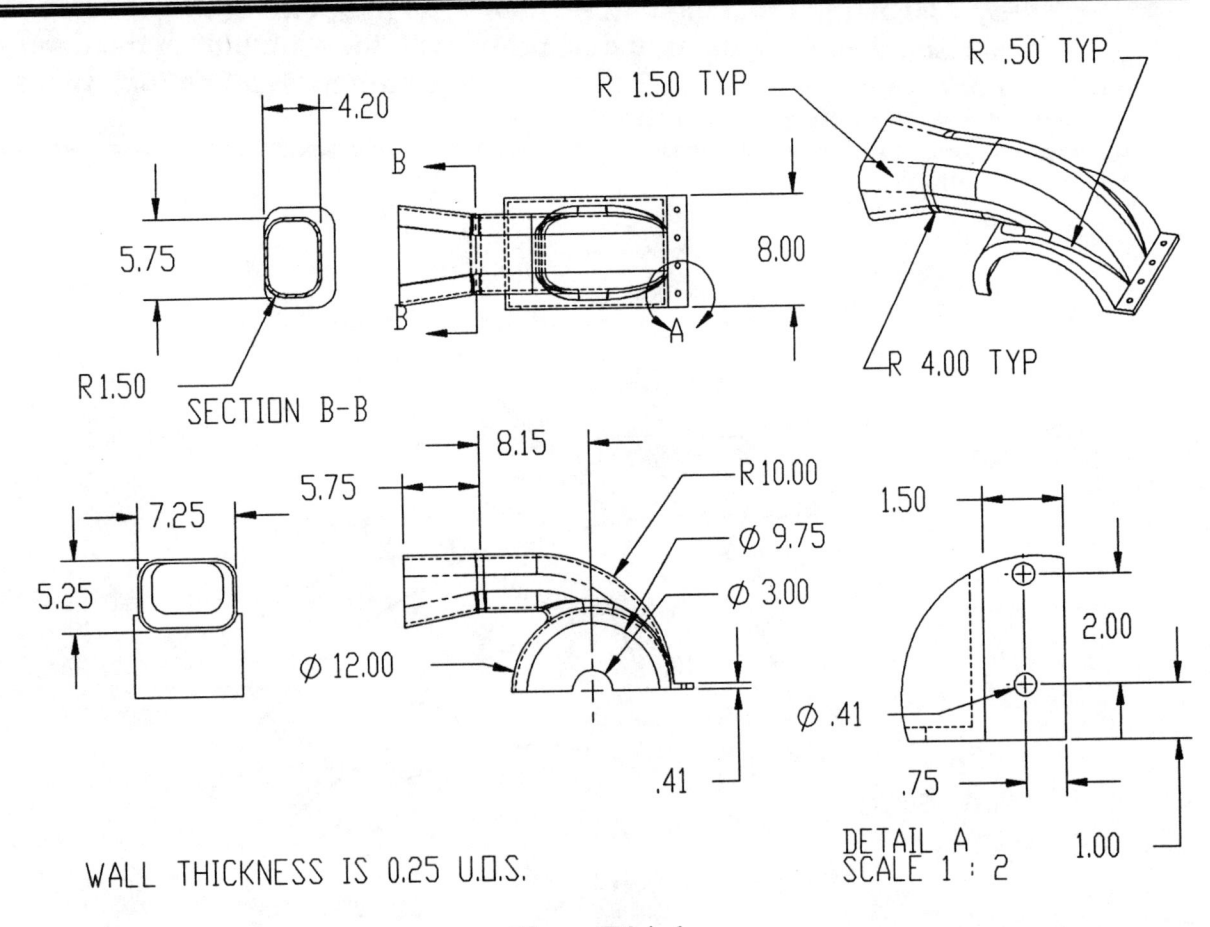

WALL THICKNESS IS 0.25 U.O.S.

Figure D3A-1

| Step 2: | Create the *base* feature. Extrude a Ø 12.00in. inverted semi-circle to a depth of 8.00 in. Using *Mid Plane* as the *Type:* of extrusion depth will greatly simplify future operations. |

DESIGN PROJECT TUTORIAL

Step 3: The first feature of the housing discharge is created using a *Sweep*, which will require two sketches. Before beginning either skecth, create a new sketching plane for the *Sweep Section* which is parallel to, and 8.15 in. to the left of, the *Right* plane--this new plane will be automatically named *Plane4*.

The *Sweep Path* is a sketch which consists of a line and an arc which lie in the *Front* plane and are tangent to one another. The arc radius is 10.00 in, and it is tangent to the *Base* feature. The endpoint of the arc is *coincident* with the *Top* plane, and the endpoint of the line is *coincident* with *Plane4*. See Figure D3A-3 for the sketch of the *Sweep Path*.

<u>Close the sketch for the *Sweep Path* before beginning the sketch for the *Sweep Section*.</u> The *Sweep Section* is a 5.75 in. wide by 4.20 in. high rectangle in *Plane 4*. The midpoint of the upper horizontal line segment is *coincident* with the endpoint of the *Sweep Path*. See Figure D3A-4 for the sketch of the *Sweep Section*. <u>Close the sketch</u>, then create the *Sweep*.

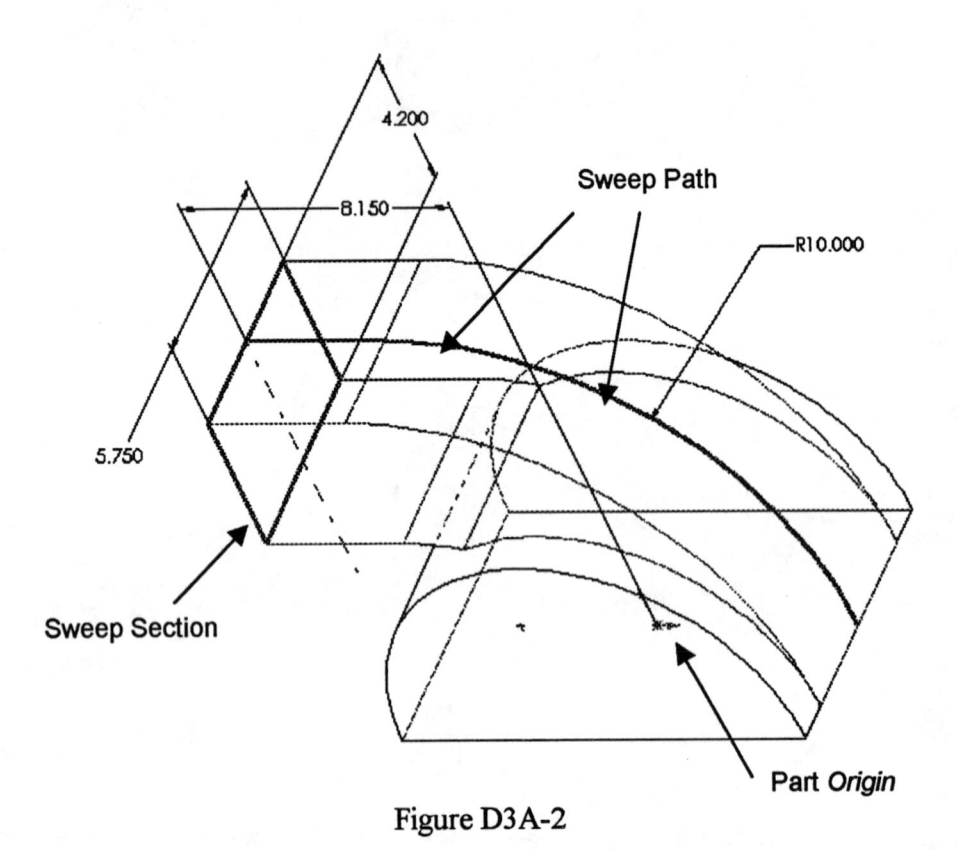

Figure D3A-2

DESIGN PROJECT TUTORIAL

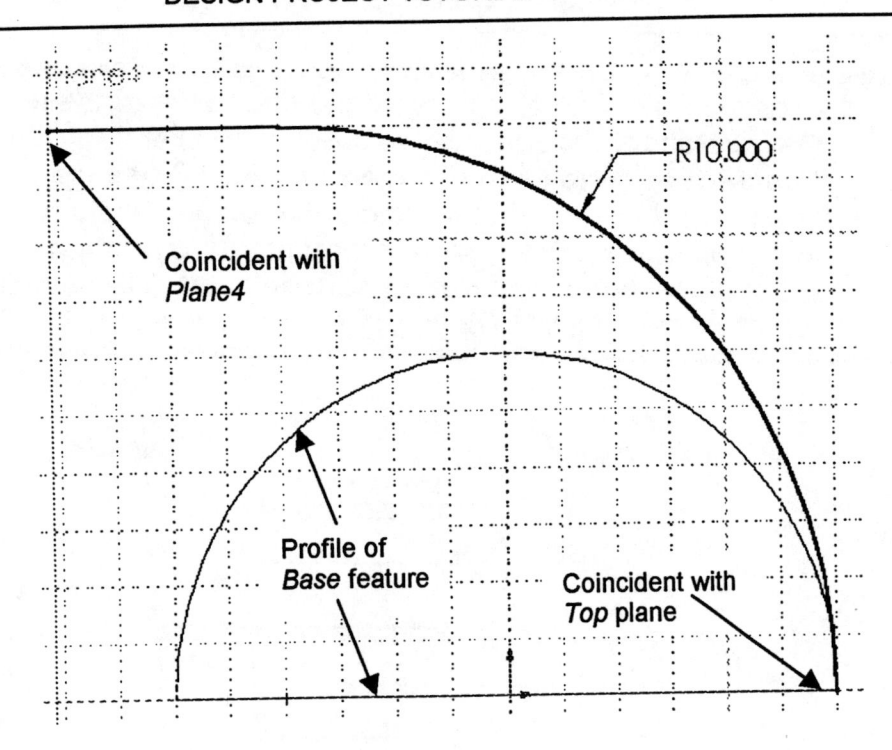

Figure D3A-3

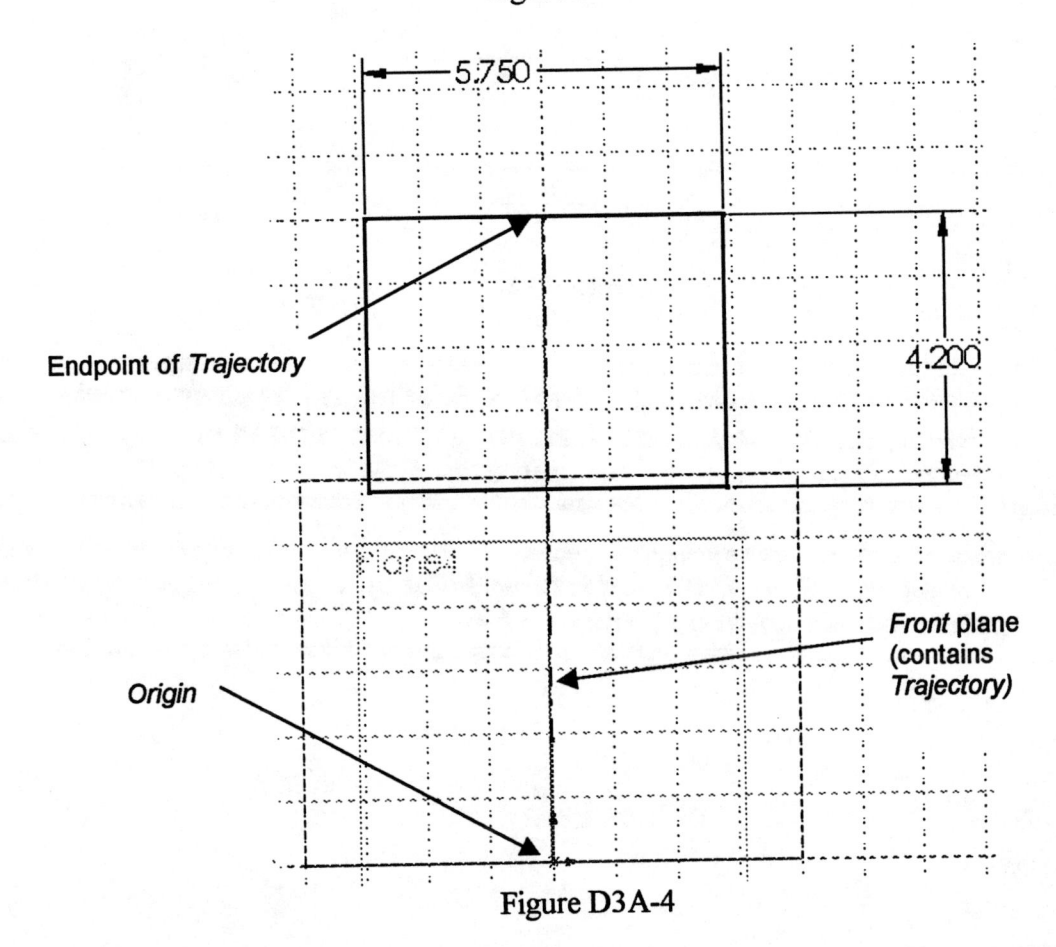

Figure D3A-4

D3-3

DESIGN PROJECT TUTORIAL

Step 4: Create a *Boss Loft* to complete the discharge of the housing. The first sketch for the *Loft* can be created by sketching on the end of *Boss-Sweep1* and using *Convert Entities*. <u>Close the sketch</u>. The second sketch should be created on a new plane which is 5.75 in. from *Plane4*. The sketch is a rectangle, *symmetrical* about the *Front* plane, and it uppermost horizontal edge is *coincident* with the top of *Boss-Sweep1*. <u>Close the sketch</u>, the create the *Boss Loft*.

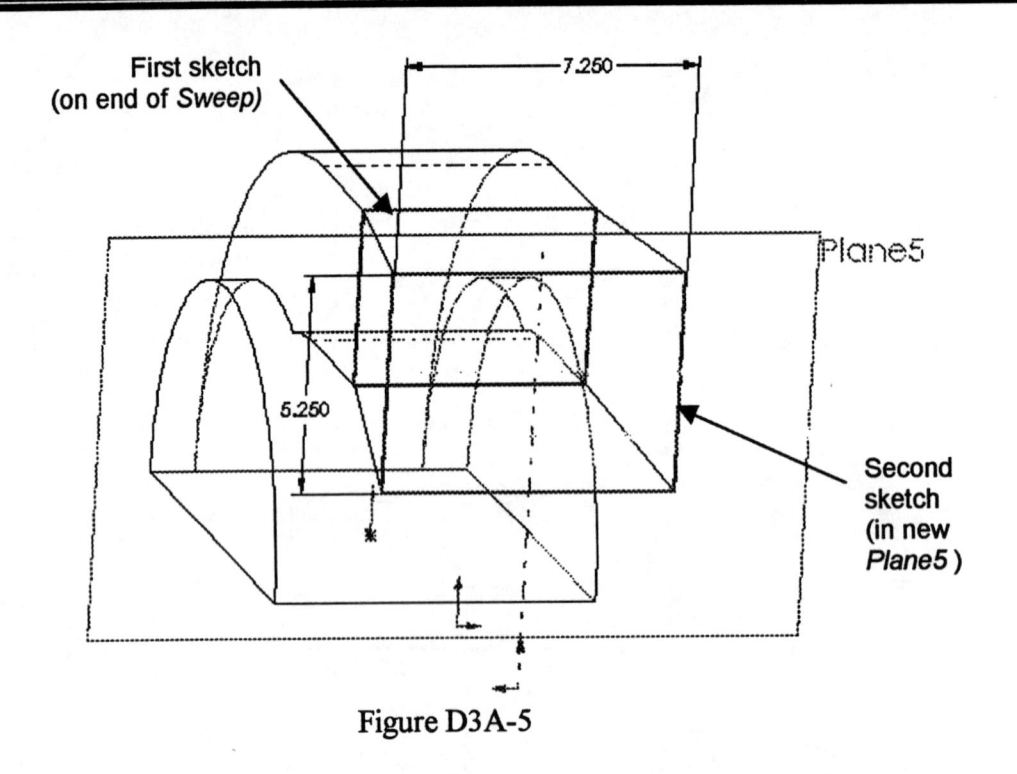

Figure D3A-5

Step 5: Create a 4.00 in. *Constant Radius Fillet* on the three edges where the *Sweep* meets the *Loft* at an angle. Turn on *Hidden in Gray* and study Figure D3A-6 before performing *Step 5*, *Step 6*, or *Step 7*.

Step 6: Create a 1.50 in. *Constant Radius Fillet* on the four edges of *Boss-Sweep1* as shown on Figure D3A-6.

DESIGN PROJECT TUTORIAL

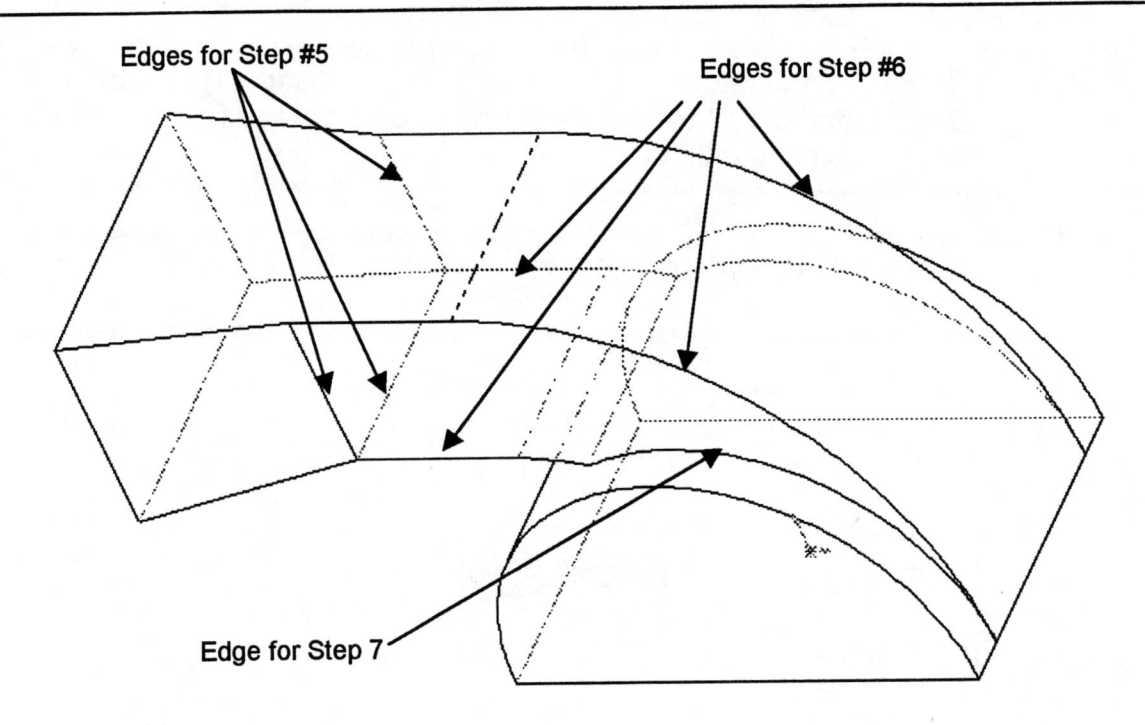

Edges for Step #5

Edges for Step #6

Edge for Step 7

Figure D3A-6

Step 7: Create a 0.50 in. *Constant Radius Fillet* on the edge where the sweep intersects the base feature. See Figure D3A-7 for the result.

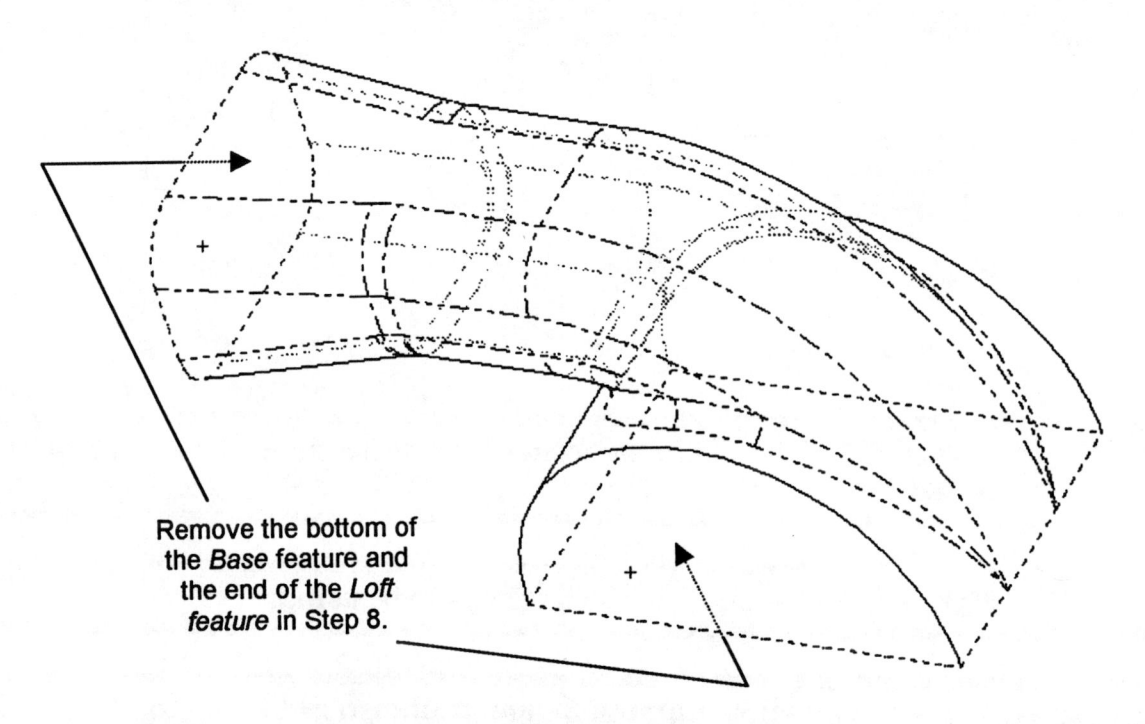

Remove the bottom of the *Base* feature and the end of the *Loft feature* in Step 8.

Figure D3A-7

DESIGN PROJECT TUTORIAL

Step 8: Create a *Shell* feature by removing two surfaces: 1) the outer end of *Boss-Loft1* and 2) the bottom surface of the *Base* feature. Make the shell thickness 0.25 in.

Step 9: Add a 1.50 in. wide by 0.41 in. high bolting flange as shown on Figure D3A-8.

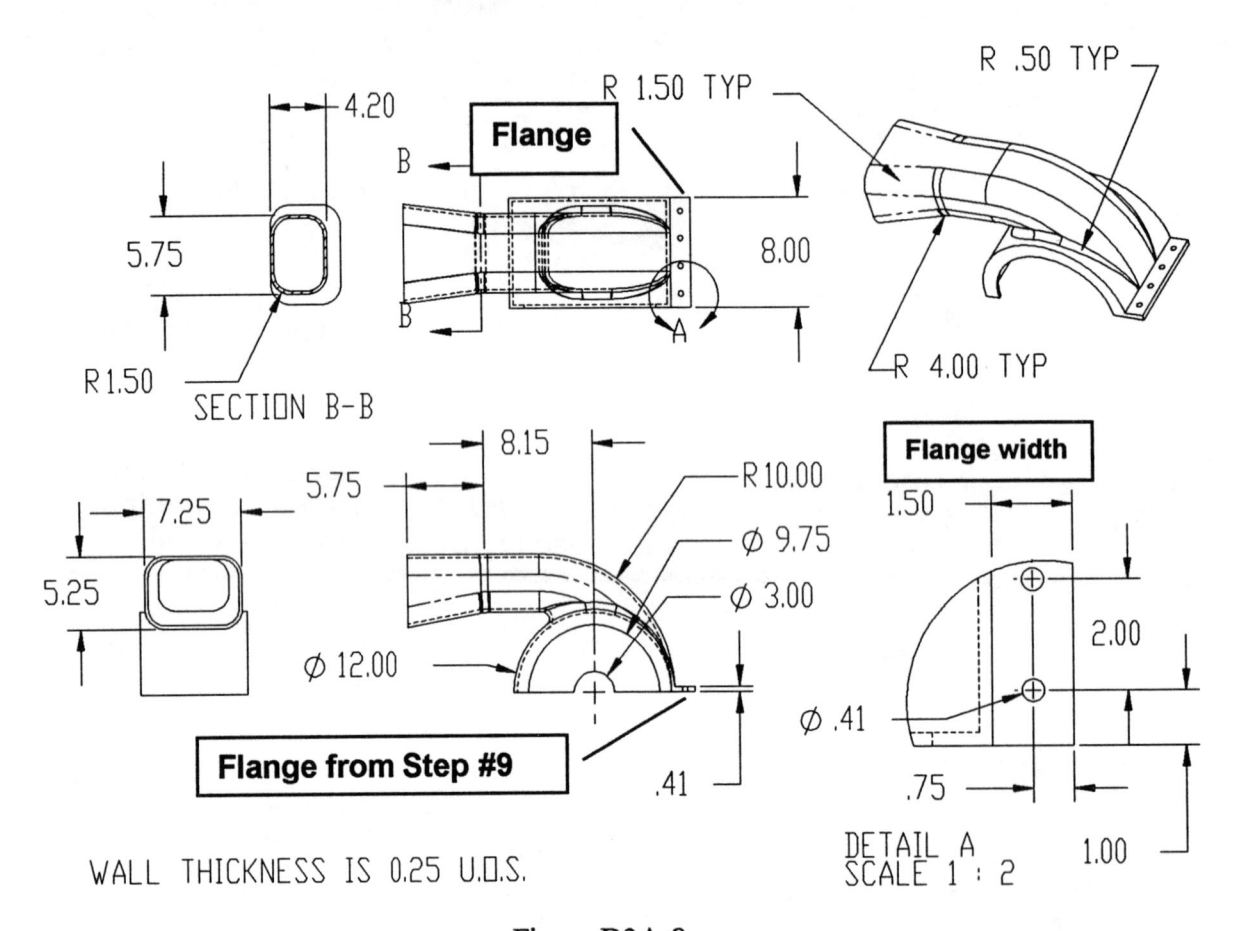

Figure D3A-8

Step 10: Make a Ø 9.75 in. cut in the front of the housing as shown in Figure D3A-8.

Step 11: Make a Ø 3.00 in. hole in the back of the housing.

Step 12: Add a straight hole thru the flange as shown in *Detail A* of Figure D3A-8.

DESIGN PROJECT TUTORIAL

Step 13: *Pattern* the hole for a total of four instances, including the original hole.

Step 14: Save the model.

Assignment 3B: Complete the COVER Part

Step 1: Open the part named COVER.

Step 2: Three bolt tabs are required for the *Cover*. Sketch on the bottom surface of the part and extrude the first bolt tab as shown in Figure D3B-1. The angular dimension originates from one of the default reference planes. It is the *characteristic* dimension for the circular patterning of the tabs. Extrude to a depth of 0.50 in.

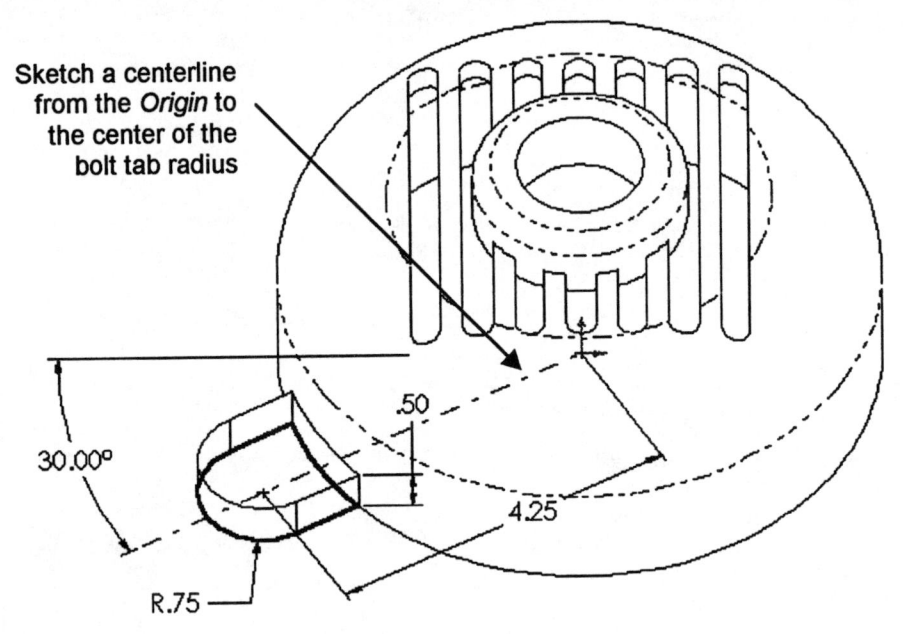

Figure D3B-1

DESIGN PROJECT TUTORIAL

Step 3: Create a Ø 0.75 in. straight hole through the first bolt tab. Use *Edit Sketch* and add a *Relation* to force the center of the hole to be *coincident* with the center of the R .75 in. outer surface of the bolt tab.

Step 4: Pattern the first bolt tab and hole to create a total of 3 equally spaced tabs. The final result should look like Figure D3B-2.

Step 5: Save the model.

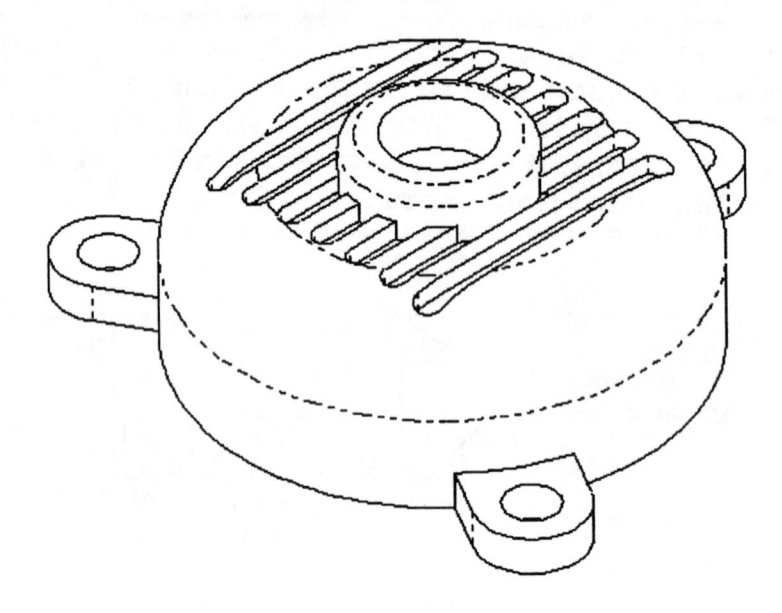

Figure D3B-2

End of Design Project Assignment 3.

DESIGN PROJECT TUTORIAL

Design Project Assignment 4

In addition to seven different part models, two sub-assemblies, and one top-level assembly three complete drawings will be created during the nine Design Project Assignments. In this fourth assignment we will complete two drawings from scratch:
- A. SNAP_RING
- B. DRIVE_SHAFT

And begin a third drawing
- C. MOTOR

Assignment 4A: Create the SNAP_RING Drawing

Step 1: Create a *New* drawing named SNAP_RING. Use *No Template* and A size paper.

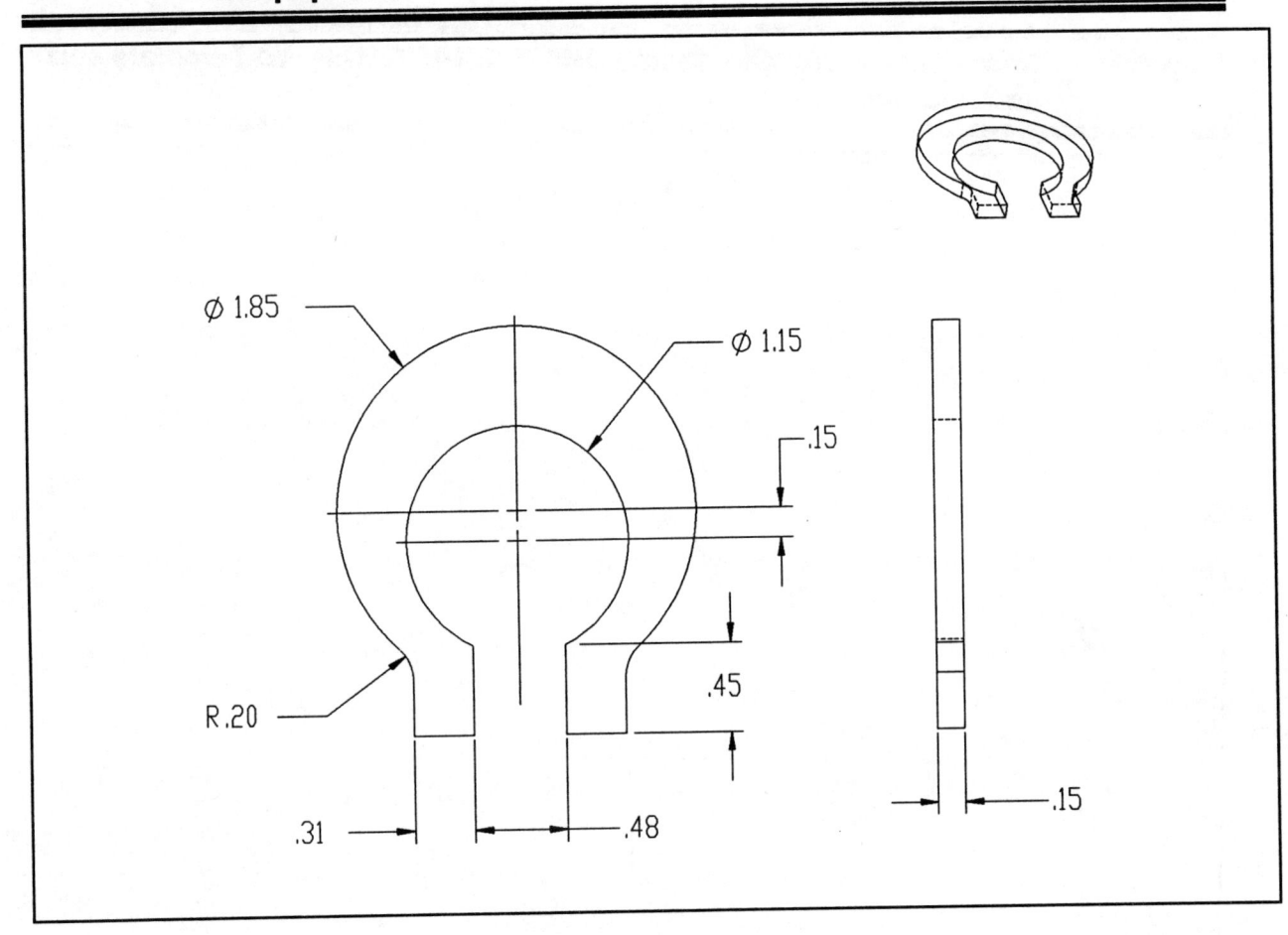

Figure D4A-1

D4-1

DESIGN PROJECT TUTORIAL

Step 2: Add the three standard orthograpic views and delete the Top View.

Step 3: Add the upper right general view with a scale of 0.75.

Step 4: Detail the drawing by adding and positioning the required dimensions.

Step 5: Save the drawing.

Assignment 4B: Create the DRIVE_SHAFT Drawing

Step 1: Create a *New* drawing named DRIVE_SHAFT. Use *No Template* and an A size sheet.

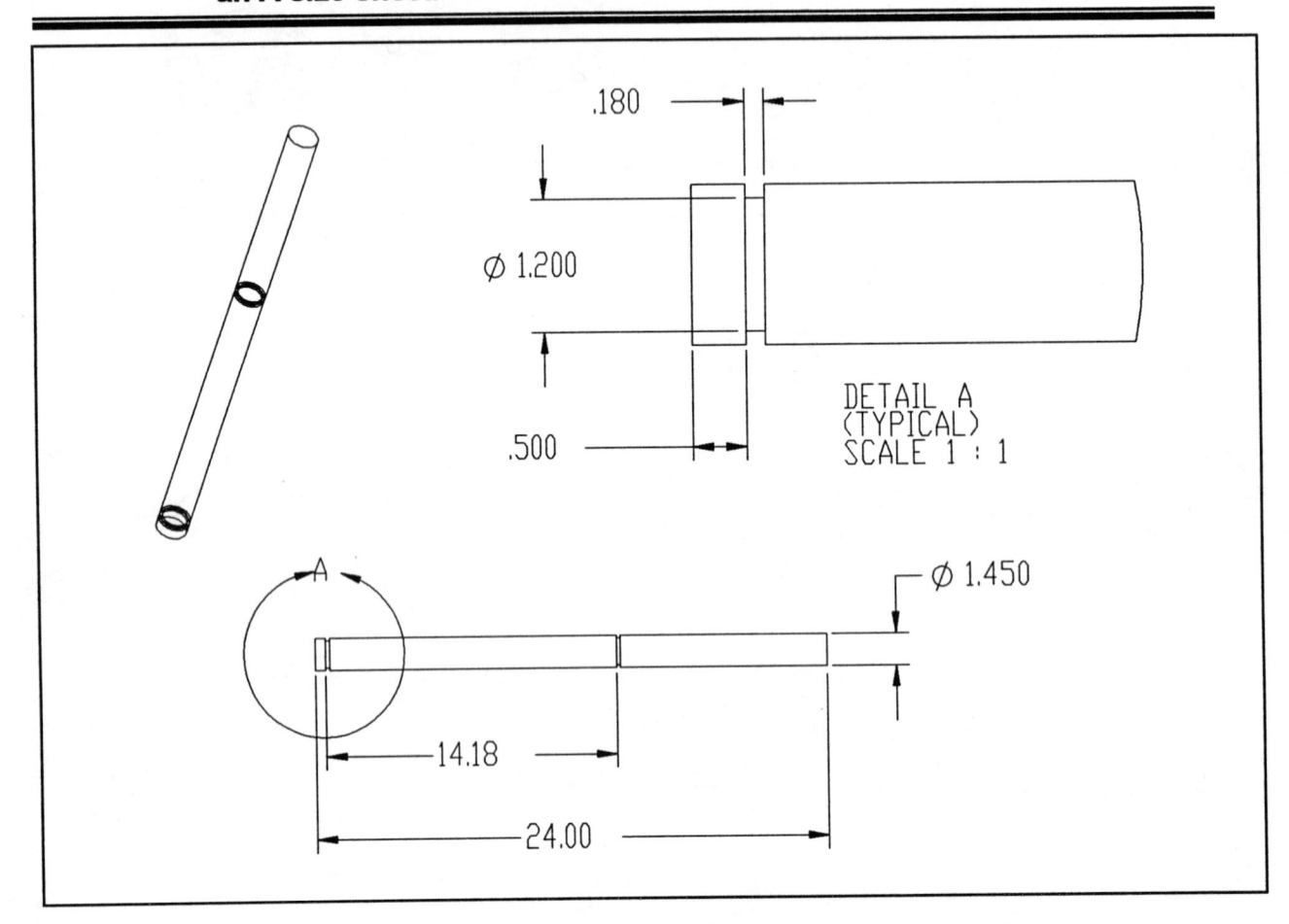

Figure D4B-1

D4-2

DESIGN PROJECT TUTORIAL

Step 2: Complete the drawing as shown and save it.

Assignment 4C: Begin the MOTOR Drawing

Step 1: Create a *New* drawing named MOTOR. Use *No Template* and an A size sheet.

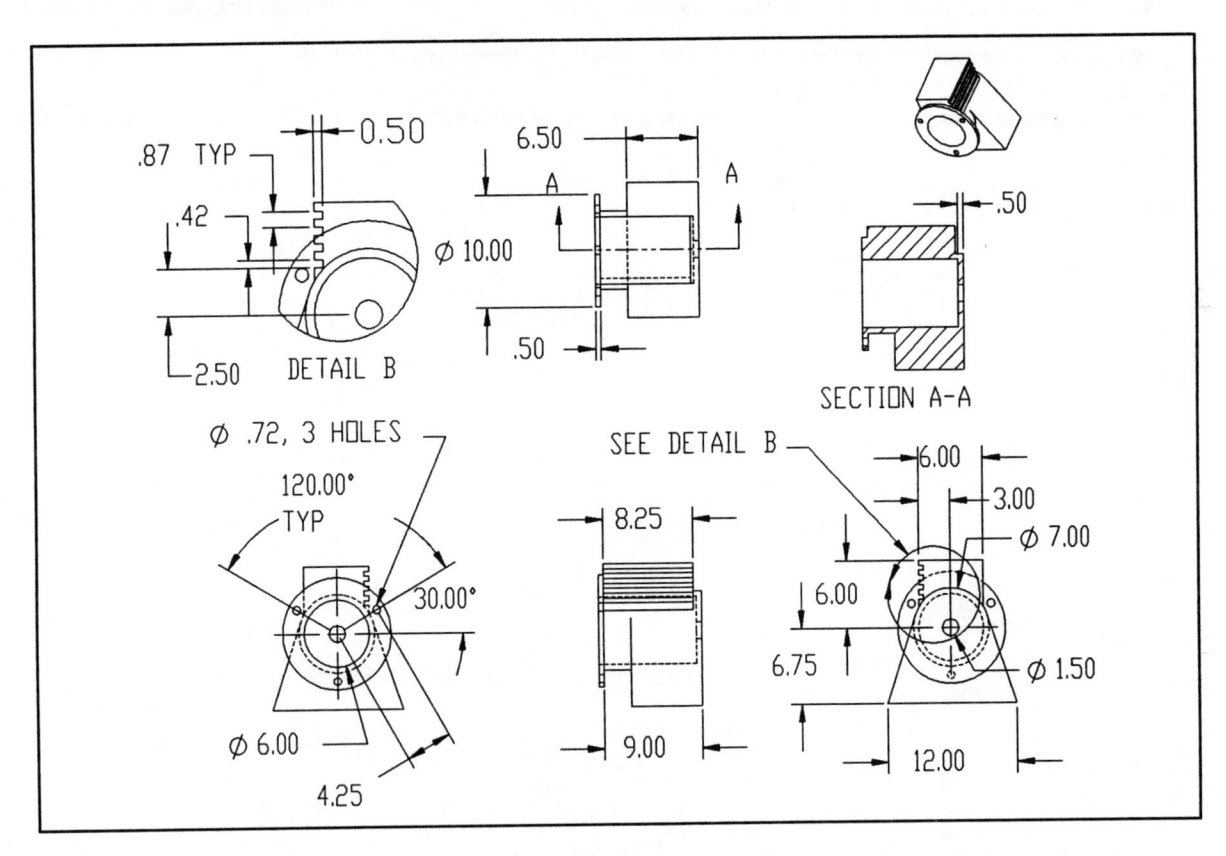

Figure D4C-1

Step 2: Add the three standard orthograpic views and delete the original Top View.

Step 3: Add a Back View, projected from the Right View, and re-create the Top View above the Right View.

D4-3

Step 4:	**Add the cross sectional view A-A.**
Step 5:	**Add the partial Detail B view.**
Step 6:	**Detail the drawing with the required dimensions.**
Step 7:	**Add a general view with a scale of 0.075.**
Step 8:	**Save the drawing.**

End of Design Project Assignment 4.

DESIGN PROJECT TUTORIAL

Exercise 21: Mirror All

In this exercise we will learn to mirror an entire part about one of its own flat surfaces. This is an extremely powerful technique for creating symmetrical parts.

Step 1: **Open the part LOCATING_FINGER. Note that one half of a symmetrical model has been built. The other half can be completed by using *Mirror All* to mirror the entire part about its own front surface.**

A. Open the part file named `locating_finger.SLDPRT`.

B. Select the front face of the part as the surface about which to mirror all features. See Figure X21-1 for clarification.

C. Select **Insert ▼ Pattern/Mirror ▶ Mirror All**, click **OK** in the *Mirror All* dialog box, and click **Zoom to Fit** to re-center the display.

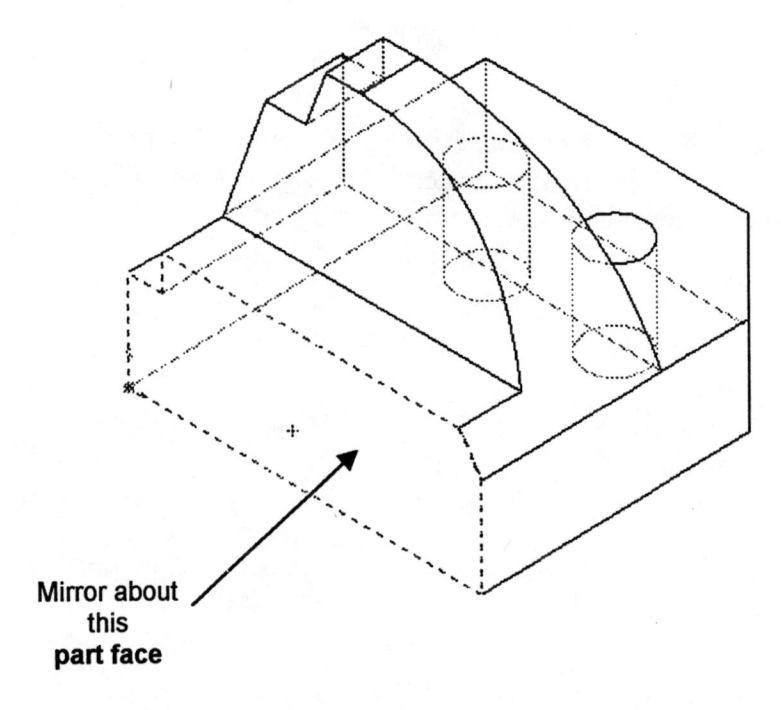

Mirror about this part face

Figure X21-1

(Configuration *before* mirroring)

21-1

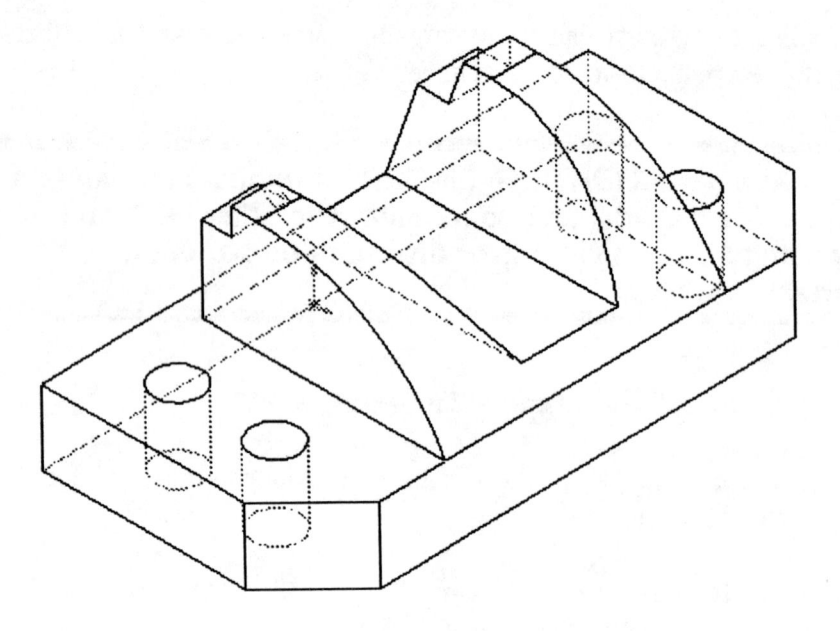

Figure X21-1

(Final configuration)

Always recall that the **Mirror All** command requires the selection of a part *surface*, never a reference plane--even if that reference plane is *Coincident* with the mirroring surface. Also, keep in mind that the **Mirror All** command can be a tremendous saver of time and effort if it is carefully and thoughtfully employed.

End of Exercise 21.

DESIGN PROJECT TUTORIAL

Exercise 22: Mirror Feature

In this exercise we will learn to mirror one or more selected features about one reference geometry plane or one flat surface of a part. The features created by a mirroring operation remain dependent upon, and related to, the original part feature. Changes to the original part feature are automatically reflected in its mirror feature.

Step 1:	A single slot is built on a model, and a second slot is desired. Copy the first slot feature using the *Mirror Feature* option.

A. Open the part file named v_stop.SLDPRT.

B. Select **Insert ▼ Pattern/Mirror ▶ Mirror Feature.**

C. Select the **Right** reference geometry plane as the *Mirror Plane* and **Slot-Straight1** as the *Item to Copy*. Note that features can be mirrored about a reference plane, but whole parts cannot.

D. Press **OK** to create the second slot.

Step 2:	Modify the angle of the parent (original) slot to show how the child (mirrored) slot will also update.

A. Double click on **Slot-Straight1** in the *FeatureManager* design tree.

B. Double click on the **30°** dimension and change the angle to **60°**.

C. **Enter** the change and **Rebuild** the model. Observe how both slots update to the modified dimension value.

Step 3:	Mirror all existing features in the model using *Mirror All*. Mirror around the *Front* plane.

A. Select the face of the part that lies coincident with the *Front* plane. To make this selection possible use *Select Other*, change to a *Back* view *before* selecting, or use *Rotate View* to spin the part *before* selecting.

22-1

DESIGN PROJECT TUTORIAL

Note that there is an important difference between a face of the part that lies coincident with the *Front* plane and the *Front* plane itself. If a reference geometry plane is selected instead of a part face the *Mirror All* option will be "grayed out" on the menu, meaning it is unavailable for execution.

B. Select **Insert ▼ Mirror/Pattern ▶ Mirror All** and click **OK** on the *Mirror All* dialog window. The completed model will look like Figure X22-1:

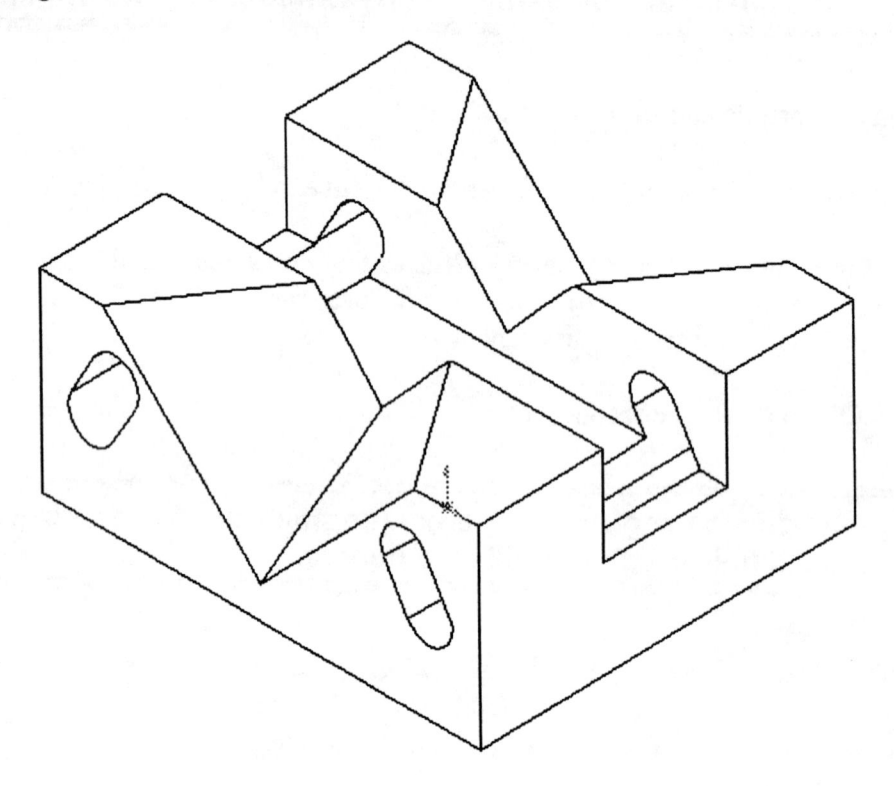

Figure 22-1

End of Exercise 22.

DESIGN PROJECT TUTORIAL

Exercise 23: Equations and Properties

In this exercise we will learn how to treat dimensions as parameters and relate them using equations.

| Step 1: | Center a hole on the top of a *base* feature using an equation and test the effect of the equation. |

A. **Open** the part file named `equations.sldprt`.

B. Choose **Tools ▼ Options** and the *General* tab. Check the option *Show dimension names* and press **OK** to activate this option.

C. Double click alternately on **Base-Extrude** and **Hole1** in the *FeatureManager* design tree to display the dimension names (or symbols) and values.

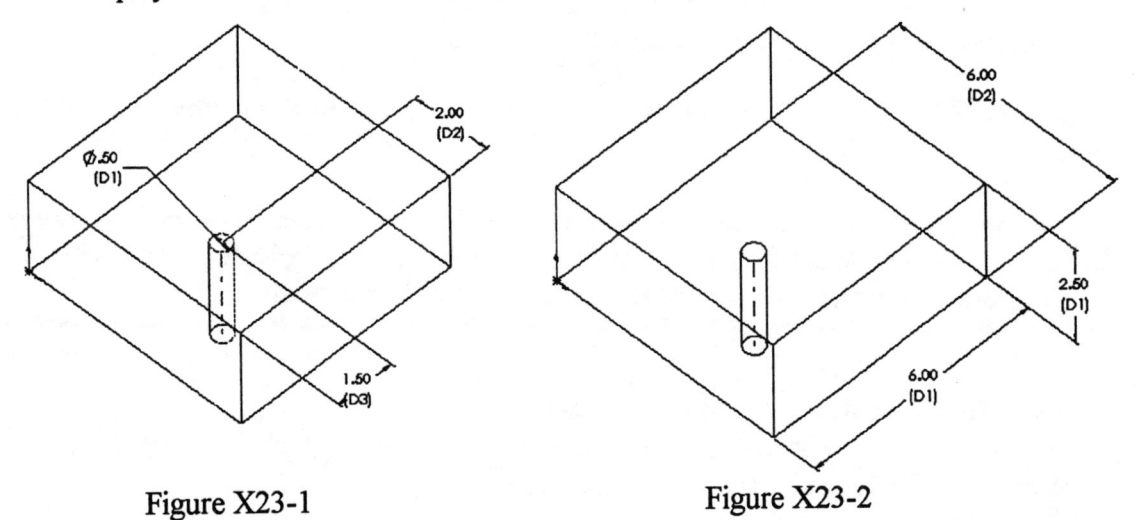

Figure X23-1   Figure X23-2

D. Choose **Tools ▼ Equations** and press the **Add** button. Double click **Hole1** in the *FeatureManager*, its **D3** dimension in the graphics window, the "=" on the calculator keypad, double-click **Base-Extrude** in the *FeatureManager*, its **D1** dimension in the graphics window, the "/" button on the *New Equation* keypad, and **2** on the *New Equation* keypad. The resulting equation must look like the following:

"D3@Sketch2" = "D1@Sketch1"/2

E. Click **OK** once, click **OK** again to activate the equation, and press **Esc** on the keyboard to clear all selections in the graphics window.

DESIGN PROJECT TUTORIAL

F. Follow a similar procedure to create the equation for the other direction:

"D2@Sketch2"="D2@Sketch1"/2

G. Click on the **Rebuild** tool to see the effect of the two equations. The hole should center on the part in both directions.

Step 2: Test the two *equations* just written for correct functioning by modifying the length and width of the *base* feature.

A. *Edit* **Sketch1** and change the two 6.00 dimensions to **7.00in.** and **9.00in.**

B. **Rebuild** the model to see the effect of the equations.

C. Double click on *Sketch2* in the *FeatureManager*.

D. Check that the two locating dimensions are 3.50 and 4.50.

E. Change the two dimensions on the *Base* feature back to **6.00in.** and **6.00in.** and **Rebuild** the model.

Step 3: This model also has two patterns of sketched hole features which are currently suppressed. *Unsuppress* them both.

A. Choose **Hole2** on the *FeatureManager* design tree.

B. Select **Edit ▼ Unsuppress with Dependents**.

Step 4: The dimensioning scheme of *Hole2* was radial around *Hole1*. In the first pattern the angle was incremented by 60° with 3 instances. A *Hole3* was dimensioned radially and at an angle from *Hole2*. In the second pattern the angle was incremented by 45° with 3 instances. Write two equations that equally space both patterns of holes around the straight hole. Use the angular pattern increment and numbers of holes in each pattern in your equation.

A. Double-click alternately on **CirPattern1** and **CirPattern2** in the *FeatureManager* to display the dimension names and values for the patterns.

B. Choose **Tools ▼ Equations** and press the **Add** button. Double click **CirPattern1** in the *FeatureManager*, its **D2** dimension in the graphics window, the "=" on the calculator keypad, **360** on the *New Equation* keypad, the "/" button on the *New Equation* keypad, and the **D1** dimension in the graphics window. The resulting equation must look like the following:

"D2@CirPattern1" = 360 / "D1@CirPattern1"

C. Click **OK** once, click **OK** again to activate the equation, and press **Esc** on the keyboard to clear all selections in the graphics window.

D. Follow a similar procedure to create the equation for the other direction:

"D2@CirPattern2" = 360 / "D1@CirPattern2"

E. Also, add an equation to stagger the two hole patterns equally:

"D1@Sketch6" = "D2@CirPattern1" / 2

F. Click on the **Rebuild** tool to see the effect of the three equations. The hole patterns should space out equally in a symmetrical, staggered arrangement as in Figure X23-3:

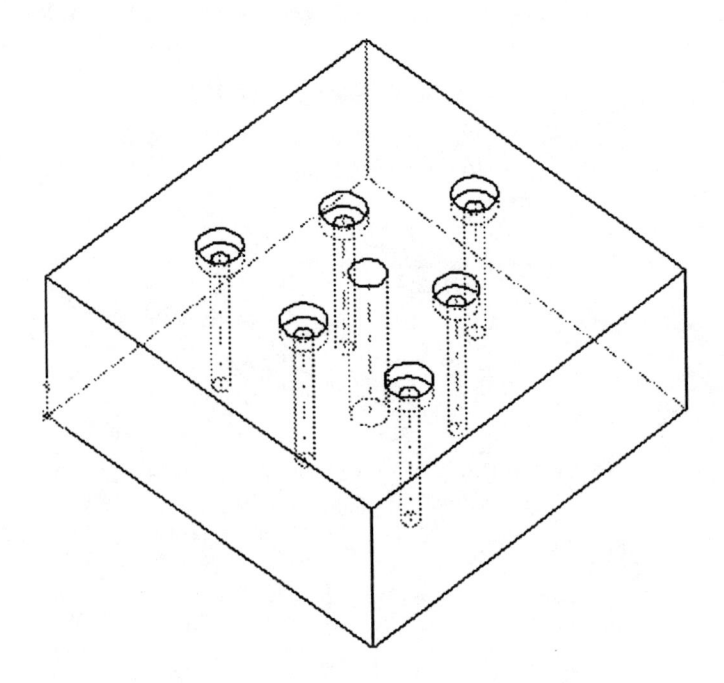

Figure X23-3

| Step 5: | Test the new equations. |

A. **Modify** the number of instances in the **CirPattern1** from 3 to **6**. This can be done by using *Edit Definition* (right click on **CirPattern1** in the *FeatureManager* design tree) or by double-clicking on **CirPattern1** in the *FeatureManager* design tree and double-clicking on the number of instances in the graphics window.

B. **Rebuild** the model. Figure X23-4 shows the resulting appearance of the part.

| Step 6: | Add a custom property for the cost of the part. |

A. Click **File ▼ Properties** and then the *Custom* tab.

B. Enter **Cost** as the *Name* of the new property.

C. Select the *Type:* as **Text.**

D. Enter a *Value:* of **375.00** and then click the **Add** button in the dialog.

E. Click **OK** in the dialog to finalize the *Property* creation.

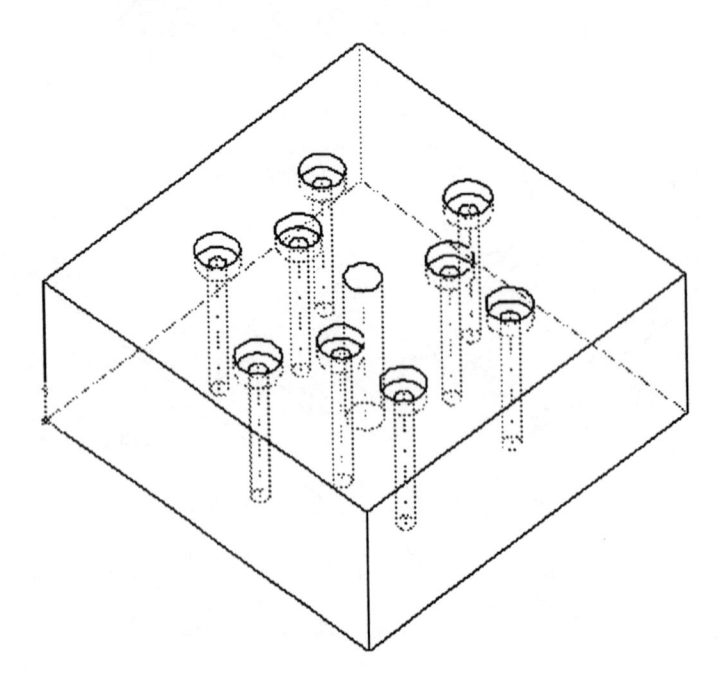

Figure X23-4

Step 7: Modify the value for the cost property.

A. Click **File ▼ Properties** and then the *Custom* tab.

B. Click on **Cost** in the *Properties* window.

C. Click inside the *Value:* window and edit the *cost* value to 425.00

D. Click the **Modify** button and then click the **OK** button to finalize the change.

End of Exercise 23.

DESIGN PROJECT TUTORIAL

Exercise 24: Part Configurations and Design Tables

In this exercise we will realize the true power of parametric solid modeling. An entire family of parts can be modeled using a single part file so long as the types and arrangement of features in each part is similar. Each individual configuration can be stored and activated with ease.

The subjects of this exercise are three families of drill jig bushings, one of which is shown on Figure X24-1:

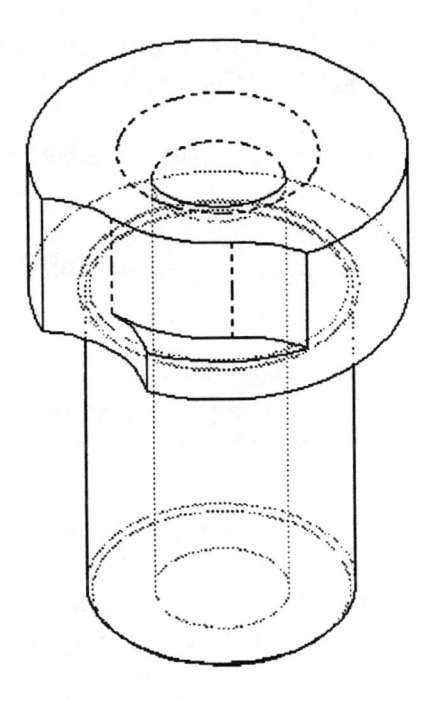

Figure X24-1

Step 1:   Open the file DRILL_BUSHING and create a *Configuration*.

A.   Open the part file named `drill_bushing.SLDPRT`. As previously mentioned, there are three families of drill jig bushings with heads on them, and the part has been modeled in the configuration of the most complex configuration, a *Slip Type Renewable* (S-type) drill bushing.

B.   At the bottom of the *FeatureManager* design tree there are three tabs. By default the *FeatureManager* is always displayed, but the other two options can be activated at any time. The one we want to activate is called *ConfigurationManager*.

See Figure X24-2:

FeatureManager tab (active) → [icons] ← *ConfigurationManager* tab (inactive)

Figure X24-2

Click on the **ConfigurationManager** tab to activate it.

C. Right click on the **drill_bushing Configuration(s)** icon at the top of the *ConfigurationManager* and select **Add Configuration** from the pop-up menu.

D. Enter **S-type** in the *Configuration Name:* field and press the **OK** button to create the configuration.

E. Right click on the **Default** configuration and select **Show Configuration** from the pop-up menu.

Step 2: *Suppress features and create two additional Configurations.*

The other two types of headed drill jig bushings are known as the *Head Type* (H-type) and the *Fixed Type Renewable* (F-type). The part model contains all features which apply to any one of the three types of bushings. Some of the features are unnecessary for the H-type and F-type bushings so we will remove them from the part display.

A. Click on the **FeatureManager** tab.

B. Click on **Cut-Extrude3** and SHIFT+pick on **Cut-Extrude4**. *Cut-Extrude3, Cut-Revolve1,* and *Cut-Extrude4* should all be highlighted.

C. Select **Edit ▼ Suppress**. The part is now in the configuration of an F-type bushing.

D. Go to the *ConfigurationManager*, right click on the **drill_bushing Configuration(s)** icon at the top of the *ConfigurationManager*, and select **Add Configuration** from the pop-up menu.

E. Enter **F-type** in the *Configuration Name:* field and press the **OK** button to create the configuration.

F. Right click on the **Default** configuration and select **Show Configuration** from the pop-up menu.

DESIGN PROJECT TUTORIAL

G. Click on the **FeatureManager** tab.

H. Click on **Cut-Extrude2**.

I. Select **Edit ▼ Suppress**. The part is now in the configuration of an H-type bushing.

J. Go to the *ConfigurationManager*, right click on the **drill_bushing Configuration(s)** icon at the top of the *ConfigurationManager*, and select **Add Configuration** from the pop-up menu.

K. Enter **H-type** in the *Configuration Name:* field and press the **OK** button to create the configuration.

L. Right click on **F-type** and select **Show Configuration**.

M. Right click on **S-type** and select **Show Configuration**.

N. Right click on **H-type** and select **Show Configuration**.

Step 3: *Modify* the part dimensions.

As modeled, the dimensions of the head and body of the bushing match those of an S-type bushing, part number S-48-16. Three of the dimensions on the head of the "cousin" part number, H-48-16, are different because no additional head thickness to allow for the locking and removal features is needed for the H-type of bushing.

A. Double click on **Base-Extrude** in the *FeatureManager* design tree.

B. Double click on the head diameter dimension and select the radio button for **This configuration**. See Figure X24-3 below.

C. **Modify** the dimension to **0.938in**, **Rebuild** the model, and **Save** the change.

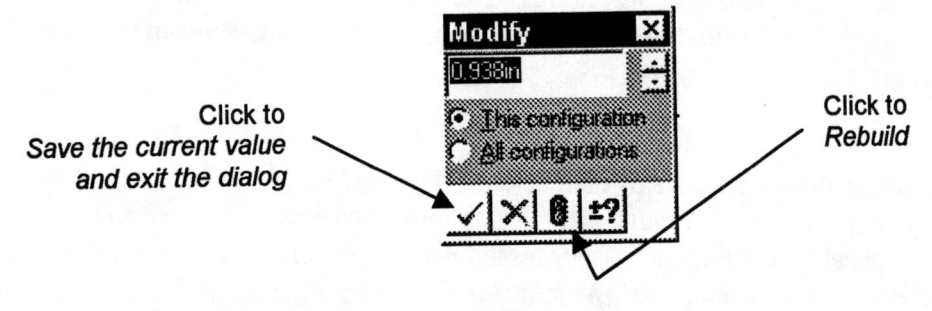

Click to *Save the current value and exit the dialog*

Click to *Rebuild*

Figure X24-3

24-3

DESIGN PROJECT TUTORIAL

D. Double click on the head thickness dimension, select the **This configuration** radio button, **Modify** the value to **0.219in.**, **Rebuild** the model, and **Save** the change.

E. Double click on **Fillet1** in the *FeatureManager*, double click on the radius dimension, select the **This configuration** radio button, **Modify** the dimension to **0.062in**, **Rebuild** the model, and **Save** the change. The model now shows catalog part number H-48-16.

You may have thought, "There has to be an easier way to arrive at standard catalog part configurations," and there is. In Step 4 we will store within this same part model a multitude of standard bushing configurations.

F. Use **File ▼ Save As...** to store the file as a new name, say `drill_bushing2.SLDPRT`.

Step 4:   **Explore and *Insert* a *Design Table*.**

Design Tables can be used to create configurations and control the size of any and all dimensions in the part model. The *Design Table* is first created in Microsoft's *Excel®* spreadsheet application and then inserted into the part file. It is best to preserve a copy of the part file before any configurations are created or *Design Tables* are inserted because configurations are slightly awkward to remove once they have been added.

Note: Obviously, if you don't have MS *Excel®* installed on your computer you cannot perform this operation. If so please continue with Exercise 25.

A. Click on the Windows 95/98/NT® **Start** button.

B. Select **Programs ▶ MSOffice2000 ▶ Microsoft Excel.**

C. Open the file `bushing99.xls`.

Notice the row headings in column "A" and the column headings in row "1." The row headings in column "A" are the names of the part configurations. The configuration names can be arbitrarily selected, but, in this case, they represent the part numbers of the bushings. The column headings are the official names of the dimensions in the part model as assigned by SolidWorks.

Also notice the headings of columns *K* through *O*. These column headings are the names of features, rather than the names of dimensions. The contents of these columns are very interesting because they are not numerical values for dimensions. Where *s* appears in this column the applicable feature will be suppressed for the specific part configuration. When a cell contains *u* it means that the feature will not be suppressed or, in other words, will be *unsuppressed*.

DESIGN PROJECT TUTORIAL

D. Close the file bushing99.xls and Exit from Microsoft *Excel®*.

E. In SolidWorks re-open the file drill_bushing.SLDPRT from the original source. It is important that the file does not contain the configurations (*F-type, H-type, and S-type*) that we created in Steps 1 and 2.

F. Select **Insert ▼ Design Table...** and browse to bushing99.xls. Select and open this file. Wait for a few seconds for the configurations to be created.

G. When an informational window appears saying, "The design table generated the following configurations," press **Yes** to see more of the list or **No** to exit from the list.

H. Maximize the drill_bushing.SLDPRT window by pressing the ☐ button.

I. Drag and drop the small black square button, circled on Figure X24-4, down and to the right.

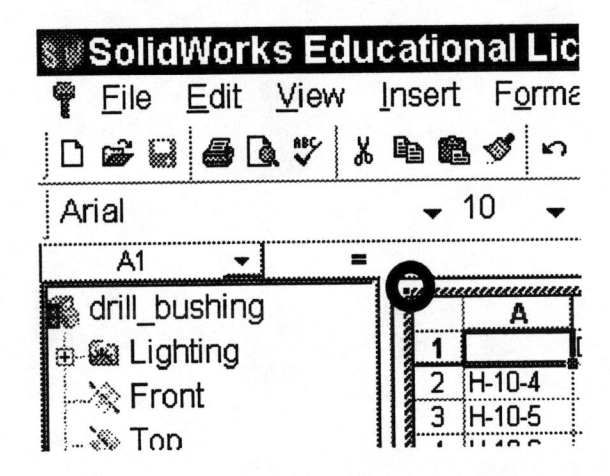

Figure X24-4

J. Click once inside the graphics window of the part (in the area exposed by operation "I") and wait momentarily while the design table is embedded in the part file.

K. **Rebuild** the model.

L. Click on the **ConfigurationManager** tab, right click on any of the listed configurations, and select **Show Configuration** to activate it. Note that feature suppression (as you performed manually in Step 2) and dimensions modification (as you performed in Step 3) are performed automatically because of the contents of columns *K* through *O* in the spreadsheet file. Also, note how radically the sizes of the bushings can vary.

M. Save the modified part file as drill_bushing3.SLDPRT.

End of Exercise 24.

DESIGN PROJECT TUTORIAL

Exercise 25 - Assembly Creation

In the grand scheme very few parts stand alone in their purpose and function without association by assembly with other parts. For this reason assembling parts is the culmination of the design process. In this exercise you will learn how to assemble parts and constrain their relationships with one another.

Step 1: Create a *New* assembly called BASE with *Millimeters* as the *Units*. This assembly will consist of one each of three components: BRACKET, BUSHING, and RING. The overall assembly will itself later become a sub-assembly for a larger assembly.

Figure X25-1 shows the desired final configuration of the `base.SLDASM`.

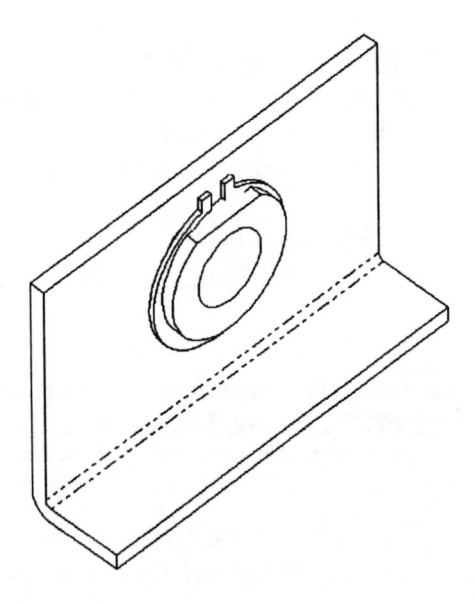

Figure X25-1

DESIGN PROJECT TUTORIAL

Step 2:   **Open all parts and assemble the BRACKET into the assembly.**

A. Open each of the following part files: `bracket.SLDPRT`, `bushing.SLDPRT`, and `ring.SLDPRT`.

B. Select **Window ▼ Tile Horizontally** to show all three parts and the new assembly at the same time.

C. Drag and drop the `bracket` icon at the top of the *FeatureManager* design tree from the `bracket.SLDPRT` window into the *FeatureManager* design tree for `base.SLDASM`.

    NOTE: The process for assembling the first part is very similar to that for subsequent parts WITH ONE VERY IMPORTANT EXCEPTION! For the second part, third part, fourth part, etc., the [part name] icon from the *FeatureManager* of that part is dragged and dropped into the GRAPHICS WINDOW area of the assembly.

          The reason for this difference is subtle but significant. The reference geometry of the first part in an assembly is automatically placed coincidentally with the reference geometry of the assembly. For instance, the *Front* plane of the first part is placed coincidentally with the *Front* plane of the assembly.

          Subsequent parts *cannot* obviously have the same relationship. The positions of these parts are determined by you through the use of *Mate* relationships. This you will see in Step 3.

Step 3:   **Assemble the BUSHING part and *Mate* it to the BRACKET.**

A. Drag and drop the `bushing` icon from the *FeatureManager* area of the `bushing.SLDPRT` window into the GRAPHICS WINDOW AREA of the assembly. After dropping the `bushing` into the assembly, note where "(-)" shows between the `bushing` icon and its name in the *FeatureManager* area of the assembly.

    This means that the position of the `bushing` is not fully constrained. The minus sign will disappear after a sufficient number of *Mates* has been added to fully constrain the position of the `bushing`.

25-2

DESIGN PROJECT TUTORIAL

B. Press the **Mate** tool: and create the three *Mates* for the bushing.SLDPRT as listed on Table X25-1.

After you select the surfaces for *Items Selected:* and the *Type:* of *Mate* the *Preview* button will appear in the *Workbench* area of the *Assembly Mating* window.

Often, the choice of *Alignment Condition (Aligned* versus *Anti-Aligned)* must be reversed, or the selection of *Flip Dimension to Other Side* must be reversed. It is a very good idea to press that **Preview** button and explore the consequences of the mate in the graphics window before pressing the **Apply** button to actually impose the *Mate* constraint.

Mate No.	Mate Type	Alignment Condition	Related Surfaces
1	Parallel		See Figure X25-2
2	Coincident	Anti-Aligned (On)	See Figure X25-2
3	Concentric		See Figure X25-2

Table X25-1

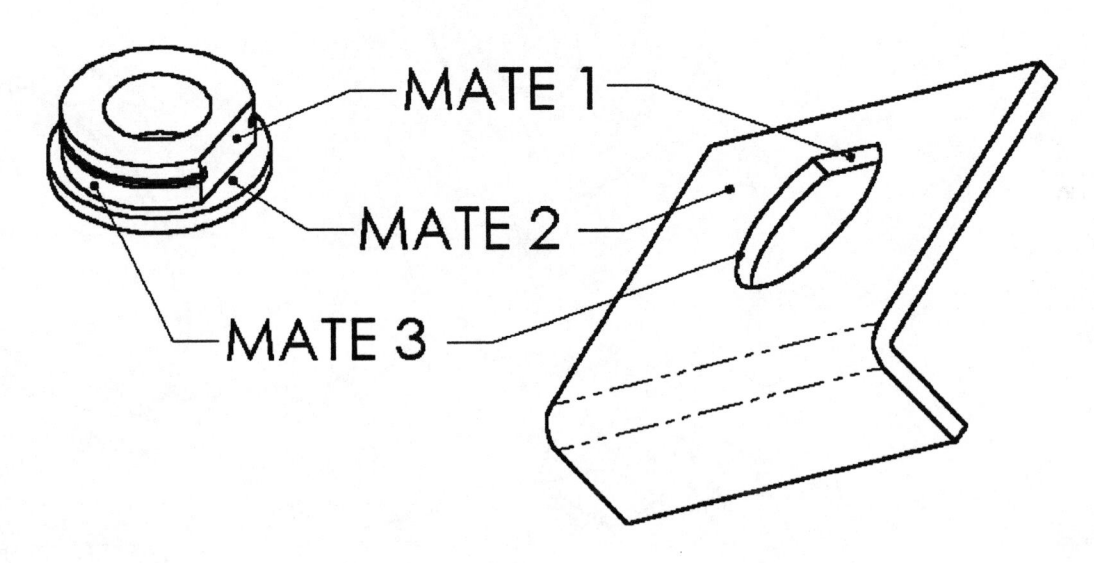

Figure X25-2

C. Note that the minus sign for the bushing has disappeared from the *FeatureManager*.

DESIGN PROJECT TUTORIAL

Step 4: Assemble the RING part and *Mate* it to the BUSHING.

A. Drag and drop the `ring` icon from the *FeatureManager* area of the `ring.SLDPRT` window into the GRAPHICS WINDOW AREA of the assembly.

B. Create the *Mates* as described in Table X25-2 and Figure X25-3. Use **Preview**.

Mate No.	Mate Type	Alignment Condition	Related Surfaces
1	Coincident		See Figure X25-3
2	Concentric		See Figure X25-3
3	Parallel	Aligned	See Figure X25-3

Table X25-2

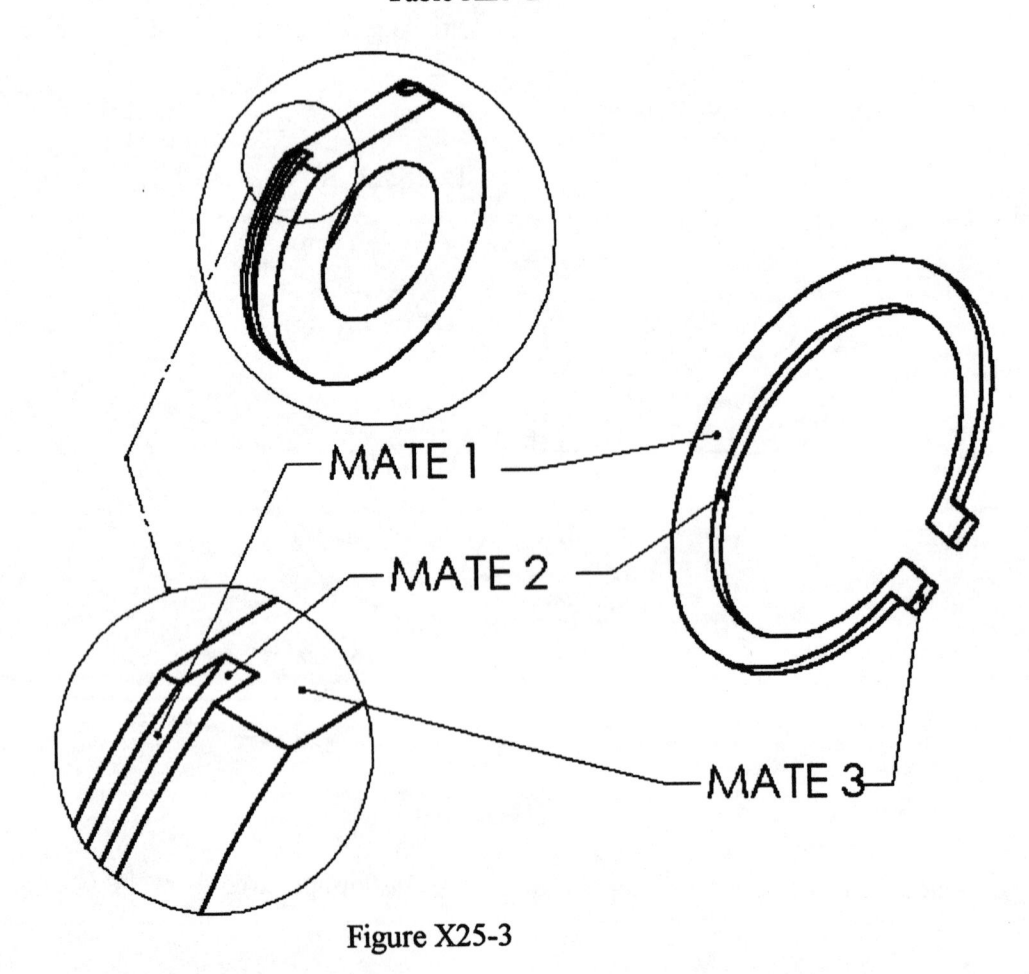

Figure X25-3

C. Save the assembly as `base.SLDASM`.

DESIGN PROJECT TUTORIAL

Step 5: **Create a new assembly called MACHINE. Assemble the BASE sub-assembly. Assemble the SHAFT part and *Mate* it to the BUSHING.**

A. Create a new assembly called machine with **millimeters** as the *Units*.

B. Drag and drop the icon base (from the previous assembly) into the *FeatureManager* area of machine.SLDASM.

C. Open the file shaft.SLDPRT. Drag and drop the shaft icon from the *FeatureManager* area of the shaft window into the GRAPHICS WINDOW AREA of the assembly.

D. Create the *Mates* as described in Table X25-3 and Figure X25-4. Use **Preview**.

Mate No.	Mate Type	Value	Comments
1	Distance	60mm.	Use *Aligned*, See Figure X25-4
2	Concentric		See Figure X25-4
3	Perpendicular		Pick Temporary Axis and Edge

Table X25-3

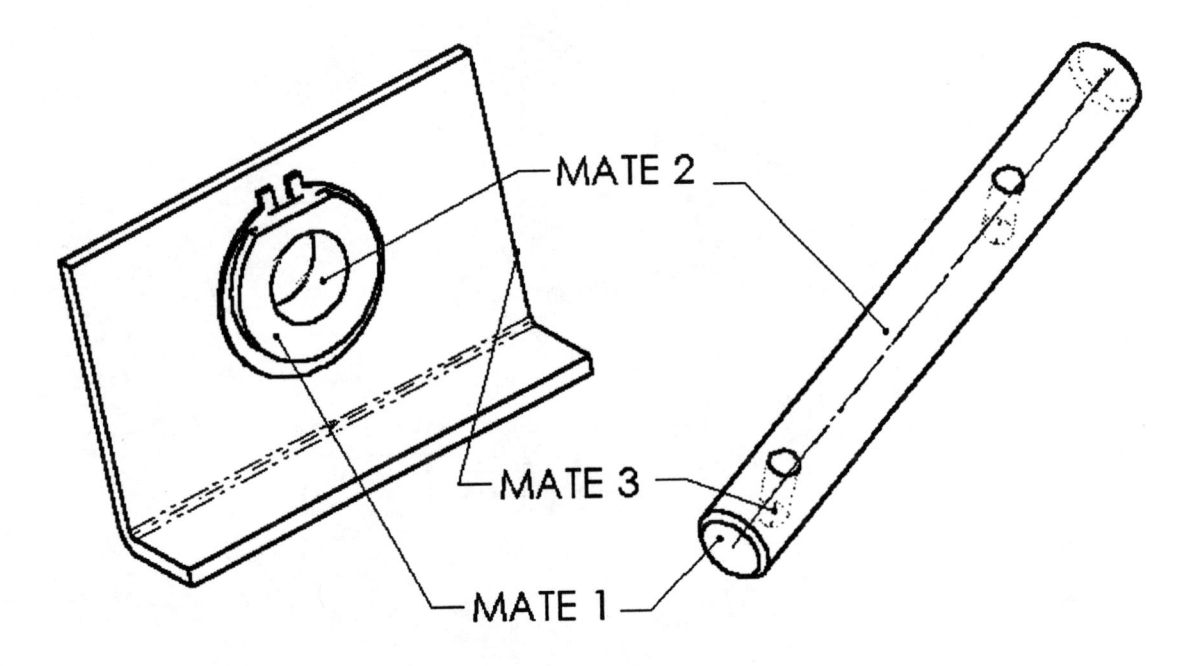

Figure X25-4

DESIGN PROJECT TUTORIAL

Step 6:   **Assemble the CRANK part and *Mate* it to the SHAFT.**

A. Open the file base_crank.SLDPRT. Drag and drop the crank icon from the *FeatureManager* area of the base_crank.SLDPRT window into the GRAPHICS WINDOW AREA of the assembly.

B. Create the *Mates* as described in Table X25-4 and Figure X25-5. Use **Preview**. Note that the end of the shaft with a hole closest to it goes on the same side of the bracket as the snap ring.

Mate No.	Mate Type	Related Surfaces
1	Parallel	See Figure X25-5
2	Concentric	See Figure X25-5
3	Concentric	See Figure X25-5

Table X25-4

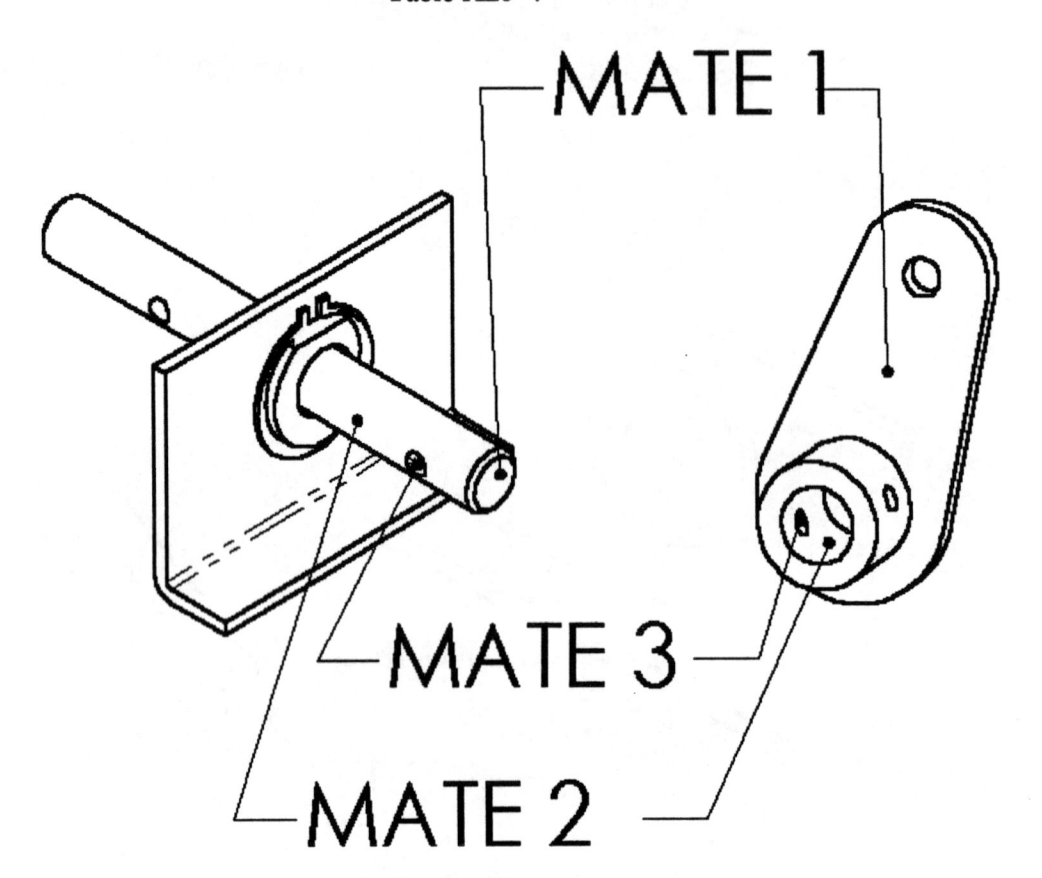

Figure X25-5

25-6

DESIGN PROJECT TUTORIAL

The resulting configuration of machine.SLDASM is as shown on Figure X25-6:

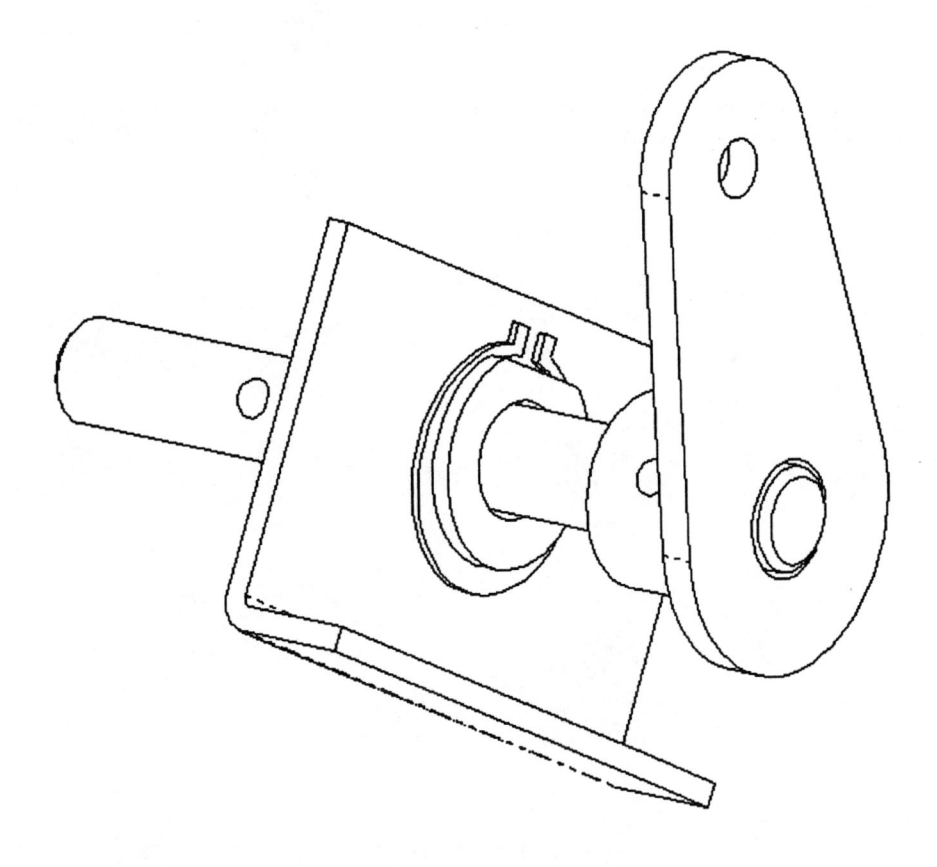

Figure X25-6

Step 7: Assemble the GEAR part and *Mate* it to the SHAFT.

A. Open the file gear.SLDPRT. Drag and drop the gear icon from the *FeatureManager* area of the gear.SLDASM window into the GRAPHICS WINDOW AREA of the machine assembly.

B. Create appropriate *Mates* for the gear to locate it as shown on Figure X26-1. After doing so, save and close all part and assembly files to your personal media (3.5" diskette, Zip® disk, etc.)

End of Exercise 25.

DESIGN PROJECT TUTORIAL

Exercise 26 - Exploded View Creation

Exploded views are often used for documentation purposes in parts and assembly manuals. They do not reflect an achievable and realistic positioning of the parts, but they are valuable for describing the inter-relationships of the parts and the order of assembly.

In this exercise you will learn how to create an exploded view from the assembly that you created during Exercise 25. Figure X26-1 shows the initial configuration of the `machine` assembly, and Figure X26-4 shows the exploded view. It is interesting to note that, once the exploded view is defined, it takes only seconds to toggle between the assembled and exploded views.

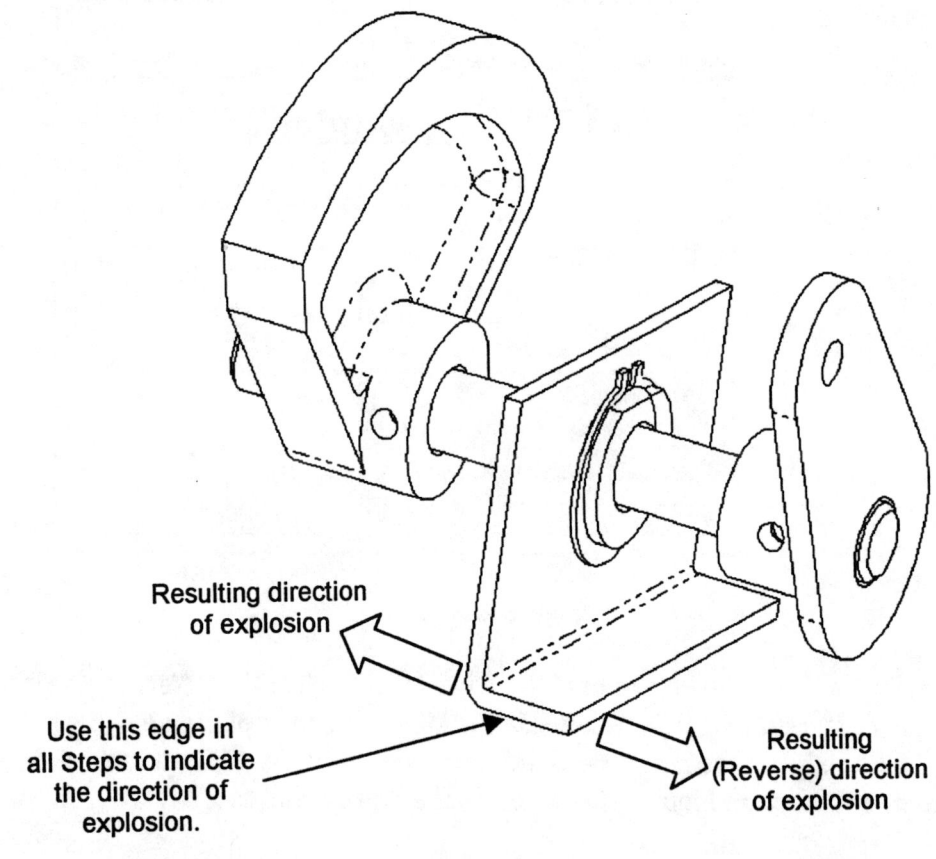

Figure X26-1

Step 1: Open the file MACHINE.SLDASM and explode the *crank* component.

A. Open your solution file `machine.SLDASM` from Exercise 25.

DESIGN PROJECT TUTORIAL

B. Select **Insert ▼ Exploded View...** to show a partial *Assembly Exploder* dialog. Press the **New Step** tool, as shown on Figure X26-2, to reveal the bottom of the dialog.

Note the *Direction to explode along:* window in the dialog. It is best to select an edge on one of the parts to specify the direction of explosion. For all of the explosion steps in this exercise we will use the front bottom edge of the `bracket` part to specify the direction of explosion. See Figure X26-1 for further explanation.

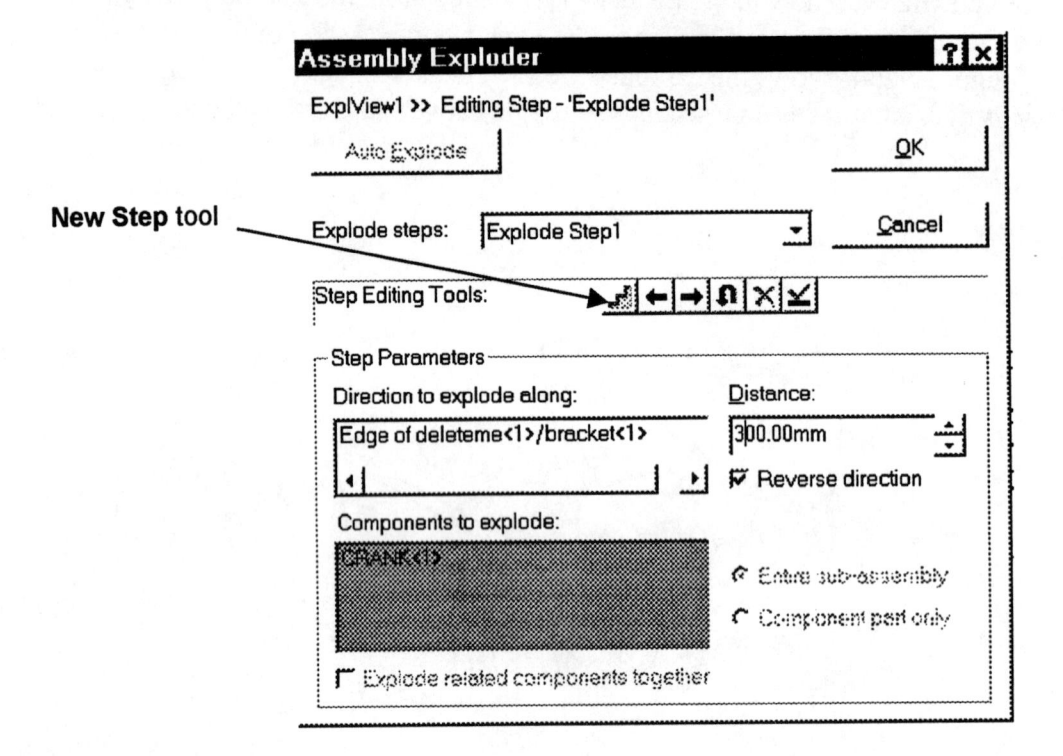

Figure X26-2

C. Click inside the **Components to explode** window and select the `base_crank` tool within the *FeatureManager*. Click inside the **Direction to explode along:** window and select the key edge of the `bracket`. Enter the *Distance:* as **275mm**. Check **Reverse direction**, as shown on Figure X26-2. Press the **Apply** tool (see Figure X26-3).

This dialog is "sticky," meaning that it will not disappear until you press the **OK** button. Right now, we do not know if the 275mm distance of explosion for the `base_crank` will be what we want after all of the other parts have been exploded, and having it perfect is not possible *or* very critical at this time. You can use the *Previous Step* tool later to return to this step, make changes, and **Apply** the changes.

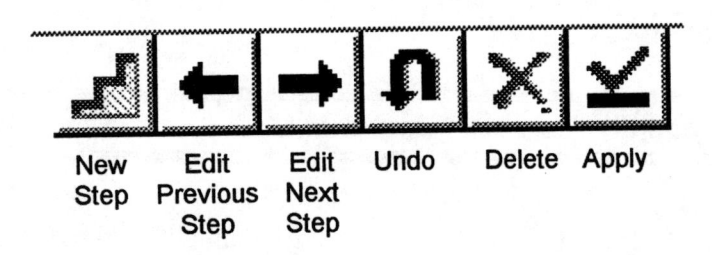

New Step   Edit Previous Step   Edit Next Step   Undo   Delete   Apply

Figure X26-3

Step 2:   Explode the *gear* component.

A. Press the **New Step** tool. Select the `gear` tool within the *FeatureManager* as the *Components to explode*. Select the key edge of the `bracket` as the *Direction to explode along:* and enter the *Distance:* as **50mm**. Press **Apply**.

B. From an *Isometric* view note that the `gear` appears a little too close to the `shaft`. Enter a new *Distance:* of **75mm**. Again, press the **Apply** tool and note the improvement.

Step 3:   Explode the *ring* component.

A. Click the **New Step** tool. Expand the `base` (sub-)assembly tool (as necessary) and select the `ring` tool within the *FeatureManager* as the *Components to explode*. Select the key edge of the `bracket` as the *Direction to explode along:* and check **Reverse direction**. Enter the *Distance:* as **100mm.**

B. Select the **Component part only** radio button and press **Apply**.

Step 4:   Explode the *shaft* component.

A. Press the **New Step** tool. Select the `shaft` tool within the *FeatureManager* as the *Component to explode*. Select the key edge of the `bracket` as the *Direction to explode along:* and check **Reverse direction**. Enter the *Distance:* as **175mm**. Press **Apply**.

B.	Note that the shaft has not passed completely through the ring as we might desire. Enter a new *Distance:* of **225mm**. Again, press the **Apply** tool.

Notice how the gear looks oddly far away from the bracket now that the shaft has been moved. Esthetically, reducing this distance will improve the appearance of the *Exploded View*, and this will be effected after the bushing has been exploded in the direction of the gear.

Step 5:	**Explode the *bushing* component.**

A.	Press the **New Step** tool. Select the bushing tool within the *FeatureManager* as the *Components to explode*. Select the key edge of the bracket as the *Direction to explode along:* and uncheck **Reverse direction** (as necessary). Enter the *Distance:* as **75mm.**

B.	Select the **Component part only** radio button and press **Apply**.

C.	From an *Isometric* view note that the bushing appears a little too far from the bracket. Enter a new *Distance:* of **60mm**. Again, press the **Apply** tool.

Step 6:	**Move each part into its final position in the *Exploded View*.**

A.	Click the **Previous Step** tool to activate *Explode Step 4*. Since the position of the ring and shaft, relative to one another, looks fine no change will be made to this step. The base_crank will be moved further away as an edit of *Explode Step 1* later.

B.	Click the **Previous Step** tool again to activate *Explode Step 3*. The position of the ring, relative to the shaft, looks fine, but it's a little too far away from the bracket. *Modify* this distance to **95mm** to center it between the two adjacent components.

C.	Click the **Previous Step** tool once again to activate *Explode Step 2*. Enter a *Distance:* of **65mm,** and press **Apply**. The position of the gear, relative to the bushing, is now final.

D.	Click the **Previous Step** tool for the final time to activate *Explode Step 1*. Enter a *Distance:* of **300mm** and press **Apply**. The relative position of all components now looks very good because there is space around each and every component and there are no apparent overlaps of components from an *Isometric* view.

DESIGN PROJECT TUTORIAL

E. Press **OK** to finalize creation of the *Exploded View*. The final result should appear much like Figure X26-4 from an *Isometric* view:

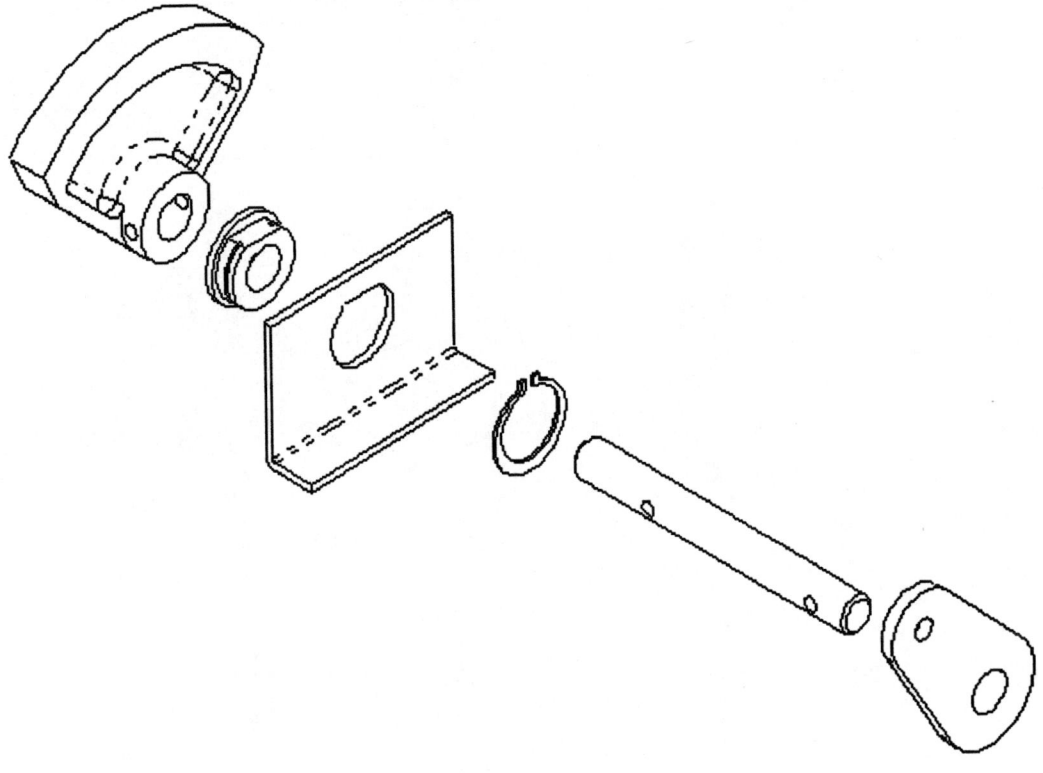

Figure X26-4

Step 7: Toggle from the exploded view to the standard assembled view.

A. At the bottom of the *FeatureManager* note the three tabs:

Figure X26-5

The one on the left indicates that the *FeatureManager* is active. Click on the one on the right, the **ConfigurationManager** tab, to activate it.

B. Click once wherever a "+" sign appears within the *ConfigurationManager* to expand all levels of the tree.

C. Right Click over **ExplView1** and select **Collapse**. Click on the **FeatureManager** tab.

D. **Save** the assembly. Note that *ExplView1* can be restored at any time by returning to the *ConfigurationManager*, expanding the tree as necessary, right clicking over **ExplView1**, and selecting **Explode.**

End of Exercise 26.

Design Project Assignment 5

Seven different parts will be created and assembled in the nine Design Project Assignments. In this fifth assignment we will modify one part:
  A. MOTOR
And complete three parts:
  B. UPPER_HOUSING
  C. LOWER_HOUSING
  D. IMPELLER, completed by adding an equation.

Assignment 5A: Change the MOTOR Part

Step 1: **Open the part named MOTOR.**

Step 2: **Change the thickness of the front flange to 1.50 in.**

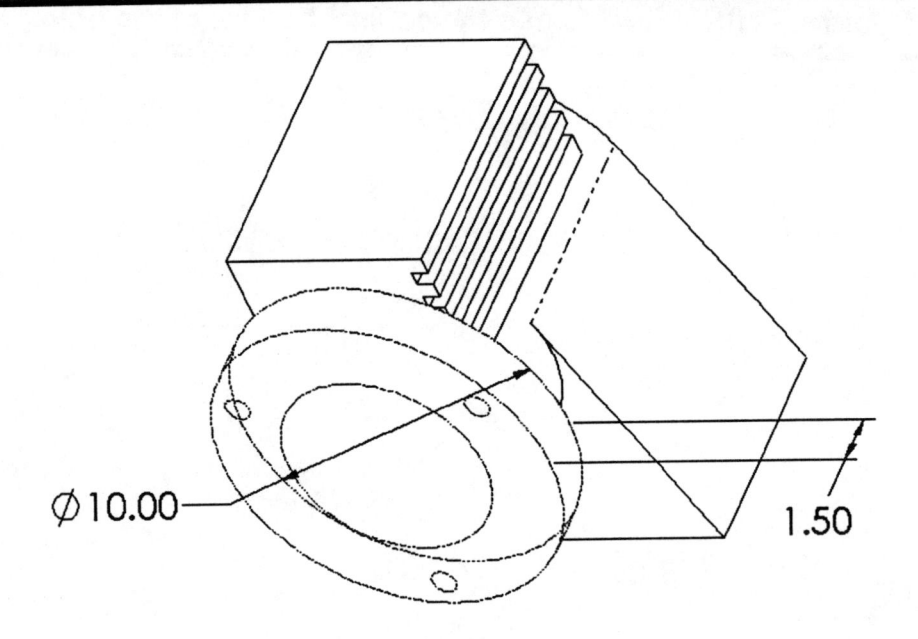

Figure D5A-1

DESIGN PROJECT TUTORIAL

Step 3: Delete the three existing holes through the flange and the sketch for the first hole. Select a point on the front of the flange at about the 2:00 position. Invoke the *Hole Wizard* by pressing its tool on the *Features* toolbar or by selecting Insert ▼ Features ▶ Hole ▶ Hole Wizard. In the *Hole Definition* window, specify the following hole characteristics:

Hole Type:	Simple Drilled
Diameter:	0.79 in.
Depth:	1.00 in.
Drill Angle:	118°

Click the **NEXT** button. With the *Hole Placement* window waiting in position sketch two center lines, and place a 4.25 in. radial dimension and 30° angular dimension as shown on Figure D5A-2. *Modify* them, as necessary, to the proper values. If your sketch does not become fully constrained at this point use *Add Relations* to fully constrain it.

Click the **FINISH** button to finalize the hole. Turn on *Hidden in Gray* and spin the model to see the conical bottom of the hole.

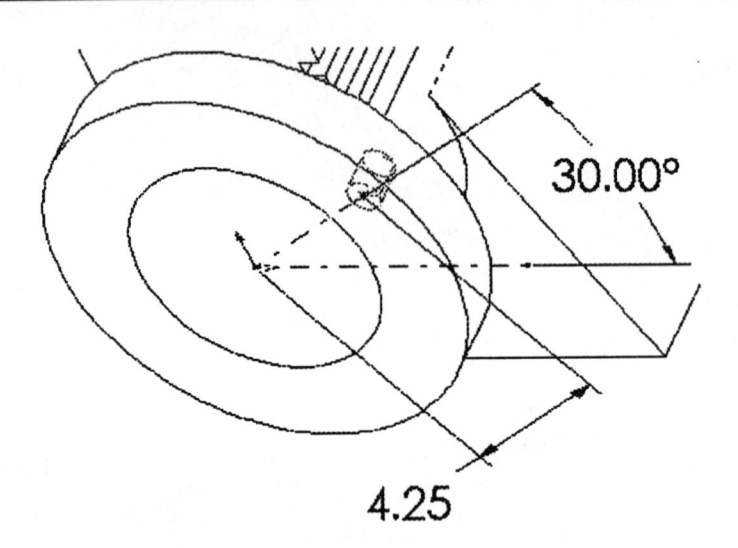

Figure D5A-2

Step 4: Create a pattern of 3 equally spaced holes from the first one.

Step 5: Save the model.

DESIGN PROJECT TUTORIAL

Assignment 5B: Complete the UPPER_HOUSING Part

Step 1: Open the UPPER_HOUSING part.

Step 2: Use *Mirror Feature* to create a bolt flange and hole pattern on the left side of the part. Before invoking the command identify write down the feature numbers of the flange, first hole instance and pattern:
  Flange   Boss-Extrude____
  First hole   Hole or Cut-Extrude_____
  Hole Pattern   LPattern_____
Mirror the three features around the *Right* plane.

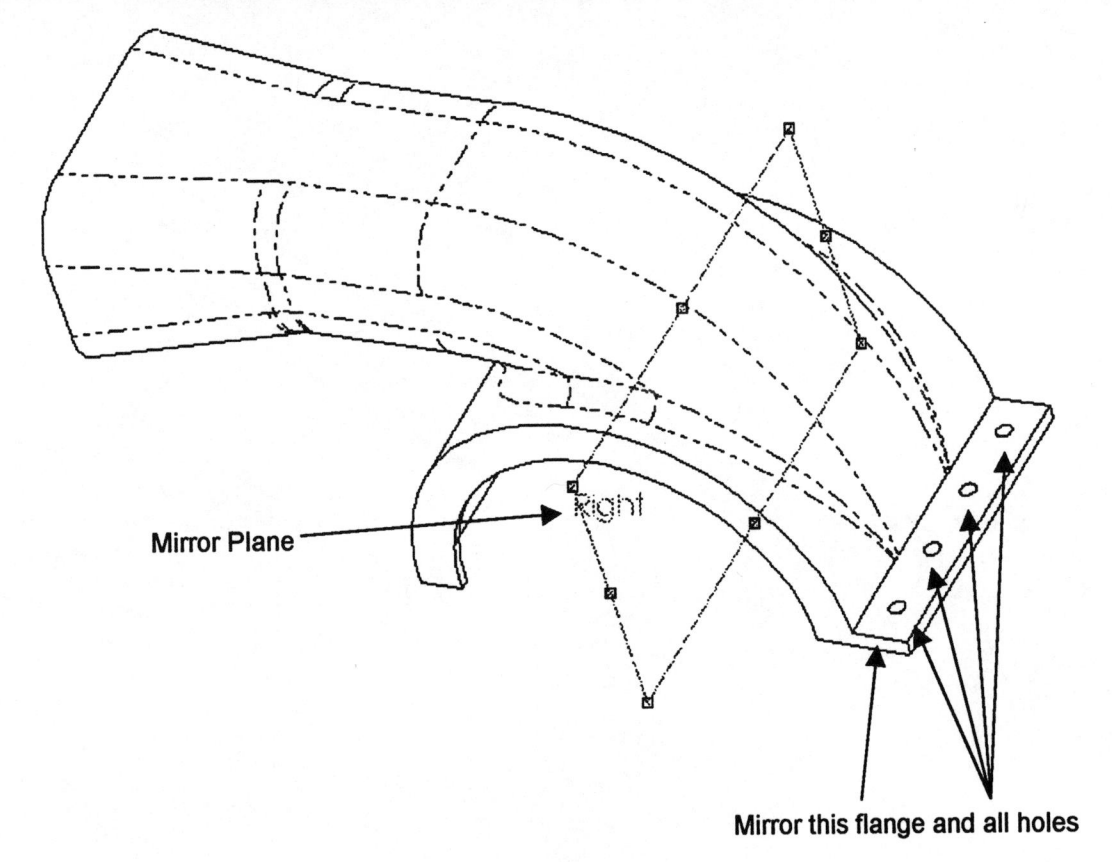

Figure D5B-1

Step 3: Save the model.

DESIGN PROJECT TUTORIAL

Assignment 5C: Complete the LOWER_HOUSING Part

Step 1: Open the LOWER_HOUSING part.

Step 2: Use *Mirror Feature* to create the bolt flange and holes on the left side of the part.

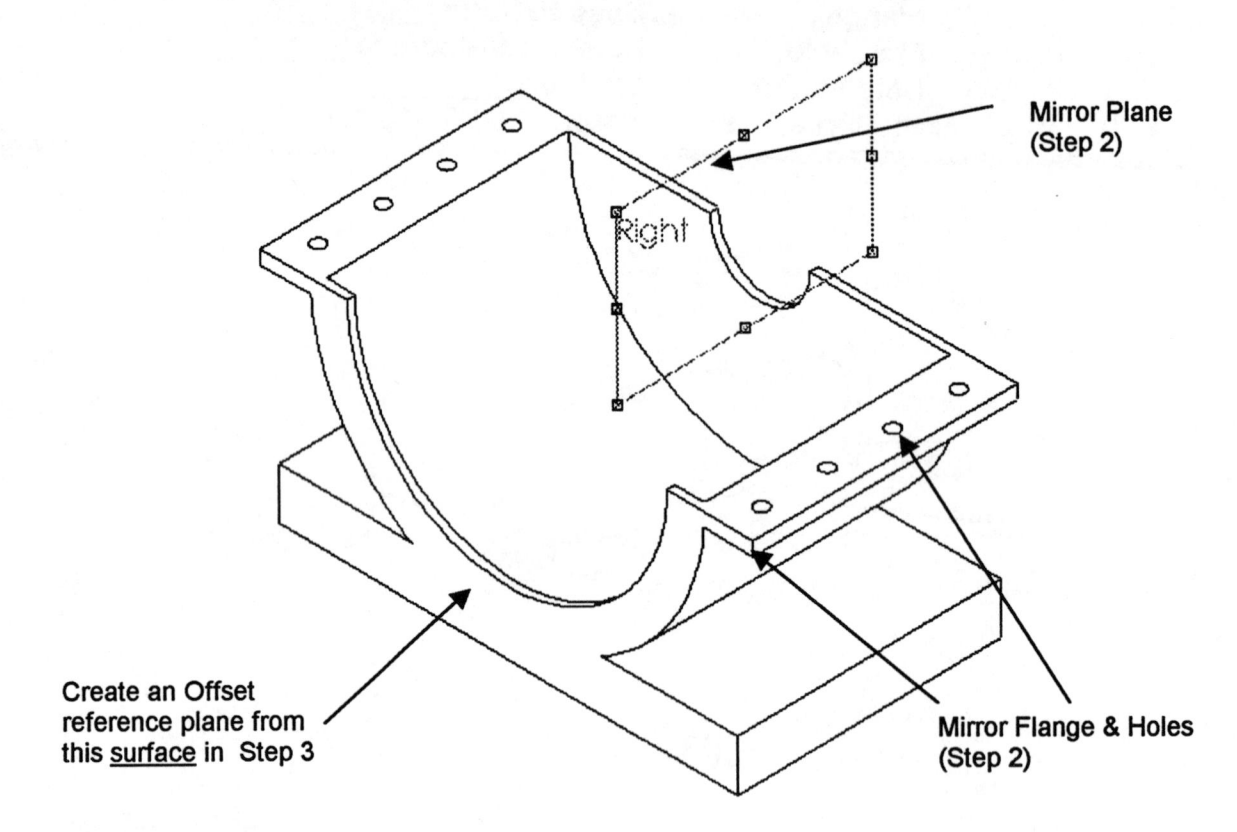

Mirror Plane (Step 2)

Create an Offset reference plane from this surface in Step 3

Mirror Flange & Holes (Step 2)

Figure D5C-1

Step 3: Add six ribs, three on each side, to the model to strengthen the part by first creating a reference plane for the sketch of the first rib--it is *Offset* from the front *surface* of the part by 2.00in. See Figure D5C-2.

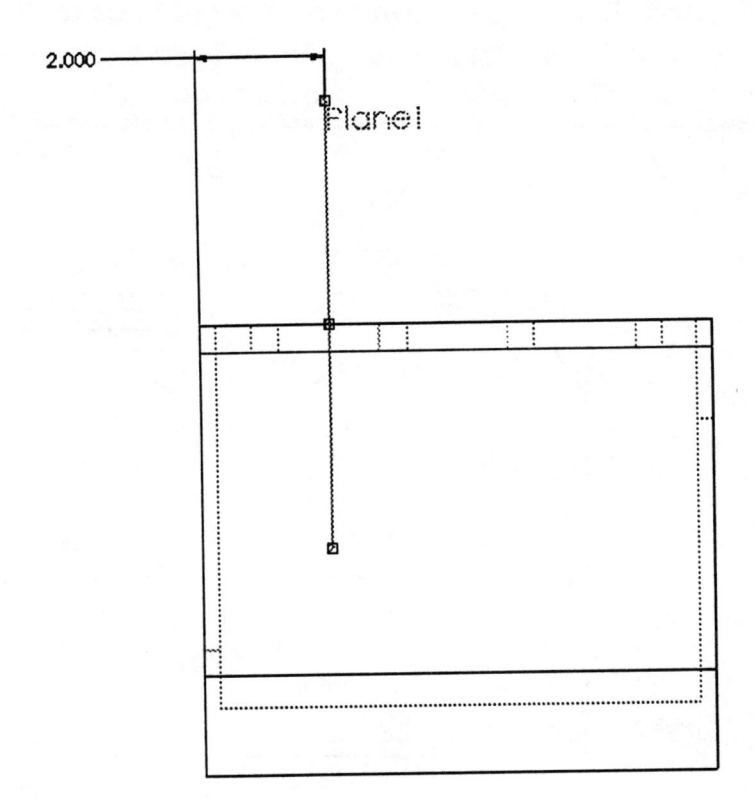

Figure D5C-2

DESIGN PROJECT TUTORIAL

Step 4: Sketch a single vertical line on the new plane as shown on Figure D5C-3. Watch for the *On Curve* inferencing indication at the top and bottom of the line and the *V* (for vertical) inferencing indication. If you recognize both of these as you sketch the line only *one* dimension will be necessary to fully constrain it.
Find and click on the *Rib* icon on the *Features* toolbar. Make the rib with a *MidPlane* thickness of 0.50in. Then click on **Next** and **Finish** (if the direction of material addition is correct).

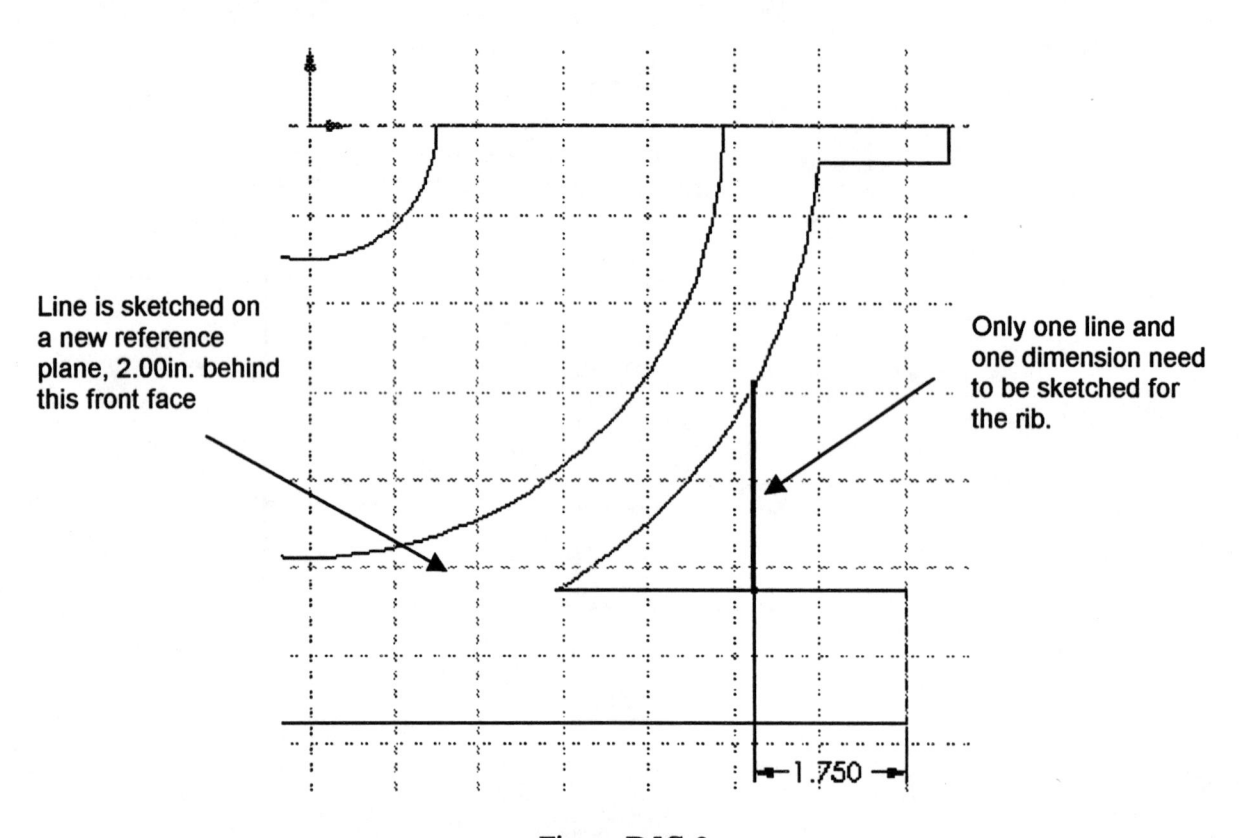

Line is sketched on a new reference plane, 2.00in. behind this front face

Only one line and one dimension need to be sketched for the rib.

1.750

Figure D5C-3

Step 5: Pattern the first rib in one direction with a spacing of 2.00in. and a total of 3 instances (including the original).

DESIGN PROJECT TUTORIAL

Step 6: Mirror all three ribs to the opposite side of the housing. Check *Geometry Pattern* in the *Mirror Pattern Features* dialog box to avoid a *Rebuild Error*.

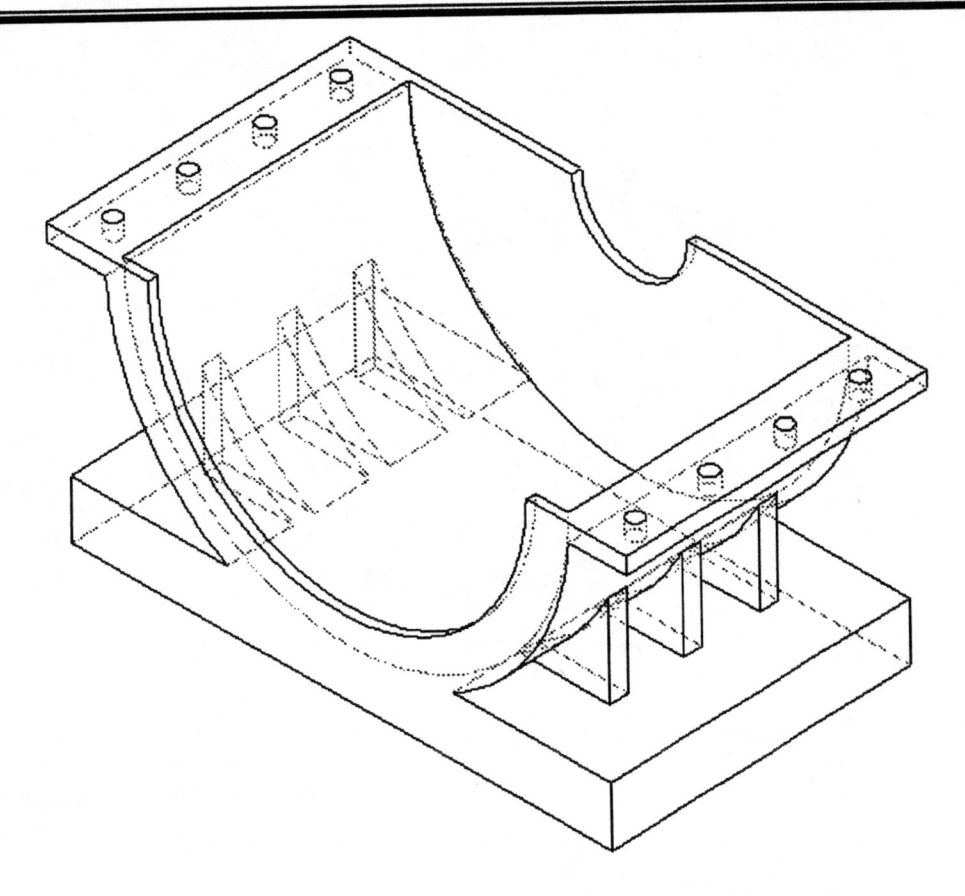

Figure D5C-4

Step 7: Save the model.

Assignment 5D: Change the IMPELLER Part

Step 1: Add an *Equation* to equally space the blades on the IMPELLER. Change the number of blades to 8 and *Rebuild* and save the model.

D5-7

End of Design Project Assignment 5.

DESIGN PROJECT TUTORIAL

Design Project Assignment 6

In addition to seven different part models, two sub-assemblies, and one top-level assembly; three complete drawings will be created during the nine Design Project Assignments. In this sixth assignment we will complete the two sub-assemblies.

Assignment 6A: Complete the MOTOR Sub-Assembly

Step 1: Create a *New* assembly named MOTOR.

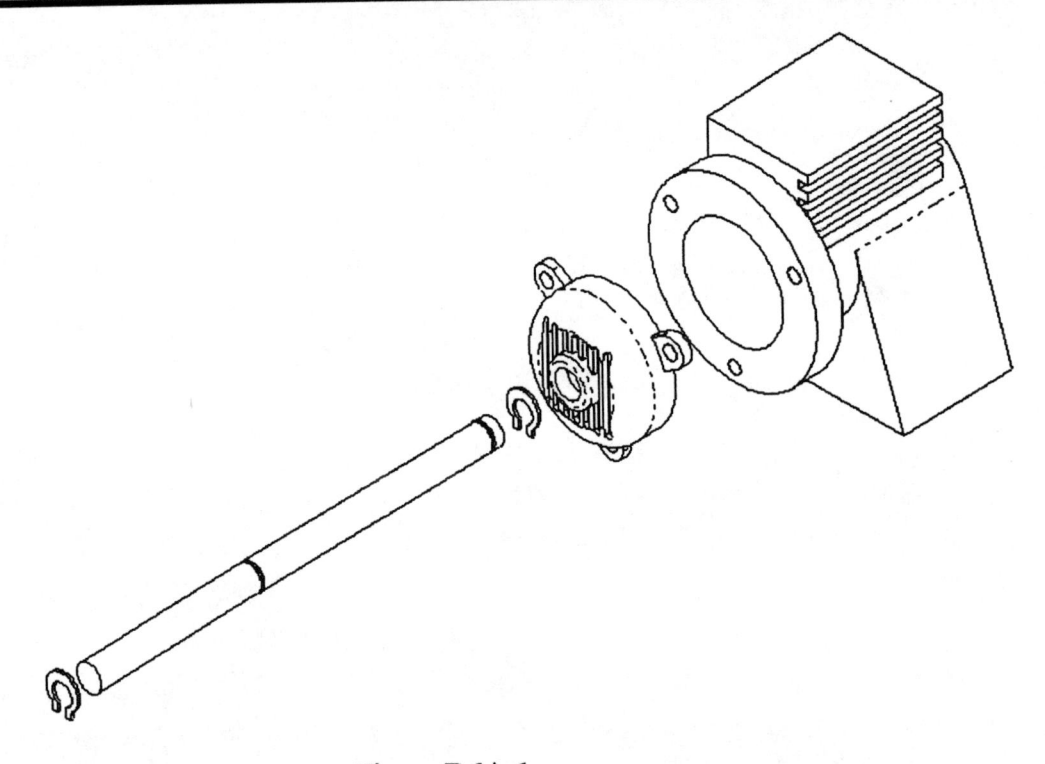

Figure D6A-1

Step 2: Open and add the MOTOR part into the assembly.

Step 3: Open and add the DRIVE_SHAFT part into the assembly. Add *Mates* to fully constrain the location of the part. See Figures D6A-2 and D6A-3.

D6-1

DESIGN PROJECT TUTORIAL

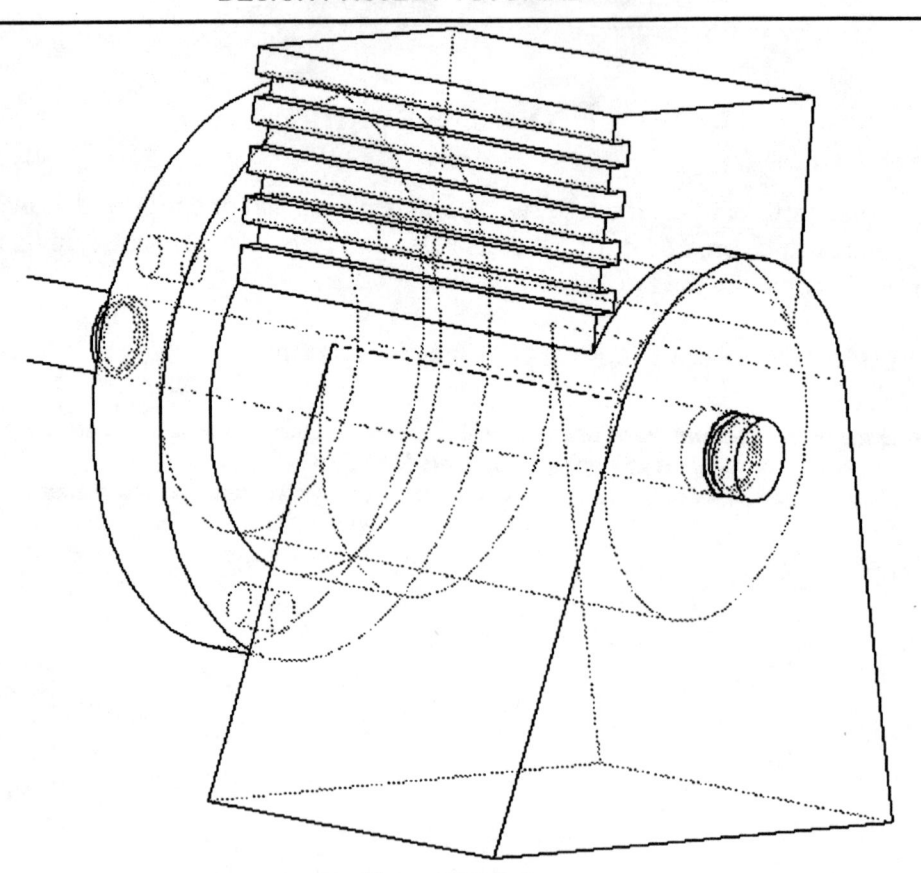

Figure D6A-2

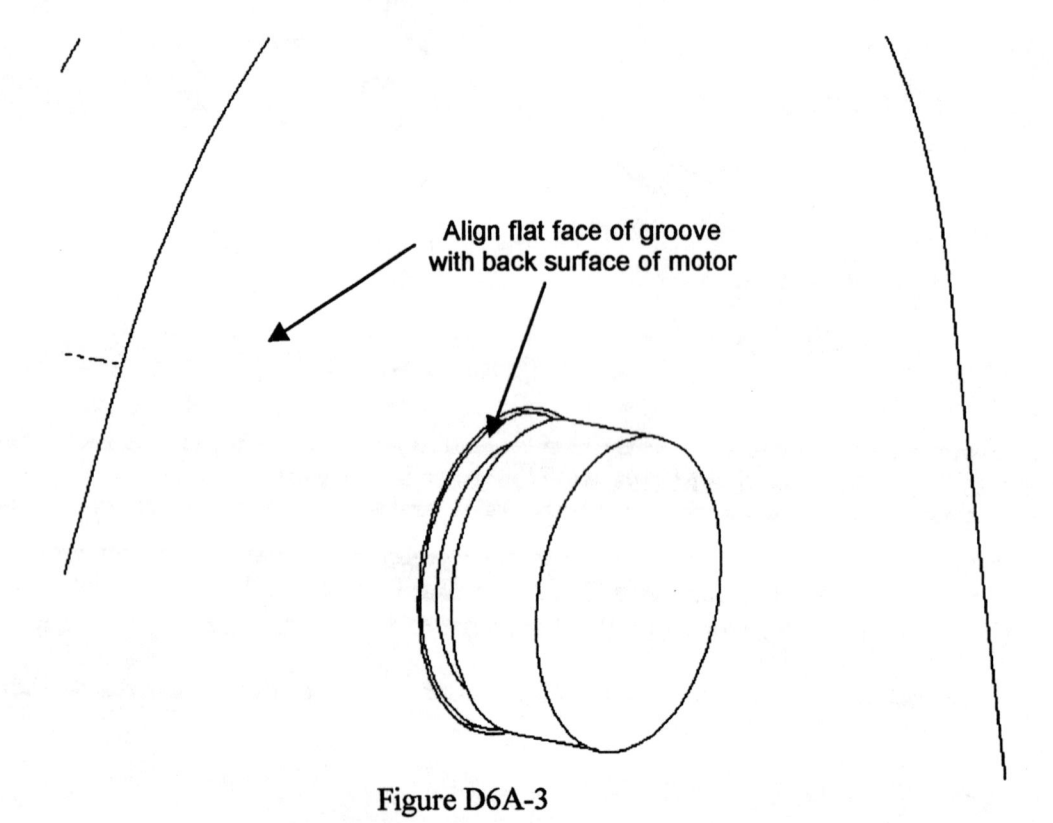

Align flat face of groove with back surface of motor

Figure D6A-3

D6-2

DESIGN PROJECT TUTORIAL

Step 4: Open and add the SNAP_RING part into the assembly. Add *Mates* to fully constrain the location of the part.

Step 5: Open and add the COVER part into the assembly. Add *Mates* to fully constrain the location of the part.

Step 6: Modify the distance between the grooves for the snap rings on the DRIVE_SHAFT part to 13.75in.

Step 7: Use *Component Pattern* to assemble a second snap ring to the shaft. Use *(Derived)* as the *Method to define the pattern*, the first SNAP_RING as the *Seed Component*, and *LPattern1* from the DRIVE_SHAFT as the *Pattern Feature*.

Step 8: Save the (sub) assembly.

Assignment 6B: Complete the BLOWER Sub-Assembly

Step 1: Create and complete the BLOWER sub-assembly. This assembly will have three components:
    1) LOWER_HOUSING
    2) UPPER_HOUSING
    3) IMPELLER
Refer to the figures in the *Design Project Introduction* section of the text (see page *iv*) for the part inter-relationships.

End of Design Project Assignment 6.

Exercise 27: Assembly Modifications, Inquiries, and Drawings

In this exercise we will explore a variety of options that are available within assembly mode. It is possible to perform operations on individual parts or analyze the assembly as a whole.

The mechanical properties of an assembly can be produced quickly, and a parts list for the assembly, also known as a *Bill of Material*, can be generated automatically. Part modifications as simple as a dimension modification or as significant as creation of a feature can also be performed.

Step 1: Within the *Machine* assembly modify an existing part feature.

A. Open your solution `machine.SLDASM` from Exercise 26.

B. Browse through the *FeatureManager* to find the base feature for the `bracket` part.

C. Double click on the **Base-Extrude** feature to display its dimensions.

D. Double click on the **25mm** width of the base and **Modify** the dimension to **50mm**.

E. Click on the **Rebuild** tool, either on the *Modify* dialog or on the *Standard* toolbar, and then click on the *Save the changes and exit...* tool (a green check mark) to exit from the *Modify* dialog box.

Step 2: Within the *Machine* assembly create a new part feature.

A. Right click on the name of the `bracket` part in the *FeatureManager*. Select **Edit Part** from the popup menu and note that many of the tools on the *Features* toolbar become available. Also, notice how the `bracket` in the graphics window and the bracket's features in the *FeatureManager* are shown in red.

B. Select the two short, parallel edges on the top of the part for filleting. See Figure X27-1.

C. Click on the **Fillet** tool on the *Features* toolbar and create a **20.00mm** *Constant Radius* round on those edges.

D. **Rebuild** the model, as necessary, to show the two new fillets.

DESIGN PROJECT TUTORIAL

E.   Right click anywhere in the graphics window and select **Edit Assembly: Machine.** or **Edit Assembly: Base**, as may be available from the popup menu. **Rebuild** again, as necessary, to change the color of the bracket from red to black.

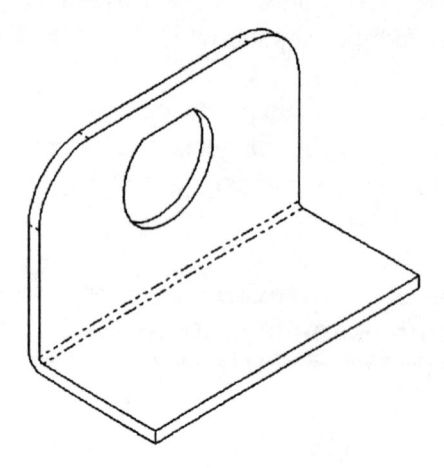

Figure X27-1

F.   Go to the *ConfigurationManager*, and right click on *ExplView1*, and select **Explode** from the popup menu.

G.   Use *Edit Definition* for the Exploded View to move the ring.SLDPRT, shaft.SLDPRT, and base_crank.SLDPRT farther from the modified bracket.SLDPRT and to remove the apparent overlap between the ring.SLDPRT and bracket.SLDPRT.

Step 3:   Inquire into the *Mass Properties* of the *Machine* assembly.

A.   *Collapse* the Exploded View and select **Tools ▼ Mass Properties...** and wait for the following report:

Mass properties for the assembly: machine.sldasm

Mass: 233.07 grams

Volume: 2.3307e+005 cubic millimeters

Surface Area: 76497 square millimeters

Center Of Mass: X = -17.443 millimeters
                 Y = 55.317 millimeters
                 Z = 1.4216 millimeters

```
Inertia Tensor:           gram * ( square millimeters )
(taken at CofM)
    Ixx = 360036      Ixy = 149894      Ixz = -27126.7
    Iyx = 149894      Iyy = 643220      Iyz = -8063.03
    Izx = -27126.7    Izy = -8063.03    Izz = 707504

Principal Axes of Inertia and their Moments:
    (0.917978, -0.393129, 0.052592)       294289
    (0.247744, 0.671874, 0.698003)        690115
    (-0.309741, -0.627722, 0.714161)      726356
```

This data is very useful for stress and fatigue analysis.

B. Note the *Copy* button in the *Mass Properties* window--this button will place the data on the clipboard for pasting into other applications.

C. Press the **Close** button to remove the *Mass Properties* window.

Step 4: Generate a *Bill of Material* for the *Machine* assembly within an assembly drawing.

A. Open your drawing `machine.SLDDRW` or create a new drawing of this assembly with a single named view, *Isometric*, and activate the drawing window. If you are creating the exploded view for the first time right click on the *Isometric* view, select **Properties...** from the popup menu, check the option **Show in exploded state**, and press the **OK** button.

B. Preset the font for the *Bill-of-Material* by selecting **Tools ▼ Options** and the *Detailing* tab. Press the **Note Font** button within the *Notes* heading, select **Points** within the *Height* heading, and select **16** as the font height setting from the scroll box. Press the **OK** button in the *Choose Font* dialog and again in the *Options* dialog.

C. Click on the *Isometric* view on the assembly drawing to activate it. Make sure that the green outline with eight grip boxes is showing before continuing to the next step.

D. Select **Insert ▼ Bill of Materials**, click the **Open** button on the *Select BOM Template* dialog, activate the **Show parts only** radio button, deselect **Use table anchor point**, and press **OK** to generate the bill of material. This will take 30 to 40 seconds.

E. After the bill of materials appears, drag it to the upper right corner of the drawing.

F. Use the **Balloon** tool on the *Annotation* toolbar to add *Part Identification Bubbles* to the assembly drawing. Notice how *SolidWorks* intelligently applies the balloon numbers to the parts in such a way as to match the item numbers within the *Bill-of-Material*.

G. If all six of the *Balloons* do not have the same type of endpoint, either a dot or an arrow, edit the ones with the arrows to make them dots. Select (with a left click while holding down the **CTRL** key if there is more than one that needs to be changed) the offending balloon(s), right click, select **Properties...** from the popup menu, deselect **Smart** within the *Leader* heading of the *Properties* dialog, and select the solid dot type of leader from the *Arrow style:* flipdown menu.

H. **Print** your drawing.

If all goes well the result will resemble Figure X27-2 on the next page:

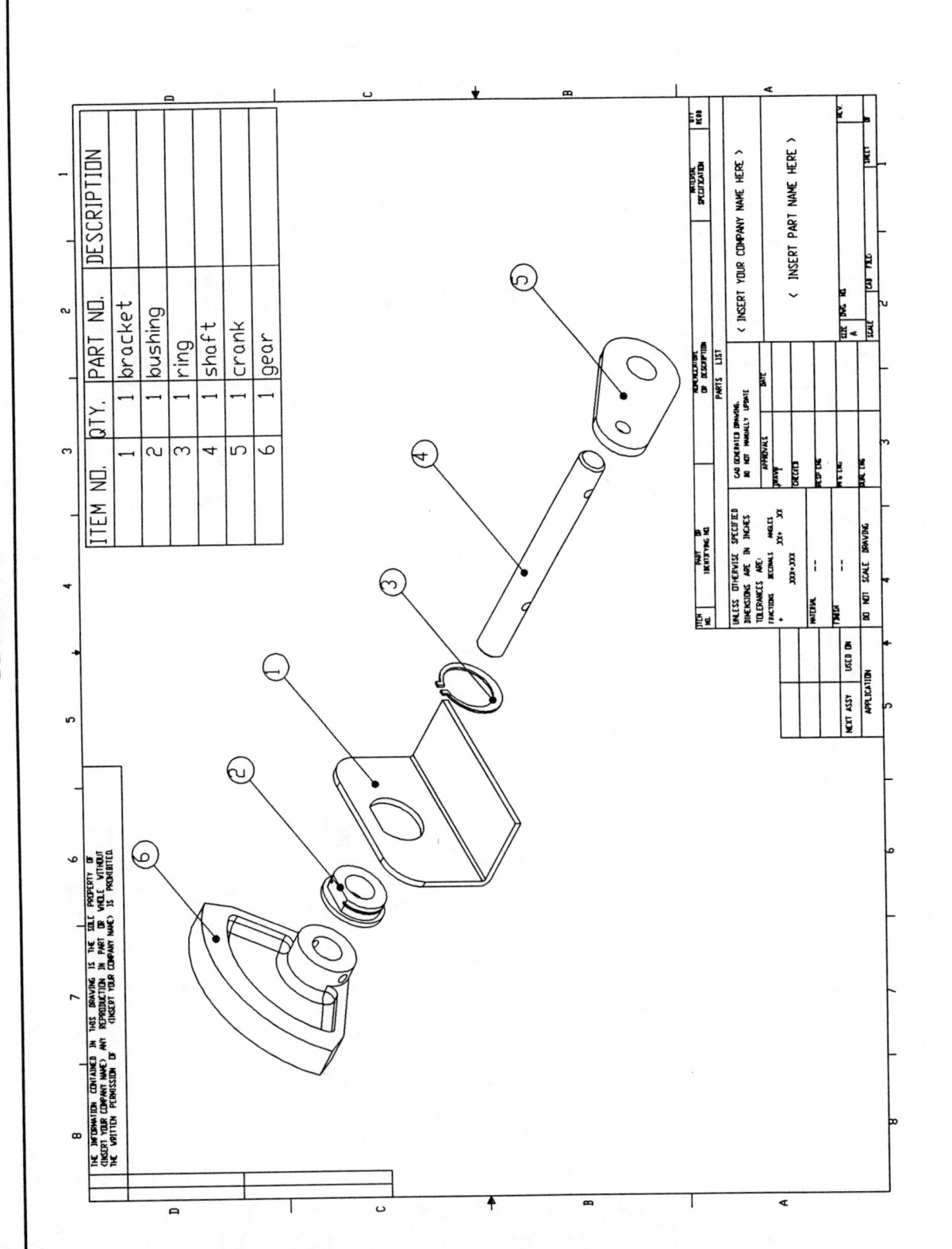

Figure X27-2

End of Exercise 27

Exercise 28 – Use of Layout Sketches and Part Creation within an Assembly

With the `base` and `machine` assemblies in previous exercises we performed "Bottom Up" assembly design. Using this method, part models are created first and separately from one another, and the final design operation collects the individual parts into an assembly. Errors and misconceptions cannot be identified until the last step in the design process when correcting them can be very costly and time consuming.

A better method is called "Top Down" assembly design. In this exercise we will design two parts from scratch directly inside an assembly model. The basic configuration of the two parts will be controlled by a *layout sketch*, which will be created before the parts. The use of this sketch helps to prevent design errors and misconceptions.

Step 1: Begin a new assembly called CRANK_PISTON and create a layout sketch within the assembly.

A. Select the **New** tool, select **Assembly**, and press **OK**. Set *inches* as the units.

B. Select **File ▼ Save As...** and name the file `crank_piston.SLDASM`.

C. Press the **Sketch** tool to begin sketching on the *Front* plane. Sketch two lines and a centerline, dimension the sketch, and modify the values as shown on Figure X28-1.

Note that the upper endpoint of the 6" long line is *Coincident* with the *Vertical* centerline, and the centerline is *Coincident* with the *Origin*. The 2" line represents the skeleton of a crankshaft, and the 6" line represents the skeleton of a connecting rod. The piston will pivot around an axis through the upper endpoint of the 6" line.

DESIGN PROJECT TUTORIAL

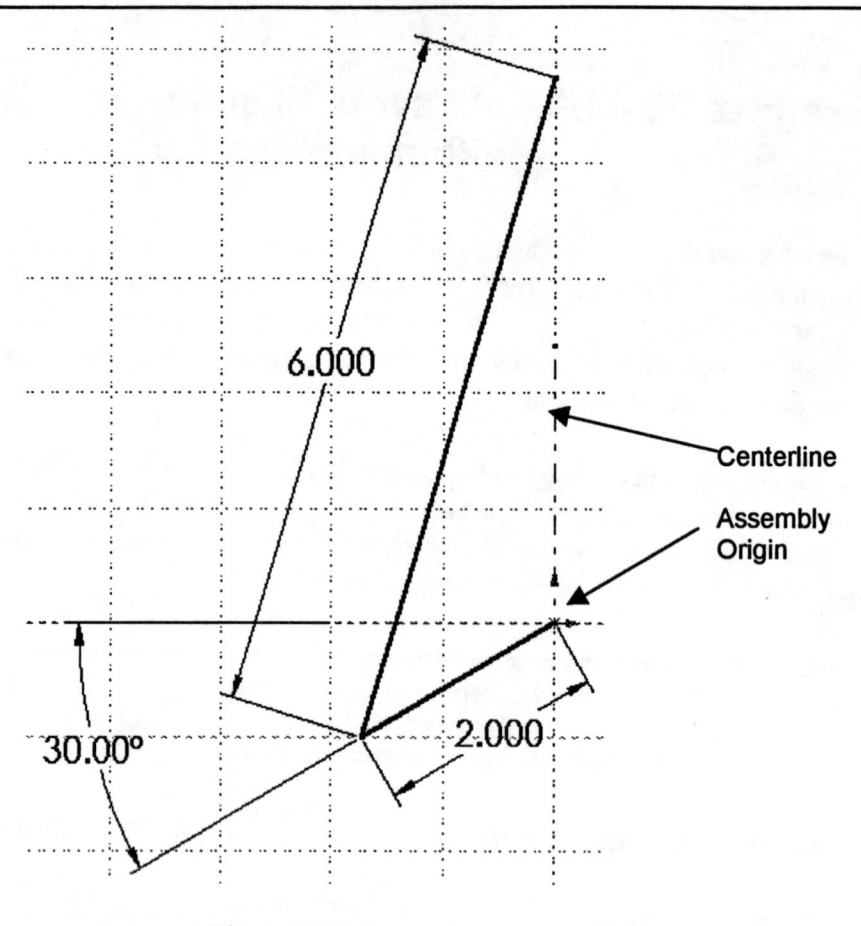

Figure X28-1

D. Press the **Sketch** tool again to close the sketch.

Step 2:   *Open* and assemble the BEARING part model.

A. Open the file `bearing.SLDPRT`.

B. Select **Window ▾ Tile Horizontally** to show both the part window and the assembly window.

C. Drag and drop the `bearing` tool from the top of the *FeatureManager* area of the part file into the *FeatureManager* area of the assembly file.

DESIGN PROJECT TUTORIAL

Step 3: Create two new part files and assemble the two empty part models into the assembly.

A. Select the **New** tool, select **Part**, and press **OK.**

B. Select **File ▼ Save As...** and name the file `crank_shaft.SLDPRT`.

C. Select the **New** tool, select **Part**, and press **OK.**

D. Select **File ▼ Save As...** and name the file `conn_rod.SLDPRT`.

E. Select **Window ▼ Tile Horizontally** to show all three active part windows and the assembly window at the same time.

F. Drag and drop the `crank_shaft` tool from the top of the *FeatureManager* area of the part file into the *FeatureManager* area of the assembly file.

G. Drag and drop the `conn_rod` tool from the top of the *FeatureManager* area of the part file into the *FeatureManager* area of the assembly file.

H. Maximize the assembly window to fill the monitor screen by clicking inside it and then pressing the ▢ tool at its upper right corner.

Step 4: Create the three features of the CRANK_SHAFT within the assembly.

A. Right click over the `crank_shaft` tool inside the *FeatureManager* area of the assembly and select **Edit Part**. The ensuing warning message means that we will have to be very careful to constrain the part as we go. Press **OK** to remove the warning message.

B. Select the **Front** plane of the assembly and press the **Sketch** tool.

C. Select the edge of the inside diameter (I.D.) of the `bearing` and press **Convert Entities**.

D. Use **Extruded Boss/Base** with a **Blind** depth of **3.00in.** Select the direction of the *Base-Extrude* so it passes through the ID of the `bearing`.

E. Again select the **Front** plane of the assembly and press the **Sketch** tool. Create a sketch like Figure X28-2 with the centers of the two semicircles related as *Coincident* with the endpoints of the short line segment in the *Layout Sketch*:

28-3

DESIGN PROJECT TUTORIAL

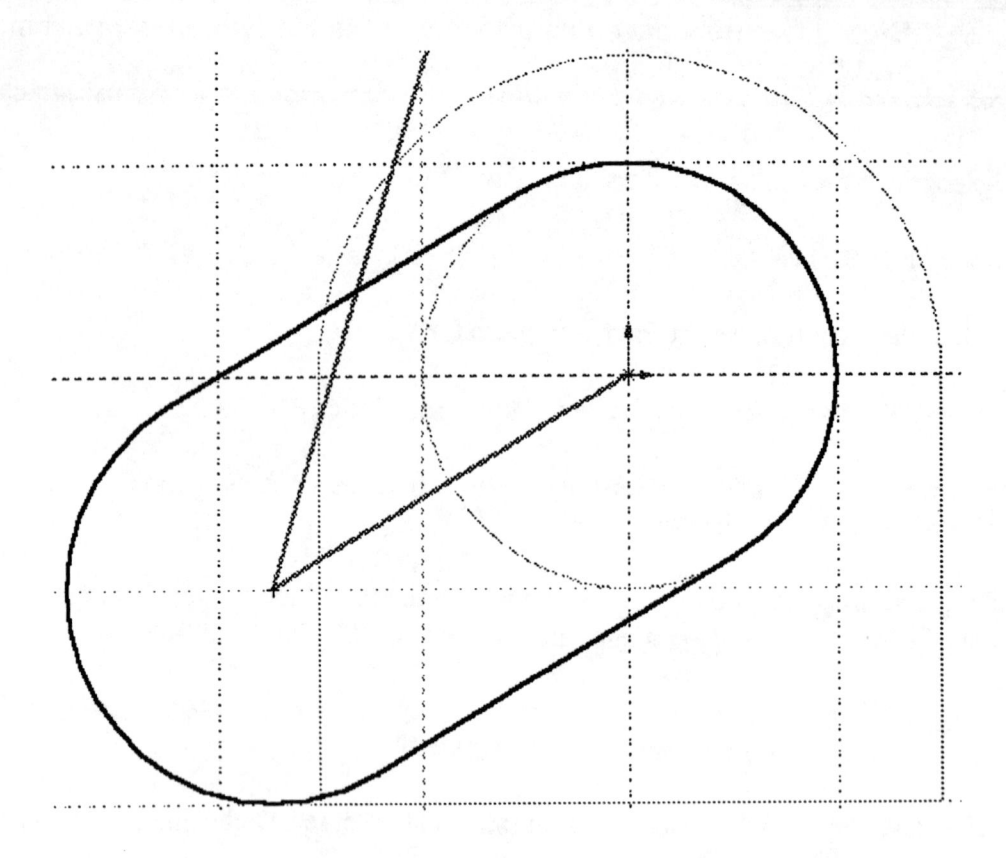

Figure X28-2

No dimensions should be necessary for the sketch. Shrewd use of *Convert Entities, Trim,* and the *Tangent, Equal,* and *Coincident* relations will allow this.

F. **Extrude** the sketch **0.75in.** forward (away from the `bearing`).

G. For a third and final time select the **Front** plane of the assembly and press the **Sketch** tool. Sketch a **Circle** with a radius that is *Equal* to the other radii on the `crank_shaft` and with a centerpoint that is *Coincident* with the elbow of the *Layout Sketch*. See Figure X28-3:

DESIGN PROJECT TUTORIAL

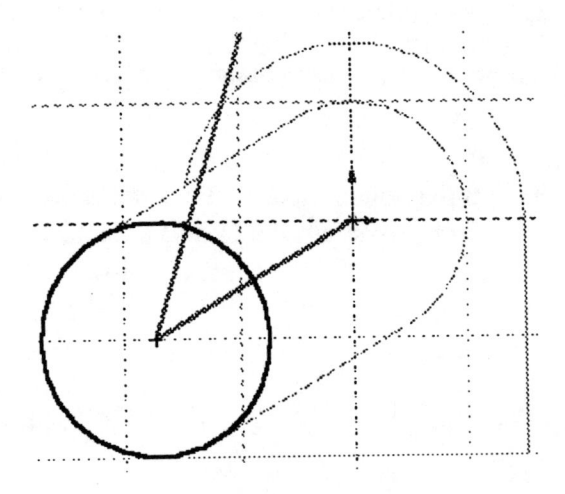

Figure X28-3

H. **Extrude** the sketch **1.75in.** forward (away from the `bearing`). The `crank_shaft` part is complete at this point, but we will need to *Mate* it to the `bearing` and to the *Layout Sketch*.

I. Right click within the graphics window of the assembly and select **Edit Assembly: Crank_Piston** to re-activate assembly editing.

J. **Rebuild**, as necessary.

K. Select **View▼** and uncheck **Temporary Axes** if it isn't already unchecked. Having these turned off will make the selection of the endpoint on the elbow of the *Layout Sketch* significantly easier. We'll turn them back on in the middle of the next substep.

L. **Mate** the *temporary axis* of the *Boss-Extrude2* for the `crank_shaft` as **Coincident** with the point at the elbow of the *Layout Sketch*. First, select the point on the elbow. Then, select **View▼**, check **Temporary Axes**, and (with the **CTRL** key held down) select the axis of **Boss-Extrude2**. **Preview** and **Apply** the *Mate*.

M. **Mate** the **Front** plane of the `crank_shaft` part as **Coincident** with the **Front** plane of the `crank_piston` assembly. The position of the `crank_shaft` should be fully constrained, as would be indicated by the disappearance of the "-" sign within parentheses, directly to the left of the name of the part in the *FeatureManager*.

N. **Rebuild**, as necessary.

DESIGN PROJECT TUTORIAL

Step 5: Create the base feature of the CONN_ROD within the assembly.

A. Right click over the `conn_rod` tool inside the *FeatureManager* area of the assembly and select **Edit Part** from the popup menu. The ensuing warning message means that we will have to be very careful to constrain the part as soon as it is created. Because we are going to sketch on a surface of the `crank_shaft` instead of on some element of reference geometry for the `conn_rod` part itself or the `crank_piston` assembly, this part can behave very erratically. Press **OK** to remove the warning message.

B. Select the front most face/surface of the `crank_shaft` as the sketching plane and press the **Sketch** tool. See Figure X28-4 for clarification:

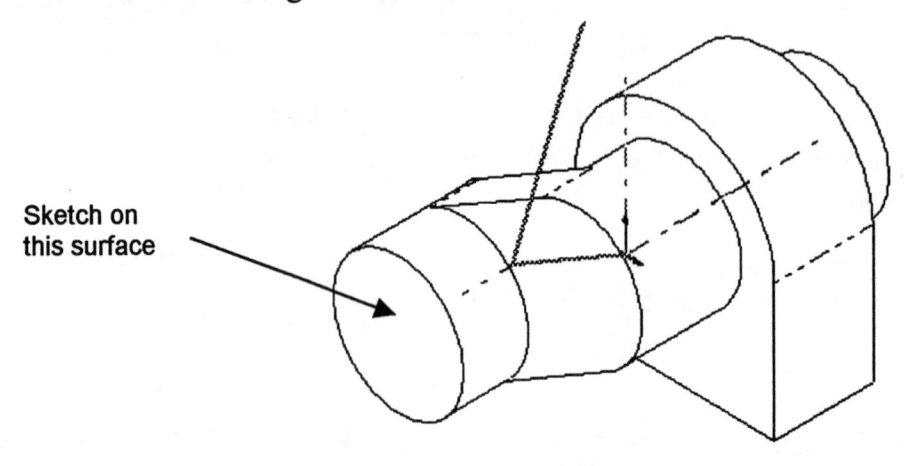

Figure X28-4

C. With the front face of the *Boss-Extrude2* of the `crank_shaft` already selected press **Convert Entities**.

D. Sketch, dimension, and relate the profile of the `conn_rod` as shown on Figure X28-5:

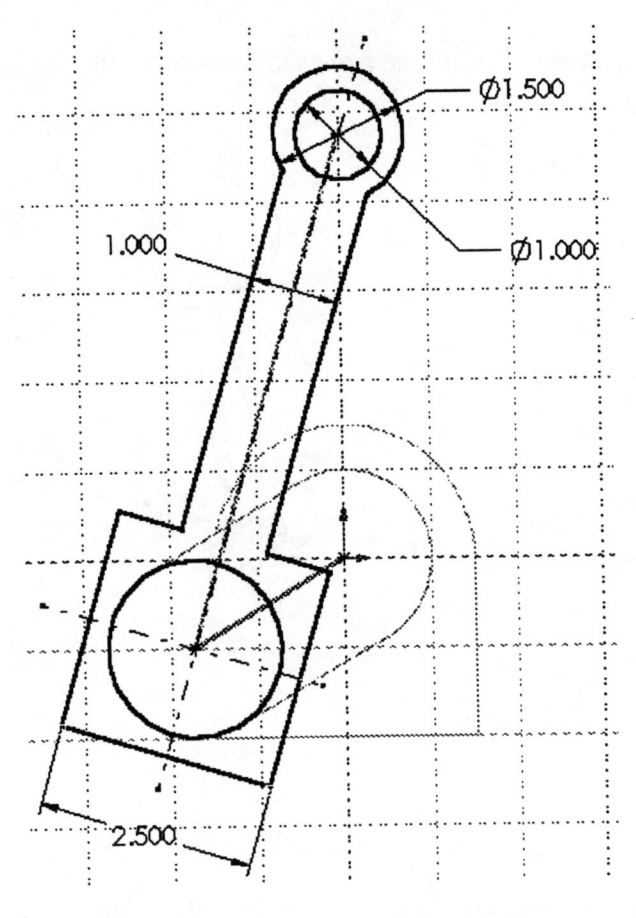

Figure X28-5

Relate the two circular holes in the sketch to the endpoints of the 6" line of the *Layout Sketch*, as necessary, to make the sketch fully constrained. The bottom of the `conn_rod` is square in shape.

E. **Extrude** the sketch **0.75in.** backward (toward the `bearing`).

F. Right click inside the graphics window and select **Edit Assembly: Crank_Piston.**

G. **Rebuild**, as necessary.

DESIGN PROJECT TUTORIAL

H. Use a **Coincident Mate** to relate the front face of the `conn_rod` and the front face of the `crank_shaft`. See Figure X28-6:

Coincident Surfaces

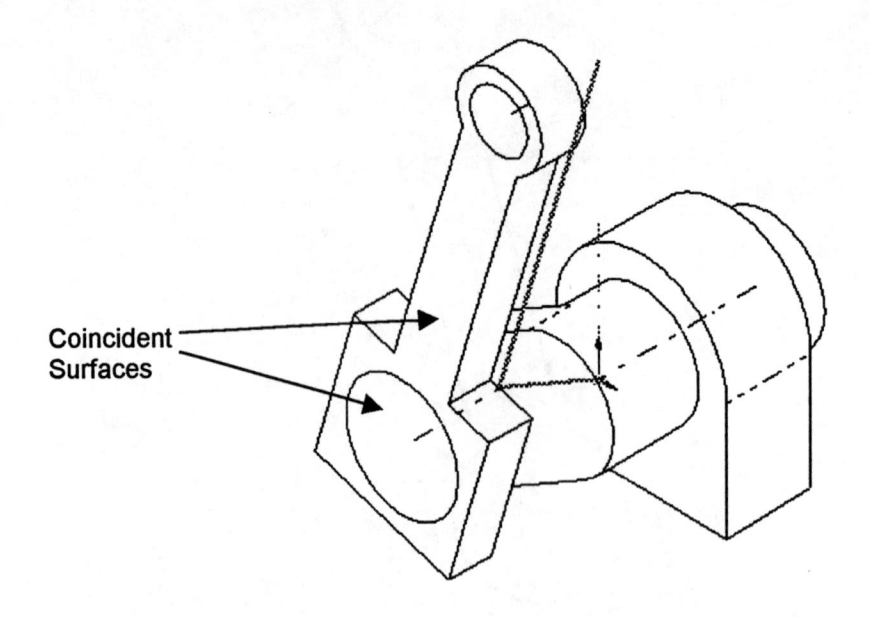

Figure X28-6

I. Use a **Coincident Mate** to relate the lower axis of the `conn_rod` and the lower vertex point of the *Layout Sketch*. See Figure X28-7.

J. Use a **Coincident Mate** to relate the upper axis of the `conn_rod` and the upper vertex of the *Layout Sketch*. See Figure X28-7. The position of the `conn_rod` should now be fully constrained.

DESIGN PROJECT TUTORIAL

Coincident Vertex and Axis

Coincident Vertex and Axis

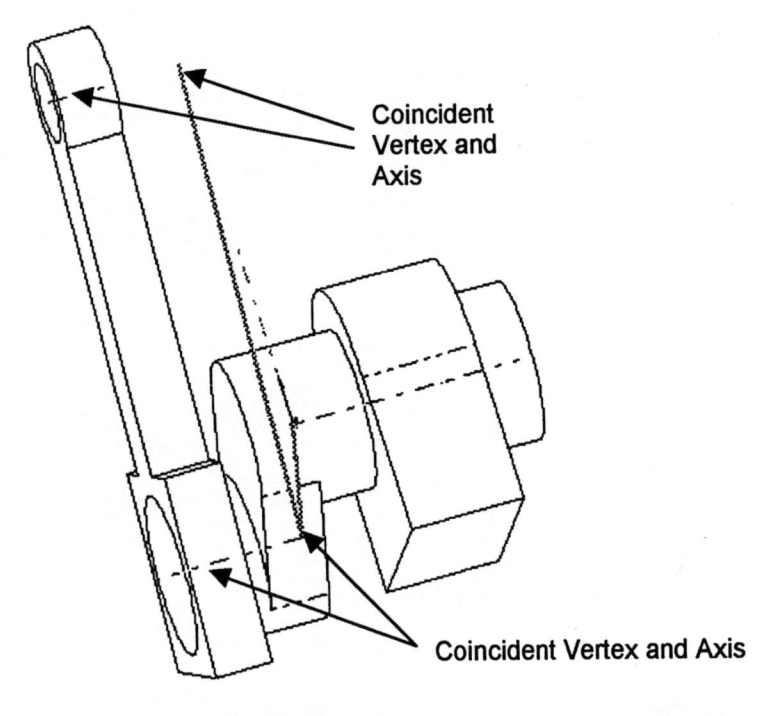

Figure X28-7

Step 6: Open, assemble, and mate the LINK_PIN part.

A. Select the **Open** tool, press **OK,** and browse to the file `link_pin.SLDPRT`.

B. Select **Window ▼ Tile Horizontally** to show all four active part windows and the assembly window at the same time.

C. **Drag and drop** the `link_pin` tool from the top of the *FeatureManager* area of the part file into the graphics window area of the assembly file.

D. **Maximize** the window of the `crank_piston` assembly.

E. Use a **Concentric Mate** to relate the outer diameter (O.D.) of `link_pin` and the ID of the upper hole in the `conn_rod`.

F. Use a **Distance Mate** to relate the front face of the `link_pin` and front face of the `conn_rod`. Set the *Distance:* as **1.625in**. See Figure X28-8.

28-9

DESIGN PROJECT TUTORIAL

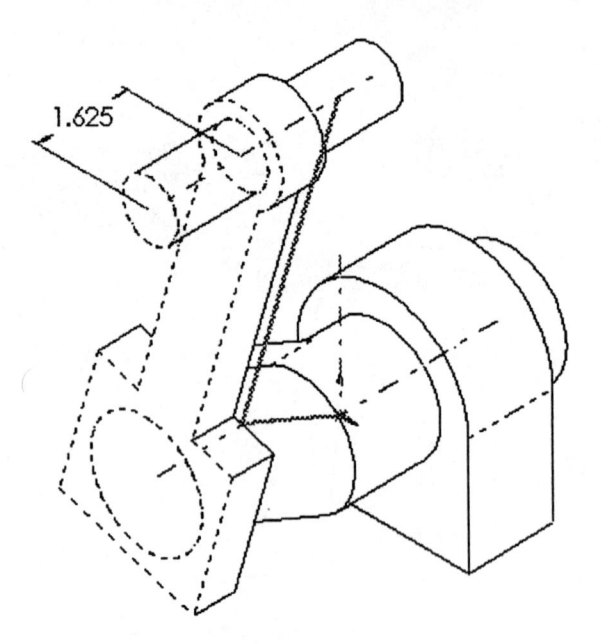

1.625

Figure X28-8

G. Use a **Parallel Mate** to relate the **Top** plane of the `link_pin` and the **Top** plane of the `crank_piston` assembly. Because the `link_pin` hasn't any radial or axial features this *Mate* is fairly trivial—it doesn't have any physical significance and its only purpose is to fully constrain the position of the `link_Pin` within *SolidWorks®*.

| Step 7: | Open, assemble, and mate the PISTON part. |

A. Select the **Open** tool and browse to the file `piston.SLDPRT`.

B. Select **Window ▾ Tile Horizontally** to show all five active part windows and the assembly window at the same time.

C. **Drag and drop** the `piston` tool from the top of the *FeatureManager* area of the part file into the graphics window area of the assembly file.

D. **Maximize** the window of the `crank_piston` assembly.

E. Use a **Concentric Mate** to relate the outer diameter (O.D.) of `link_pin` and the ID of the hole in the `piston`.

F. Use a **Coincident Mate** to relate the face of the inner slot of the `piston` and front face of the `conn_rod`. See Figure X28-9:

28-10

DESIGN PROJECT TUTORIAL

Coincident Surface (Hidden)

Coincident Surface

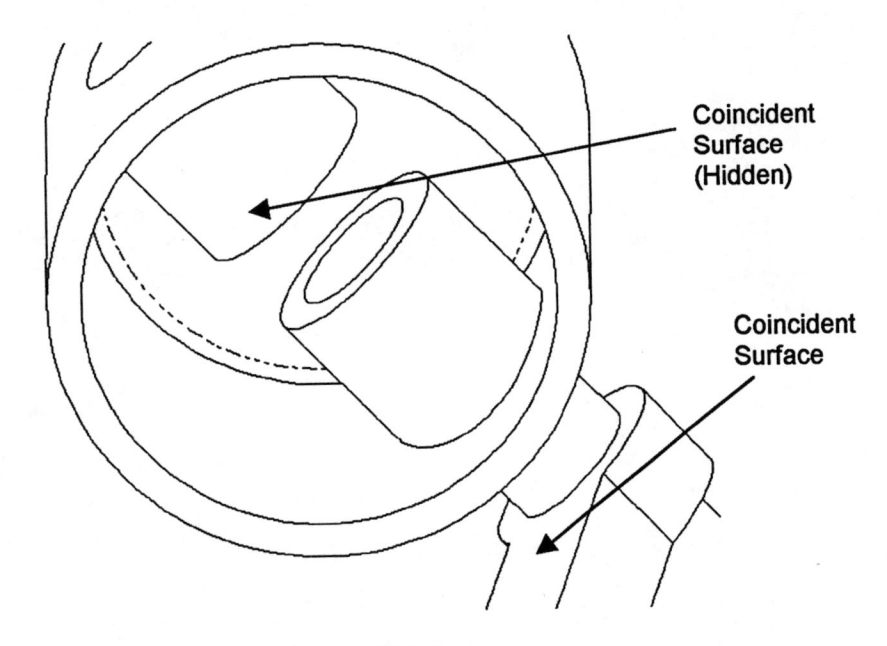

Figure X28-9

G. Use a **Parallel Mate** to relate the bottom surface of the `piston` and the bottom surface of the `bearing`. This mate will keep the top of the `piston` horizontal.

Step 7: **Play with the completed assembly to see the value and effect of the *Layout Sketch*.**

A. Change to a **Front** view of the assembly. **Shade** the assembly.

B. Double click on **Sketch1** of the `crank_piston` assembly.

C. Double click on the **30°** dimension to expose the **Modify** dialog box. Drag this dialog box out of the way, as necessary.

D. Click on the **Reset Spin Increment Value** tool:

E. Enter **30deg** and press the **Enter** key on the keyboard.

F. Alternately, click on the **Spin Up (▲)** button and **Rebuild** tool. The entire assembly should move. At certain positions (such as 180°) some of the mates become *indeterminate*, meaning that they cannot be resolved mathematically. Depending upon your mates they should rebuild probably on the next movement.

G. Save and close all open files.

28-11

End of Exercise 28.

Exercise 29 - Creating an SLA File

Stereolithography is also known as *Three Dimensional (3D) Printing*. In essence, a CAD design can be output through a Stereolithography Apparatus (S.L.A.) instead of through a common two-dimensional paper printer for later fabrication. SLA allows design prototypes to be ready very rapidly for engineering evaluation and analysis. In this exercise we will learn how simple it is to create an SLA program file.

One type of Stereolithography Apparatus (SLA) translates CAD designs into solid objects through a combination of laser, photochemistry and software technologies. A computer-driven laser solidifies a vat of liquid resin, layer by layer, into a three-dimensional epoxy prototype part. This SLA technology offers excellent small feature definition and accuracy, and the epoxy resin provides rigidity and strength.

Another type of SLA ejects a small (in diameter) liquid stream of plastic from a slowly moving nozzle. The nozzle moves in a 3D fashion that is very similar to the motion of a cutting tool in any common Computer-Numerically Controlled (C.N.C.) machine tool, only very much slower.

Step 1: Open the file *widget*.SLDPRT. Set the export options.

A. Open the part file `widget.SLDPRT`.

Step 2: Create and *Preview* the STL file.

A. Select **File ▼ Save As...** and, under the *Save as Type:* flipdown selector, choose **STL Files (*.stl)**.

B. Click the **Options** button at the bottom right of the *Save As* dialog box.

C. Enable the **Preview** checkbox and press the **OK** button on the *STL Export Options* dialog box.

D. Press the **SAVE** button on the *Save As* dialog box.

E. Read the question in the *SolidWorks 99* information window, note the storage location for the STL file, and move the dialog box out of the way by dragging and dropping its *Title Bar*.

F.	Briefly, observe the screen image of the STL file. This faceted model image can be translated by the Stereolithography Apparatus (S.L.A.) and its supporting software into a three-dimensional part prototype without any production planning or tooling.

G.	Press **Yes** on the *SolidWorks 99* information window to conclude the process.

**Step 3:	Close the *widget* part file.**

End of Exercise 29.

DESIGN PROJECT TUTORIAL

Exercise 30 - Part Modeling Review

It is impossible to design or model a part without knowing its function, surface-by-surface and feature-by-feature. This is true because there are as many different ways to create a model and to dimension it as there are people to perform the modeling. Once function is known there is only one completely logical and appropriate way to create and dimension the part model.

For example, if the dimensioning scheme shown on Figure X30-1 is ignored, the part can be created a number of different ways, and we will explore these. The four holes suggest that there are mating parts, but you have no indication how the part is mounted or used.

In general, dimensioning schemes on mating features of assembled parts should be complementary, if not identical. In the absence of this knowledge each model or modeling technique is as good as any other.

1) Discounting the given dimensioning scheme what are the different ways that the model can be created, exclusive of the holes:

_____
_____
_____
_____
_____
_____
_____

2) If the dimensions shown on Figure X30-1 are all *parametric* dimensions, inserted automatically from the part file, indicate which of your answers to question #1 is or are still possible.

3) What are the different ways that the hole shown on Section B-B be created:

_____
_____
_____
_____

DESIGN PROJECT TUTORIAL

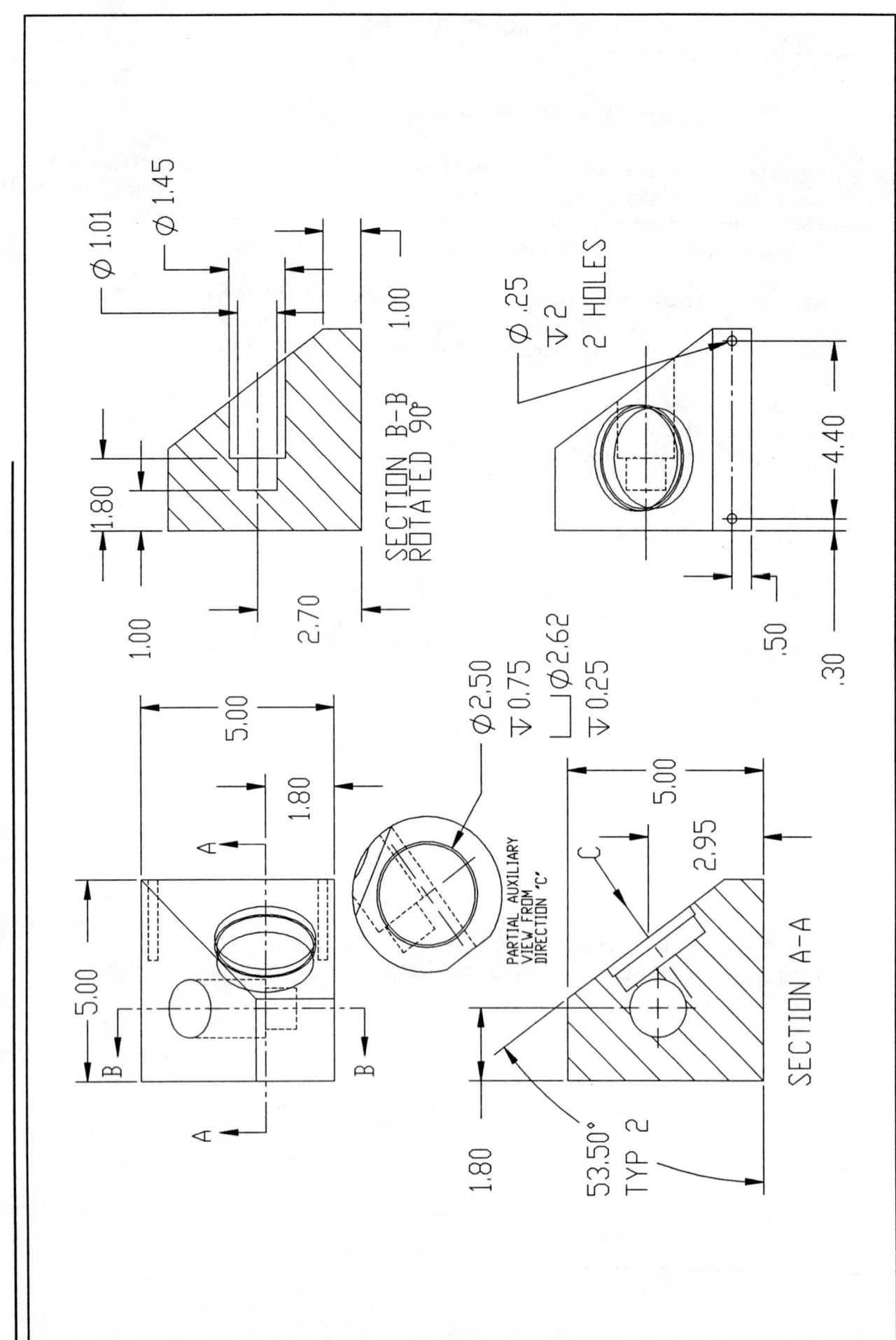

Figure X30-1

Design Project Assignment 7

Seven different parts will be created and assembled in the nine Design Project Assignments. In this seventh assignment we will modify and finish the MOTOR part

Assignment 7A: Complete the MOTOR part.

Step 1: Open the MOTOR part.

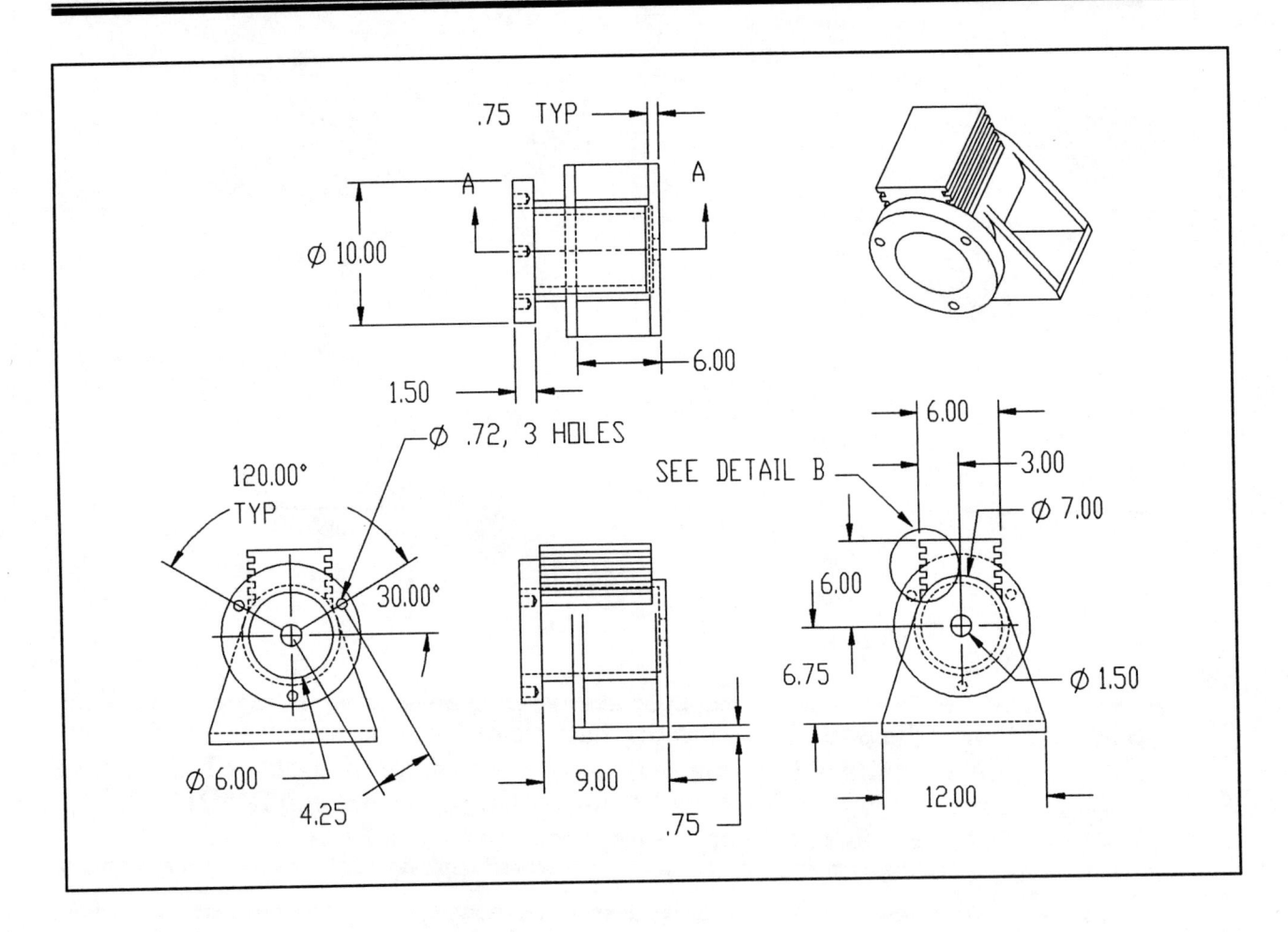

Figure D7A-1

DESIGN PROJECT TUTORIAL

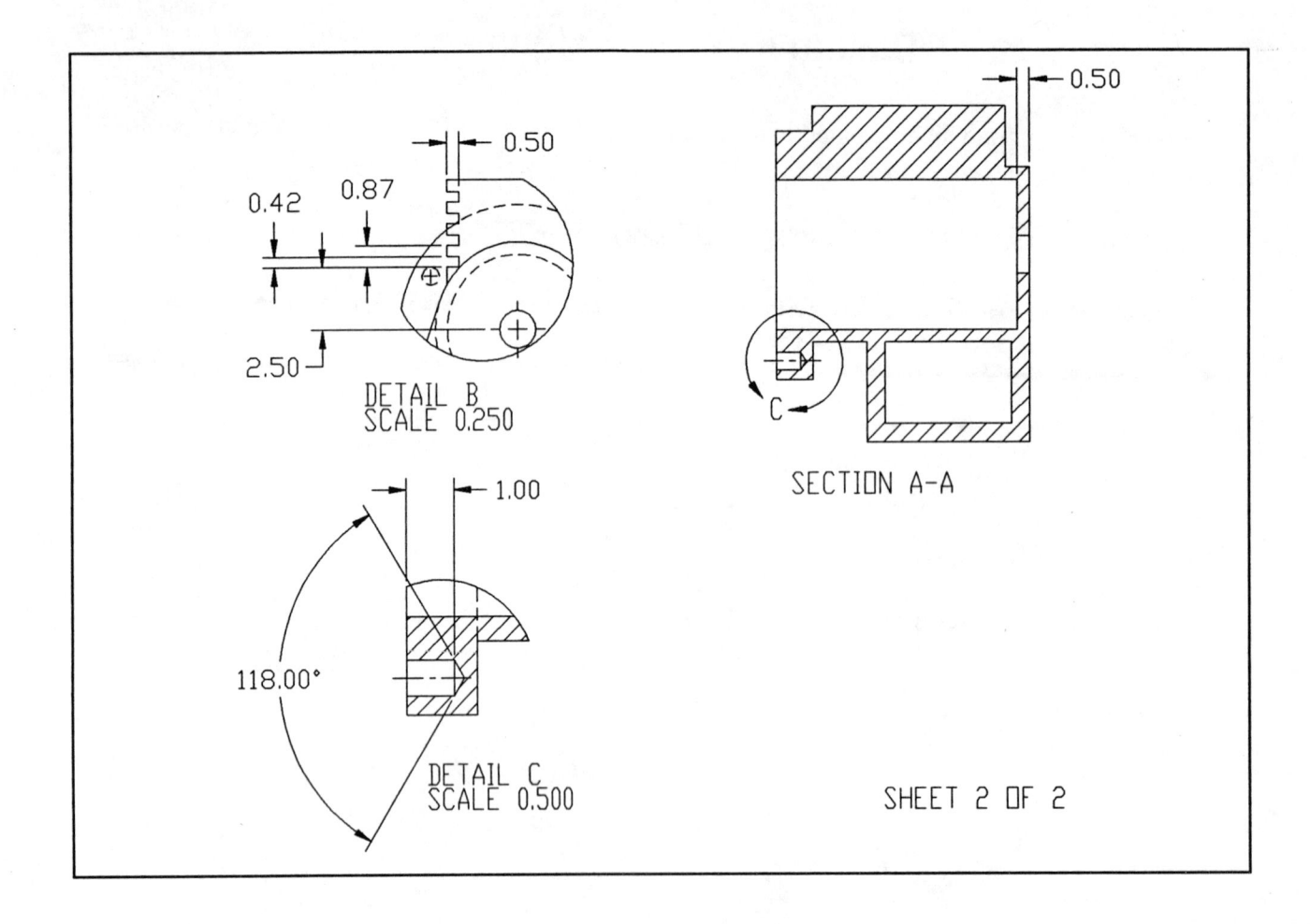

Figure D7A-2

| Step 2: | Mirror the patterned cuts on the side of the electronics foundation to the opposite side of the part. *NOTE:* An error may occur if the depth definition of the cut is something other than *Through All*. Use *Edit Definition* as necessary to redefine the *Depth Type*. |

| Step 3: | Since the support for the Motor would be very heavy as currently designed we will take action to lighten it without reducing its effective strength. First, *Modify* the depth of the motor support from 6.50in. to 0.75 in. |

DESIGN PROJECT TUTORIAL

Step 4: Pattern the (relatively) thin motor support to create a second support 6.00 in. from the first. In this case an edge must be selected to indicate the direction of the pattern. Pick the edge shown on Figure D7A-3.

Pick this short edge in Step 4 to indicate the direction of the pattern.

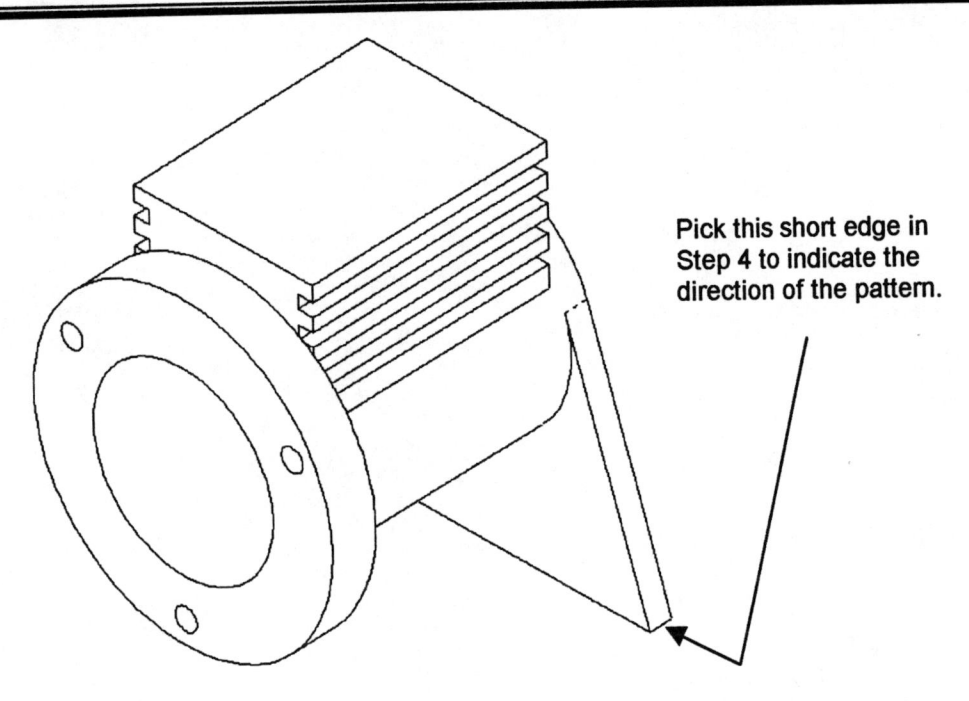

Figure D7A-3

Step 5: Create a 0.75in. thick extrusion on the bottom of the supports (see Figure D7A-1). It is advisable to sketch with a *Bottom* direction of viewing the part. Wise use of inferencing will preclude the need for *any* dimensions in this sketch!

Step 6: Save the model.

End of Design Project Assignment 7.

DESIGN PROJECT TUTORIAL

Design Project Assignment 8

In addition to seven different part models, two sub-assemblies, and one top-level assembly; three complete drawings will be created during the nine Design Project Assignments. In this eight assignment we will complete the final drawing for the MOTOR part.

Assignment 8: Complete the MOTOR Drawing

Step 1:	Retrieve the drawing MOTOR.SLDDRW.
Step 2:	Move Detail B and Section A-A to a new sheet number two, as shown on Figure D7A-2.
Step 3:	Add Detail C to sheet 2, as shown on Figure D7A-2.
Step 4:	Add the parametric notes and dimensions for the *Simple Drilled* hole.
Step 5:	Complete the detailing of the drawing.
Step 6:	Save the drawing.

End of Design Project Assignment 8.

DESIGN PROJECT TUTORIAL

Design Project Assignment 9

The purpose of creating the seven different part models and two sub-assemblies in the previous assignments was to achieve the top-level assembly. In this ninth assignment we will culminate the entire design process by creating and modifying the AIR_HANDLER assembly.

Assignment 9A: Create the AIR_HANDLER Assembly

| Step 1: | Create a *New* assembly called AIR_HANDLER. |

| Step 2: | Open the MOTOR sub-assembly and add it to the AIR_HANDLER. |

| Step 3: | Open the BLOWER sub-assembly and add it to the AIR_HANDLER. Add *Mates* to constrain its position. |

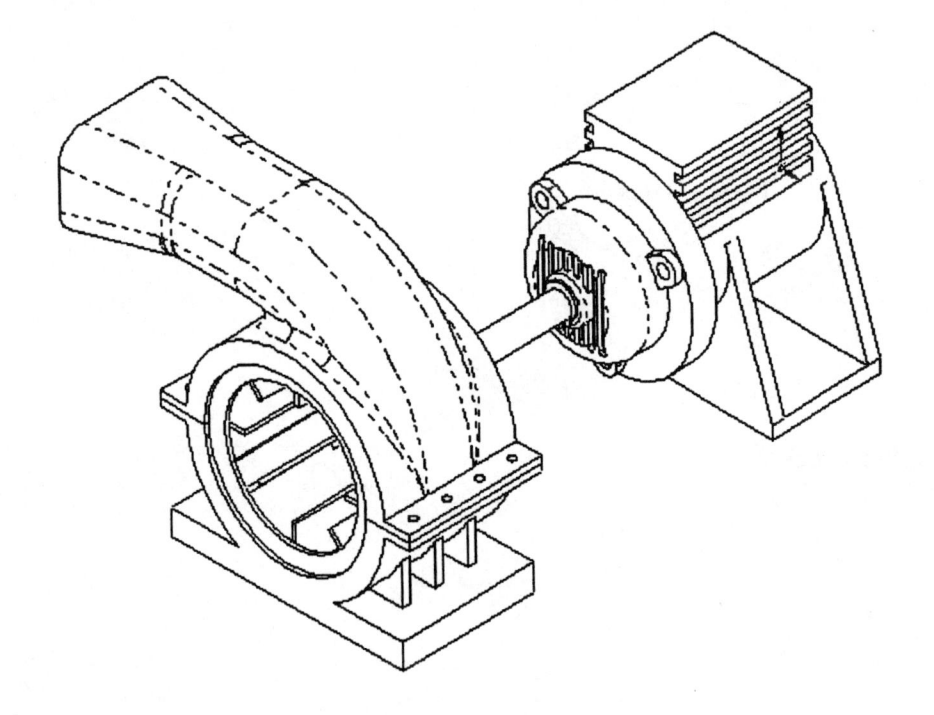

Figure D9A-1

Step 4: Modify the height of the MOTOR part's foundation so that its bottom surface will be at the same level as the bottom surface of the LOWER_HOUSING part.

Step 5: Save the AIR_HANDLER assembly.

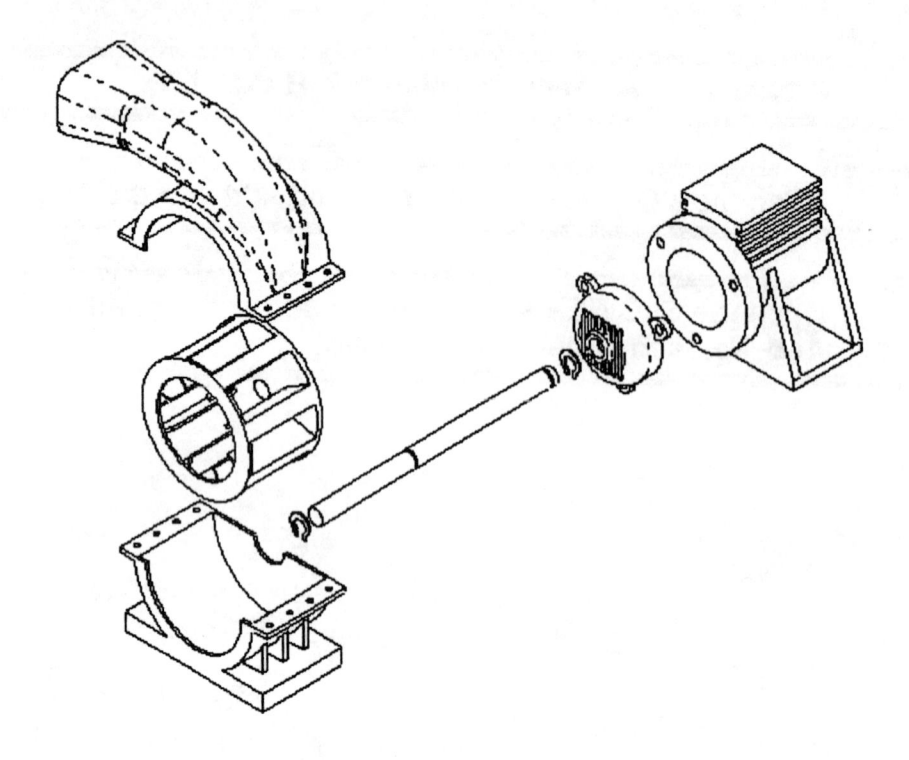

Figure D9A-2

End of Design Project Assignment 9.

Appendix A

LIST OF SolidWorks 99 PULLDOWN MENU OPTIONS
WITH PATH TO GET THERE (AND SHORTCUTS)

3 point arc <== sketch Entity <== Tools
3d sketch <== Insert
Add <== relatiOns <== Tools
aDd-ins <== Tools
aliGn grid <== sketch Tools <== Tools
aNnotation <== Toolbars <== View
Arrange icons <== Window
Assembly <== Toolbars <== View
automatic Inferencing lines <== sketch Tools <== Tools
aUtomatic relations <== sketch Tools <== Tools
automatic solVe <== sketch Tools <== Tools
Axes <== View
Axis <== Reference geometry <== Insert
bAlloon <== Annotations <== Insert
bAse part <== Insert
Bends <== sheet Metal <== Features <== Insert
Cascade <== Window
cavIty <== Features <== Insert
ceNterline <== sketch Entity <== Tools
centerpoint Arc <== sketch Entity <== Tools
centerpoInt ellipse <== sketch Entity <== Tools
Chamfer <== Features <== Insert
Check <== Tools
checK sketch for feature <== sketch Tools <== Tools
Circle <== sketch Entity <== Tools
Circular pattern <== pattErn/mirror <== Insert
Circular step and repeat <== sketch Tools <== Tools
Close <== File
close aLl <== Window
cLose sketch to model <== sketch Tools <== Tools
Composite <== cUrve <== Insert
Constrain all <== relatiOns <== Tools
convert Entities <== sketch Tools <== Tools
Coordinate system <== Reference geometry <== Insert
Coordinate systems <== View
Copy <== Edit (Ctrl-C)
Copy material <== Photoworks
cOsmetic thread <== Annotations <== Insert
Curvature <== Display <== View
curve through Free points <== cUrve <== Insert

curve Through reference points <== cUrve <== Insert
Customize <== Toolbars <== View
customiZe <== Tools

cuT <== Edit (Ctrl-X)
Cut Material <== Photoworks
datUm feature symbol <== Annotations <== Insert
Datum target <== Annotations <== Insert
Decals <== Photoworks
deFinition <== Edit
Delete <== Edit (Del)
deleTe <== pictUre <== Modify <== View
delete desIgn table <== Edit
deriVed sketch <== Insert
desiGn table <== Edit
Design table <== Insert
detacH segment on drag <== sketch Tools <== Tools
display as Icon <== Object <== Edit
Display content <== Object <== Edit
Display/delete <== relatiOns <== Tools
dOme <== Features <== Insert
Draft <== Features <== Insert
Drawing <== Toolbars <== View
Edit <== mAcro <== Tools
edit sketch plAne <== Edit
Ellipse <== sketch Entity <== Tools
Equations <== Tools
eXit <== File
eXtend <== sketch Tools <== Tools
Extrude <== Cut <== Insert
Extrude <== Boss/Base <== Insert
Extrude <== surface <== Insert
Feature palette <== Tools
Features <== Toolbars <== View
Fillet <== sketch Tools <== Tools
Fillet/round <== Features <== Insert
Find references <== File
fOnt <== Toolbars <== View
geometric Tolerance <== Annotations <== Insert

Helix/spiral <== cUrve <== Insert
hidden in Gray <== Display <== View
Hidden lines removed <== Display <== View
Hole <== Features <== Insert
Horizontal <== dimensionS <== Tools
hYperlink <== Insert
Imported <== Surface <== Insert
inseRt spline point <== sketch Tools <== Tools
Interactive rendering <== Photoworks
Join <== Features <== Insert
Knit <== Surface <== Insert
Library feature <== Insert
Lighting <== View
Line <== sketch Entity <== Tools
Line format <== Toolbars <== View
Linear pattern <== pattErn/mirror <== Insert
Linear step and repeat <== sketch Tools <== Tools
Loft <== Cut <== Insert
Loft <== Boss/Base <== Insert
Lof <== Surface <== Insert
Macro <== Toolbars <== View
Mass properties <== Tools
Materials <== Photoworks
mate refereNce <== Tools
measuRe <== Tools
Mirror <== sketch Tools <== Tools
mirror All <== pattErn/mirror <== Insert
Mirror feature <== pattErn/mirror <== Insert
Mirror part <== Insert
modifY <== sketch Tools <== Tools
No solve more <== sketch Tools <== Tools
New <== File (Ctrl-N)
neW design table <== Insert
New window <== Window
Note <== Annotations <== Insert
Object <== Insert
Offset entities <== sketch Tools <== Tools
Offset <== Surface <== Insert
Open <== File (Ctrl-O)
Options <== Photoworks
oPtions <== Tools
Orientation <== View (Space bar)
orIgins <== View
override Dims on drag <== sketch Tools <== Tools
page setup <== File
Page setup <== Photoworks
paN <== Modify <== View
paraBola <== sketch Entities <== Tools
Parallel <== dimensionS <== Tools

parallelograM <== sketch Entity <== Tools
Paste <== Edit (Ctrl-V)
Paste Material <== Photoworks
Perspective <== Display <== View
Perspective <== Modify <== View
Photoworks <== Toolbars <== View
pictUre <== Modify <== View
pictUre <== Display <== View
Picture <== Insert
Planar <== Surface <== Insert
Plane <== Reference geometry <== Insert
Planes <== View
Point <== sketch Entity <== Tools
Points <== View
Print <== Photoworks
Print <== File (Ctrl-P)
print preView <== File
Projected <== cUrve <== Insert
propertiEs <== Edit
properties <== File
Radiate <== Surface <== Insert
Rebuild <== Edit (Ctrl-B)
Record <== mAcro <== Tools
Rectangle <== sketch Entity <== Tools
Redraw <== View (Ctrl-R)
reference Geometry <== Toolbars <== View
Reload <== File
Render <== Photoworks
replaCe <== pictUre <== Modify <== View
Reset size <== Object <== Edit
Revolve <== Cut <== Insert
Revolve <== Boss/Base <== Insert
Revolve <== Surface <== Insert
Rib <== sheet Metal <== Features <== Insert
roLlback <== Edit
rotatE <== Modify <== View
rotate about screen Center <== Modify <== View
rUn <== mAcro <== Tools
Save <== File (Ctrl-S)
save As <== File
scAle <== Features <== Insert
Scan equal <== relatiOns <== Tools
sectIon properties <== Tools

section View <== Display <== View
section View <== Modify <== View
seLect <== Tools

selection fIlter <== Toolbars <== View
senD to <== File
Shaded <== Display <== View
shaPe <== Features <== Insert
Shell <== Features <== Insert
Simple <== Hole <== Features <== Insert
Simplify spline <== sketch Tools <== Tools
sKetch <== Edit
sKetch <== Insert
sKetch <== Toolbars <== View
skeTch from drawing <== Insert
sketch Relations <== Toolbars <== View
sketch Tools <== Toolbars <== View
Spline <== sketch Entity <== Tools
spLit curve <== skethc Entity <== Tools
Split liNe <== cUrve <== Insert
Standard <== Toolbars <== View
standard viEs <== Toolbars <== View
status Bar <== View
Stop <== mAcro <== Tools
Suppress <== Edit
surface Finish symbol <== Annotations <== Insert
Sweep <== Cut <== Insert
Sweep <== Boss/Base <== Insert
Swept surface <== reference Geometry <== Insert
tanGent arc <== sketch Entity <== Tools
tangent edges as phantoM <== Display <== View
tangent edges Removed <== Display <== View
tangent eDges visible <== Display <== View
temporary aXes <== View
Text <== sketch Entity <== Tools
Thicken <== Cut <== Insert
Thicken <== Boss/Base <== Insert
tile Horizontally <== Window
tile Vertically <== Window
Trim <== sketch Tools <== Tools
undo <== Edit (Ctrl-Z)
Undo view change <== Modify <== View
uNsuppress <== Edit
unsuppress With dependents <== Edit
Vertical <== dimensionS <== Tools
View image file <== Photoworks
View <== Toolbars <== View
Web <== Toolbars <== View
Weld symbol <== Annotations <== Insert
Wireframe <== Display <== View
With surface <== Cut <== Insert
Wizard <== Hole <== Features <== Insert
zoom In/out <== Modify <== View

Zoom to area <== Modify <== View
zoom to Fit <== Modify <== View
zoom to Selection <== Modify <== View

Appendix B

SOFTWARE CONFIGURATION

This text assumes that several changes have been made to the factory default software settings. The use of descriptive names for the three primary reference planes is especially important for aiding spatial visualization. For instance, *Front, Top,* and *Right* are extremely more suggestive of a viewing direction than are *Plane1, Plane2,* and *Plane3*.

Effect the configuration changes as follows:

A. Without a single part, drawing, or assembly file open select **Tools ▼ Options** and **click** on the **Reference Geometry** tab. Re-name the Plane Default Names as follows:

        Plane1:   Front

        Plane2:   Top

        Plane3:   Right

B. On the **Grid/Units** tab disable under *Snap Behaviour:* disable **Snap to Points (or Grid).**

C. On the **Grid/Units** tab set the *Length Unit:* as **millimeters** with **2 decimal places.**

    NOTE: All Design Project Assignments use **inches** as the units.

D. Press the **OK** button to activate the changes.

E. Select **View ▼ Toolbars** and check only the following options:
    Standard
    View
    Annotation
    Features
    Sketch
    Standard Views

In the event that you wish to revert to factory default software settings simply press the **Reset All** button at the bottom of the *Options* dialog window.

Appendix C

DOWNLOAD SUPPLEMENTAL FILES from http://www.schroff1.com/solidworks/suppfiles/

Exercise Number	File Name
1 & 2 & 29	widget.SLDPRT
3	holes.SLDPRT
4	boss_cut.SLDPRT
7	con_plane.SLDPRT
10	geo_relations.SLDPRT
11	crank.SLDPRT
12	idler_arm.SLDPRT
13	widget_x13.SLDPRT
14	pattern1.SLDPRT
15	pattern2.SLDPRT
17	clevis.SLDPRT
18	gear.SLDPRT
21	locating_finger.SLDPRT
22	v_stop.SLDPRT
23	equations.SLDPRT
24	drill_bushing.SLDPRT bushing99.xls
25	bracket.SLDPRT ring.SLDPRT bushing.SLDPRT shaft.SLDPRT base_crank.SLDPRT gear.SLDPRT
28	bearing.SLDPRT piston.SLDPRT link_pin.SLDPRT